Clear and Queer Thinking

Clear and Queer Thinking

Wittgenstein's Development and His Relevance to Modern Thought

Laurence Goldstein

ROWMAN & LITTLEFIELD PUBLISHERS, INC.

Lanham • Boulder • New York

ROWMAN & LITTLEFIELD PUBLISHERS, INC.

First published in the United States of America
by Rowman & Littlefield Publishers, Inc.
4720 Boston Way, Lanham, Maryland 20706

ISBN 0-8476-9545-X (cloth)
ISBN 0-8476-9546-8 (pbk.)

Printed in Great Britain

Contents

Aletheia to me:

'Where, what universe were you kidnapped to,
to write like this – so deep, so pensive.'

This book is dedicated, with
reciprocal admiration, to her.

Preface

Bergen, a remarkably beautiful romantic old city, mostly drenched in rain when not swept with snow, was where the 24-year-old Wittgenstein spent two nights at the Hotel Norge before setting off, with his companion David Pinsent, for the small village of Östersö (now spelled Øystese) on his first visit to Norway. They strolled and sailed; Pinsent played the piano and studied Law, Wittgenstein worked on Logic. That was at the beginning of September 1913. Wittgenstein visited Norway on seven further occasions. He produced some of his best ideas in Norway, working for extended periods of virtually solitary confinement. He had a hut built for him on a mountain by a lake outside the tiny village of Skjolden to the north of Bergen on the breathtaking Sognefjord, where sleepy clouds hang low over the clear still waters. Wittgenstein admired what he called the 'quiet seriousness' of this landscape.

The University of Bergen now houses the Wittgenstein Archive and it is here that Wittgenstein's *Nachlaß*, a collection of manuscripts totalling around 20,000 pages, is being painstakingly transcribed into an electronic database (Huitfeldt, 1994; Stern, 1996). Wittgenstein wrote in exercise books, rewriting extensively and, from time to time, cutting up fragments, reassembling, refining, and dictating the resulting text to a typist. It is fascinating to track some of his enigmatic remarks back to their original manuscript sources. Widespread misinterpretations in the secondary literature can frequently be corrected once we locate the context in which a certain thought was born, and trace the sometimes convoluted path of its development. I am grateful to those colleagues, Claus Huitfeldt, Knut Åmås, Peter Cripps, Franz Hespe, Wilhelm Krüger and Angela Requate, who were good to me during my two stays at the Archive. And to Harald Vatne in Skjolden for making vivid the way that Wittgenstein lived there.

This book has two aims. The first is to give philosophers a thorough appreciation of the development of Wittgenstein's central ideas. Even today, after many books and thousands of articles have been written on Wittgenstein's work (Shanker and Shanker, 1986; Frongia and McGuinness, 1990), there is still no proper appreciation of how and why his

vii

ideas changed as they did. There is still a neglect of his work on the philosophy of mathematics, as if this were some excrescence foreign to his central philosophical concerns. Some commentators completely ignore these writings, quite disregarding the facts that Wittgenstein spent at least half of his 'transitional' and 'late' periods working on the subject, felt that his own most lasting contribution to philosophy lay in this area, and treated general topics within philosophy often more perspicuously and illuminatingly in his writings on mathematics. There is also still little appreciation (although I exempt Hacker, von Wright and Zemach from this accusation) that the last six years of his life is a distinctive, creative, imaginative phase in which Wittgenstein approaches many problems in a new way, overturning views which are themselves an overturning of views maintained in his early work. I have paid particular attention to this last phase, the culmination of his career, with the exception of his writing on *certainty*, which just doesn't turn my crank – although the book *On Certainty* contains some indisputable gems – and I refer readers to other authors who have been more fired by that writing, such as Joachim Schulte (1992, ch. 6), Avrum Stroll (1994) and Michael Kober (1996).

The second aim is to indicate to people working in disciplines outside philosophy how an understanding of Wittgenstein's thought may be relevant to the way in which they pursue their own subjects. Marie McGinn (1997, p. 7) says that Wittgenstein 'remains an isolated thinker, whose distinctively intense and individual voice is ultimately inimitable'. And in her book she discusses themes from Wittgenstein's later writings without making any real attempt to connect these to the views of other philosophers, or to the views of anyone else, thus perpetuating this sense of 'isolation'. Inimitable Wittgenstein may be, but isolated, no. Wittgenstein was a great thinker not because he created a private world of ideas, but because so many of his ideas engage most forcibly with the views of others. There are few significant modern writers working in the theory of mind or the philosophy of language who have not been profoundly influenced by him. Typically, he takes a view which is an alternative to opposing positions, not in the sense of being midway between them, but in the sense of revealing and rejecting presuppositions common to both. He fought the temptation to give alternative *theories*, for he came to think that there is no place for theory in philosophy. Yet his is not exclusively destructive work. I believe that Wittgenstein supplies us with the tools for enlightened constructive work *outside* philosophy and, like Hintikka (1996, p. xi), I contend that Wittgenstein's ideas and problems are of great topical interest – they provide a refreshing viewpoint that ought to affect people working in linguistics, psychology and various of the sciences (including cognitive science and neuroscience) and also people working at living a decent life.

My two-fold aim has created something of a headache; a slave to two masters is liable to satisfy neither, and to end up getting a kicking from both. What I have done in order to accommodate both philosophers and also those not specialist in philosophy is to make the body of the text as straightforward as possible. Where I have had to use a term or a notion that may not be familiar to a non-specialist reader, I have supplied explanatory notes. And at those points in the text where I judge that a specialist reader might find the argument wild, or not properly supported, I have supplied notes indicated by numerals in square brackets, in which I elaborate and give references.

Much of Wittgenstein scholarship is sycophantic; many writers (including the authors of the four-volume *Analytical Commentary* on the *Philosophical Investigations*) think that Wittgenstein, in his late writings, was right about just about everything. (Adrian Moore astutely points out that to toe the Wittgensteinian line too willingly will often mean failing to feel the allure, which Wittgenstein himself felt, for the views he was opposing (Moore, 1997, p. 244).) A few commentators, by contrast, are blindly hostile. On many issues, my own philosophical thinking has been shaped by Wittgenstein. Yet, at several points, I hold that he is too quickly dismissive, or is premature in thinking that he has successfully killed off certain traditional problems. Here, I believe, he should be wrestled to the ground. It is therefore in a loincloth rather than a sackcloth that I confront him in this book, while at the same time, I hope, making readers properly aware that we are in the ring with one of the all-time greats. A sense of fair play dictates that one not score too many points by attacking manuscript material that Wittgenstein had not worked up with an eye to publication. In these, Wittgenstein is frequently pulled in opposite directions (as one usually is with interesting questions) so it is all too easy to find contradictions that he had not yet resolved – *On Certainty*, compiled from five late manuscripts, is a good example (Grayling, 1998). My policy here has been to applaud (what I take to be) the good moves and to ignore (what I take to be) the lapses.

Unlike Wittgenstein, who believed in leaving the hard work to the reader, I seek to give a clear and simple account of his thought, and, where other commentators have conducted the discussion at a highly abstract level, I have tried to give easy, even simple-minded illustrations. What I wish, above all else, is to achieve an exposition free from verbiage, jargon and opacity. Reading a lot of the secondary literature which tends to shroud his ideas in darkness and mystery, you might be forgiven for thinking that such an ambition is not achievable. One strategy that I have employed is to ensure that I have conversations on Wittgenstein with friends who are just too dumb to cope with anything too complicated. Among those from conversing with whom my style of presentation has benefited in this regard, I'd like to thank José Bermudez, Deborah Brown, Stewart Candlish, Pascal Engel, Paul Fletcher, Newton Garver, Leonard Goddard, Peter Hacker, Oswald Hanfling, Joe Lau, Tim Moore, Martine Nida-Rümelin, Colin Radford, Hartley Slater, and Eddy Zemach. Thanks too to Vivian Chu and Loletta Li for great secretarial assistance, and to Aletheia Goldstein for help in compiling the bibliography. Anthony Grayling read the whole manuscript with great care, and any infelicities which remain in the text are doubtless traceable to those outbursts of arrogant assertiveness when I refused to act on one or two of his excellent suggestions.

Abbreviations

Wittgenstein's published works, listed in rough chronological order of composition, are referred to by the following abbreviations. The ordering is rough because many of these works include material composed at different times. In those works in which sections are numbered, reference will be made to section number rather than page number (Part I of the *Philosophical Investigations* will be referred to by section number, Part II by page). Unpublished material in the Wittgenstein *Nachlaß* is referred to by the labels that Georg Henrik von Wright assigned in his *Catalogue* (von Wright, 1982). For listings of the unpublished sources of the published texts and diagrams, see Biggs and Pichler (1993).

RC = 'Review of P. Coffey *The Science of Logic*', *Cambridge Review* 34 (1913), p. 351.

N = *Notebooks 1914-16*, eds G.H. von Wright and G.E.M. Anscombe, trans. G.E.M. Anscombe (Blackwell, 1961)

T = *Tractatus Logico-Philosophicus*, trans. D.F. Pears and B.F. McGuinness (Routledge and Kegan Paul, 1961)

LO = *Letters to C.K. Ogden with Comment on the English Translation of the Tractatus Logico-philosophicus*, edited with an Introduction by G.H. von Wright (Blackwell and Routledge & Kegan Paul, 1973)

LRKM = *Letters to Russell, Keynes and Moore*, eds G.H. von Wright and B.F. McGuinness (Blackwell, 1974)

LF = *Briefe an Ludwig von Ficker*, ed. G.H. von Wright (Otto Müller Verlag, 1969). English version in (Luckhardt, 1979) to which all references in the text are made.

RLF = 'Some Remarks on Logical Form', *Proceedings of the Aristotelian Society*, supp. vol. 9 (1929), pp. 162-71.

LE = 'A Lecture on Ethics' (Heretics Club, Cambridge, 1930) *Philosophical Review* 77 (1965), pp. 3-12; also in *PO*, pp. 37-44.

WVC = *Wittgenstein and the Vienna Circle* (Blackwell, 1979)

PR = *Philosophical Remarks*, ed. R. Rhees, trans. R. Hargreaves and R. White (Blackwell, 1975)

DL = *Wittgenstein's Lectures, Cambridge 1930-32*, from the notes of John King and Desmond Lee, ed. D. Lee (Blackwell, 1980)

M = 'Wittgenstein's Lectures in 1930-33', in G.E. Moore, *Philosophical Papers* (Allen and Unwin, 1959)

PG = Philosophical Grammar, ed. R. Rhees, trans. A.J.P. Kenny (Blackwell, 1974)

A = Wittgenstein's Lectures, Cambridge 1932-35, from the notes of Alice Am--brose and Margaret MacDonald, ed. A. Ambrose (Blackwell, 1979)

BB = The Blue and Brown Books (Blackwell, 1958)

NL = 'Notes for Lectures on "Private Experience" and "Sense Data"', *Philosophical Review* 77 (1968), pp. 275-320; reprinted with corrections and additions in *PO*, pp. 201-88.

LSD = 'The Language of Sense-Data and Private Experience' (Notes taken by Rush Rhees of Wittgenstein's Lectures, 1936', *Philosophical Investigations* 7 (1984) 2-45, 101-40; reprinted in *PO*, pp. 290-367.

RFM = Remarks on the Foundations of Mathematics, revised edition, ed. G.H. von Wright, R. Rhees, G.E.M. Anscombe (Blackwell, 1978)

LA = Lectures and Conversations on Aesthetics, Psychology and Religious Beliefs, ed. C. Barrett (Blackwell 1970)

LFM = Wittgenstein's Lectures on the Foundations of Mathematics, Cambridge, 1939, ed. C. Diamond (Harvester Press, 1976)

PI = Philosophical Investigations, 2nd edition, ed. G.E.M. Anscombe and R. Rhees, trans. G.E.M. Anscombe (Blackwell, 1958)

NPL = Notes for the 'Philosophical Lecture' (MS 166, probably composed around 1941) in *PO*, pp. 447-58.

Z = Zettel, ed. G.E.M. Anscombe (Blackwell, 1967)

RPP I = Remarks on the Philosophy of Psychology, vol. I, ed. G.E.M. Anscombe and G.H. von Wright, trans. G.E.M. Anscombe (Blackwell 1980)

RPP II = Remarks on the Philosophy of Psychology, vol. II, ed. G.H. von Wright and H. Nyman, trans. C.G. Luckhardt and M.A.E. Aue (Blackwell, 1980)

LPP = Wittgenstein's Lectures on Philosophy of Psychology 1946-7 – notes by P.T. Geach, K.J. Shah, A.C. Shah, A.C. Jackson, ed. P.T. Geach (Harvester, 1988)

LW I = Last Writings on the Philosophy of Psychology, vol. I, ed. G.H. von Wright and H. Nyman, trans. C.G. Luckhardt and M.A.E. Aue (Blackwell, 1982)

LW II = Last Writings on the Philosophy of Psychology, vol. II, ed. G.H. von Wright and H. Nyman, trans. C.G. Luckhardt and M.A.E. Aue (Blackwell, 1992)

OC = On Certainty, ed. G.E.M. Anscombe and G.H. von Wright, trans. D. Paul and G.E.M. Anscombe (Blackwell, 1969)

CV = Culture and Value, ed. G.H. Von Wright in collaboration with H. Nyman, trans. P. Winch (Blackwell, 1980)

LW-GW = 'Some Hitherto Unpublished Letters from Ludwig Wittgenstein to Georg Henrik von Wright', *Cambridge Review* (28 February 1983) 56-65, reprinted in *PO*, 459-79.

RoC = Remarks on Colour, ed. G.E.M. Anscombe (Blackwell, 1977)

PO = Philosophical Occasions 1912-1951, ed. J. Klagge and A. Nordmann (Hackett, 1993)

Introduction

Ludwig Wittgenstein (26 April 1889 – 29 April 1951) was one of the central figures (many would say he was *the* central figure) in twentieth-century philosophy. A student of philosophy who has no knowledge of Wittgenstein is no student of philosophy. Although he was very much a philosopher's philosopher, and was careful to confine his attention to conceptual enquiry, his fame has spread way outside the confines of academic philosophy, and one finds his name being tossed about in the most unlikely places. The name – 'Wittgenstein' – does have a pleasing resonance. Many people have used that name in attempting to give their own work a certain cachet, even when their own work has absolutely nothing to do with anything on which Wittgenstein ever wrote. Those with little knowledge of the man and little understanding of what he wrote have regarded his words as deep and his character as intriguingly dark. Propositions from his early *Tractatus Logico-Philosophicus* have been set to music. A play (an amazingly silly one) has been written about his life, and works of fiction have had him as their hero.

This book studies Wittgenstein's thought in the main areas on which he wrote – meaning, mind and mathematics. Although he did not write much on the subject, he agonised a great deal about ethics, and there is, in the final chapter, a discussion of his moral attitudes and conduct. I have concentrated on central themes within core areas of Wittgenstein's work and have traced the development of his thinking on these from early to late. This strategy is useful for illustrating the nature of the radical difference between the early style of his thinking and the later. Getting clear on some central doctrines doesn't exactly guarantee that the rest will simply fall into place, but it's a good start. My aim is to give those who, when reading Wittgenstein, find themselves floundering (I don't think this excludes anyone), something firm onto which to cling.

People new to his works should be warned that, very frequently, Wittgenstein writes as if addressing an imaginary interlocutor, sometimes himself. This is not (just) for literary effect. When a phenomenon is puzzling, he himself is tempted to say such and such – but then his

1

alter ego steps in and says: 'No, wait a minute ....' Readers often get confused because they think he is setting out a definite position, but very often he is just, as he once put it, having a conversation with himself, *tête à tête*. Like any good, creative philosopher, he also asks a lot of questions (for example, I haven't counted, but there seem to be more questions than assertions in his very late work *Remarks on Colour*). Occasionally his questions are meant rhetorically, as the surrounding text makes clear, but frequently they are just a record of his restless inquisitiveness.

Most books on Wittgenstein start off with some biographical information, go on to discuss what is unique about Wittgenstein's conception of philosophy and the way he pursued it, and then get down to the business of discussing his works, typically in their chronological order. This may sound perfectly logical. But that is not what I am going to do; I'll be discussing Wittgenstein the man last. The particular question in which I'm interested is whether understanding the man's personality can help us to understand his philosophy – can light be thrown on the interpretation of various of his views if one knows the kind of person Wittgenstein was? Obviously before asking whether the interpretion of what he wrote is aided by knowing what kind of character he was, one needs first to be reasonably well acquainted with what he wrote. Only then can we sensibly discuss whether he wrote it not just because that was where reason would have guided anyone as smart as him, but because, being the sort of person he was, that was the sort of thing that he would say. In good Freudian style, we shall try to interpret the views and behaviour of a person by delving into his childhood and adolescence (Gay, 1985), which, in Wittgenstein's case, means the first forty-odd (forty very odd) years of his life.

The gist of the five chapters is as follows:

Method
A reading of *Philosophical Investigations* and the other late writings will not make any sense at all without some preliminary intercourse with the *Tractatus*. Why? Because the late works are in large part a reaction against the preconceptions that informed Wittgenstein's earlier philosophy. '[The new thoughts] could be seen in the right light only by contrast with and against the background of my old way of thinking' (*PI* Preface, p. viii). There are several explicit critical references to the *Tractatus* in the late writings. In his book *Nothing is Hidden* (subtitled 'Wittgenstein's Criticism of his Early Thought'), Norman Malcolm rightly says that in Wittgenstein's later period there is a 'massive attack' on the principal ideas of the *Tractatus*. He lists fifteen positions

2

that are taken in the *Tractatus* and rejected in Wittgenstein's later writings (Malcolm, 1986, p. viii). In this chapter, I offer a quick sketch of central doctrines of the *Tractatus*, and give a more detailed treatment of certain themes in the chapters that follow.

Wittgenstein believed that, in the *Tractatus*, he had succeeded in establishing, on all essential points, the final solution of the problems of philosophy. The reader needs to absorb his discussion of the limits of thought, then to recognize that the very propositions which constitute that discussion are nonsensical, 'and then he will see the world aright' (6.54). No such grand ambition informs the *Philosophical Investigations*. Here there is no question of producing theories to answer long-standing philosophical problems. In fact, Wittgenstein's view is that these problems are just the result of philosophers' attempts to theorize, for frequently such attempts commit what Wittgenstein calls 'grammatical' errors which come about through embracing false assumptions about how language works, e.g. that the sole function of language is to convey thoughts, or that a word applies to X because X satisfies certain conditions necessary and suffient for the application of that word. The proper method in philosophy is to diagnose these errors, not to advance theories of one's own. This so-called 'quietism' of Wittgenstein's is an important contribution to a historical debate over how philosophy ought to be pursued. Does philosophy have only this humble rôle to play or can philosophical theorizing make a contribution to such tasks as gaining a scientific understanding of how humans feel and think?

Meaning

A good route into the *Tractatus* theory of meaning starts at a consideration of tautologies and contradictions, which are *sinnlos* (lacking sense). This leads to an understanding of what constitutes a fully-fledged (*sinnvoll*) proposition. The theory of meaning construed as answering the question of how language is connected with the world, is the core of the *Tractatus*. By the early 1930s Wittgenstein had abandoned that theory completely, recognizing that its central tenets (e.g. that the meaning of a sentence is a function of the meaning of its parts) were based on a misguided conception of what the problem requires. For example, he had thought that one of the things needed was an analysis of propositions (rather like the chemical analysis of a compound substance), but he later recognised that this was just one of those tempting but unfounded suppositions that theorists are so prone to make.

In his later writings, Wittgenstein came to realize how a proper study of language depends on recognizing how intimately our language is bound up with various human activities and that what a given expression means is to be equated with how it is used in such activities. People complain about the doctrine that meaning is use. Some say that it is just a slogan, too vague to be of any use; others that it is a theory, and that this sits ill with Wittgenstein's disavowal of theories in philosophy. One decisive way of rebutting these charges is to show how acceptance of the simple claim that meaning is use can have serious consequential effects for theorizing outside philosophy. I try to show how a superior alternative to standard theories of first language acquisition is to be had by following Wittgenstein's lead.

Mind

There is a clutch of propositions in the *Tractatus* on the soul and on the self. Wittgenstein holds that it is incorrect to construe belief as a relation between a proposition and an incorporeal soul, although what construal he himself favours is none too clear. In the later writings on the philosophy of psychology, there is a good deal of discussion about belief and other so-called 'propositional attitudes' including hope and expectation. Such attitudes make themselves manifest in the ways we act (we shouldn't wish, as behaviourists might, to deny the existence of these attitudes), but we must resist conceiving them as inner things or episodes which, as it were, burst to the surface from time to time.

Moore's paradox (which concerns the absurdity of someone saying something like 'It isn't raining, but I believe that it is') was the impetus for important reflections on belief in Wittgenstein's last period. We consider the solution he offers to Moore's paradox. Also, in the last phase of his work, he investigates various kinds of sensation. His reflections are inconclusive, but suggestive, and his view that certain of these phenomena lie outside the bounds of scientific enquiry needs to be looked at quite carefully. These discussions, which occur in Part II of the *Philosophical Investigations* and in other writings from the last six years of Wittgenstein's life are fascinating, but are woefully neglected in the literature. So I try to make partial amends.

Mathematics

Frege thought it a disgrace that mathematicians of his time did not have a defensible account of what a number is. He devoted an entire book to providing such an account. Wittgenstein offers an ingenious alternative in the *Tractatus*. His theory that numbers are formal concepts is one aspect of the important doctrine of what is unsayable (but can only be shown). The structure of the world, he claims, is shown in equations. With his subsequent abandonment of grandiose metaphysics, Wittgenstein rejects as 'nebulous' the search for an answer to the question about the nature of number, but other concerns in the philosophy of mathematics occupied the major part of his time for about fifteen years. The views that emerged have met with a generally unsympathetic response from both philosophers and mathematicians; many have found outrageous such claims as that consistency in mathematics is not a desideratum, that a mathematical proof determines the sense of the theorem proved, that there is nothing particularly interesting in the theory of transfinite numbers developed by Cantor etc. We look at the question of whether these views are crazy or fertile (or both).

Man

Is there some close relationship between a commitment to philosophy and the quality of one's moral character? One famous extreme view is that the devoted study of the subject uniquely gives the philosopher access to the Good, a necessary qualification for being in a position to rule a state justly. Wittgenstein too accords the philosopher an elevated status. He holds that 'working in philosophy ... is really a working on oneself', a painful process which few can undertake, and one which results in a deepening of one's moral character.

Ray Monk (1990) remarks that many people who read Wittgenstein instinctively feel the unity of his philosophical concerns with his emotional and spiritual life. This sounds all very fine, until we reflect on how Wittgenstein actually lived his life – brutalizing schoolchildren, victimizing students, vilifying colleagues .... The man was clearly arrogant, petulant and plain nasty, yet he was revered almost as a saint by some of the great people who knew him. This is a paradox that needs resolving.

That Wittgenstein was full of self-loathing is clear. He subjected himself to a variety of punishing regimes in order to improve his character – working in solitude for long periods, exposing himself to mortal danger at the war front, schoolmastering in primitive rural areas, living in a kitchen, a toolshed and other kinds of unprepossessing dwelling. After a long, hard struggle he did succeed in making a better person of himself, and from this effort emerges a conception of ethics not as a theoretical discipline but as a form of experimentation on oneself, a process of trial and error – in his case, mostly error.

1

Method

The intellectual ancestry of the *Tractatus*

Apart from a small 'Wörterbuch' (word book) for schoolchildren, the *Tractatus Logico-Philosophicus* was the only book that Wittgenstein published in his lifetime. It is a great, elegant and highly distinctive work. Although very short (75 pages) it ranges over a wide variety of big subjects, including the structure of the world, the nature of language, logic and mathematics, probability, causation, ethics, solipsism and death. The text is a series of remarks, concise and oracular, beginning with the pronouncement 'The world is everything that is the case'. The propositions of the *Tractatus* have a certain austere beauty. The writing is spare, with no ornamentation; the argumentation is lean and mean. The work is so intellectually rich that it was the centre of philosophical discussion in Cambridge and Vienna for ten years after its publication; it is a landmark work in the history of philosophy.

Immediately after the 'Contents' page of the *Tractatus* is an 'Introduction' written by Bertrand Russell (1872-1970). When the *Tractatus* was first offered for publication, the text was regarded as so obscure that publishers were unwilling to risk investing in it. Only through the inclusion of Russell's Introduction did the book get published. Wittgenstein thought that Russell had badly misunderstood the work, and at one stage was adamant that his Introduction not be printed even at the cost of jeopardizing the book's chances of publication.[1] After Russell's Introduction comes a dedication, followed by the author's Preface, a curious mixture of arrogance and false modesty. Wittgenstein says that the 'whole sense of the book might be summed up in the following words: what can be said at all can be said clearly, and what we cannot talk about, we must pass over in silence'. Conversely, to try saying the unsayable is just to indulge in 'gassing'.[2] He continues with some humble words about the limitations of the work and of his own intellectual powers, but his final paragraph begins: 'On the other hand, the *truth* of the thoughts that are here set forth seems to me unassailable and definitive. I therefore believe myself to have found, on all essential points, the final solution of the problems.' So, consistently, he then retired from philosophy. He came out of this retirement only after about six years, when he became aware that cracks in the structure of the *Tractatus* spelled the collapse of the entire edifice.

The *Tractatus* has seven pivotal propositions, numbered 1 to 7; every proposition is assigned a decimal number according to its logical importance. Thus the second proposition of the *Tractatus* is numbered 1.1, showing that it is a comment on proposition number 1; and, for example, proposition 3.1432 is the second comment on 3.143 which, in turn, is the third comment on 3.14. The closing proposition, number 7, repeats the prefatory caution: 'Whereof one cannot speak, thereof one must remain silent.'[3]

No book, even one as singular as the *Tractatus*, appears out of thin air, and to begin to understand it, we need to know why it came into being. A text in philosophy inherits an argumentative tradition in which different problems and different methods have become prominent from time to time. One must be aware of the context in which it was written to appreciate the questions a particular work seeks to answer. For many philosophers, and Wittgenstein is a prime example, it would be rash to offer an interpretation of their writings without a thorough appreciation of their background. We must avoid the error of 'reading back' into the writings of an author our own philosophical preconceptions and our own perspective, which have been shaped by developments *subsequent* to that author's work.[4] Fortunately, in the case of the *Tractatus*, it is reasonably easy to identify the problems that Wittgenstein was attempting to confront. He began intensive work on the book when he was 23 years old. His philosophical reading up to that point was strictly limited (his subsequent philosophical reading was strictly limited too) and research into his life and his early cultural milieu has now disclosed a fairly comprehensive picture of the very heterogeneous collection of writers, artists and scientists whom he admired and who exercised an influence on him.

Vienna, in the early years of the twentieth century when the Habsburg Empire was in its death throes, was a political, scientific and cultural melting pot. One of the great catalysts of this prodigious interanimation was the Wittgenstein family mansion in the Alleegasse which housed the finest furniture and tapestries, traditional portraits, paintings by contemporary artists including Klimt, sculptures by Rodin and Mestrovic, and several grand pianos, and was the venue for musical evenings at which Brahms, Mahler and Bruno Walter were frequent guests. It is obvious from his manuscripts how strong and lifelong was the influence upon Wittgenstein of thinkers who either attended or were the subjects of discussion at the family home. Among those whom he names as influencing his thought are Immanuel Kant, Arthur Schopenhauer, Ludwig Bolzmann, Heinrich Hertz, Karl Kraus, Adolf Loos, Otto Weininger and Oswald Spengler. He was intimately familiar with the writings of Goethe, Schiller, Mörike and Lessing, representatives of the 'high' German culture, and he greatly admired Tolstoy and Dostoevsky.

Certainly, the questions discussed by Viennese intellectuals shaped Wittgenstein's outlook, and it might be tempting to search for the provenance of the doctrines of the *Tractatus* in that Germanic tradition in which Wittgenstein was so thoroughly immersed. But that would be a mistake. While there can be no denying that the shades of Kant, Schopenhauer, Bolzano and, particularly, Hertz[5] hover above the pages of the *Tractatus*, it is quite clear that the work is principally the culmination of Wittgenstein's adventure in mathematical logic, which began in earnest only after he had left Austria to begin his studies abroad.

What must be remembered is that, at the age of 19, Wittgenstein took a decisive step away from all that civilization and culture of Kakania[6] and went to fly experimental kites in Glossop and to study aeronautical engineering at Manchester University, at the time when powered flight was just taking off. He left behind him the stifling atmosphere of Vienna and sought fresh stimulation, first in the bleak and ugly industrial north of England, then at Cambridge where a logical revolution fomented by Russell was in full swing. The *Tractatus* is best seen as a response to a set of logical conundrums bequeathed by Russell and the 'father of modern logic', the German mathematician Gottlob Frege (1848-1925).[7] Wittgenstein was dissatisfied with the various answers that his two distinguished predecessors had proposed, and he offered not piecemeal counter-suggestions but an all-embracing theory which, so he says in the Preface, solves all the problems. That theory is known as the picture theory of language, which I shall outline below and develop more fully in Chapters 2 and 3.

It was in Manchester, or even just before his time there, that Wittgenstein began studying the writings of Frege and Russell (apparently learning some passages from Frege's *Grundgesetze* almost by heart).[8] He visited Frege in Jena, probably in the summer of 1911 (Frege 'wiped the floor' with him, so he reported), attended Russell's lectures in Cambridge during the Michaelmas Term of 1911, and returned to study as an undergraduate with Russell during the academic year 1912-13. In September of 1913, after his short holiday there with Pinsent, Wittgenstein decided to return to Norway for two years, to live

9

alone and work on logic. Russell sought to discourage him, but Wittgenstein was resolute:

> I said it would be dark, and he said he hated daylight. I said it would be lonely, and he said he prostituted his mind talking to intelligent people. I said he was mad and he said God preserve him from sanity. (God certainly will.) (Letter from Russell to Lucy Donnelly, 19.10.13)

Russell wasn't joking. He believed that if Wittgenstein subjected himself to this punishing regime he would lose either his mind or (following a family tradition of suicide) his life. Russell had, by this time, formed an extremely high opinion of Wittgenstein's ideas on logic and, though he could not quite prevail on Wittgenstein to write them down, was instrumental in securing a written record by asking questions of Wittgenstein in the presence of a secretary who took notes, in shorthand, of the responses. This formed the basis of the 'Notes on Logic', now published in the *Notebooks* (*N*). Wittgenstein then went off to Norway and spent a year in Skjolden, reflecting intensively both on himself and on logic. This may have been the most productive period of his philosophical life, when his mind, as he later described it, was 'on fire' (Monk, 1990, p. 94). We have, from that year, a dictation to G.E. Moore, who visited him for two weeks in late March to early April 1914.[9] The central ideas of the *Tractatus* were forged during that year. Towards the end of June, Wittgenstein left for Austria, intending to return to Norway after a summer vacation. But, when the First World War broke out, he enlisted, on August 7, as a volunteer in the Austrian army, and was not to return to Norway for almost seven years.

In the Preface to the *Tractatus*, Wittgenstein says 'what I have written here makes no claim to novelty in detail, and the reason why I give no sources is that it is a matter of indifference to me whether the thoughts that I have had have been anticipated by someone else'. He does, however, mention that he is 'indebted to Frege's great works and to the writings of my friend Mr. Bertrand Russell'. (Whether he intended, by this choice of words, to belittle Russell, nobody knows.) The *Tractatus* is informed not just by the problems with which Frege and Russell were grappling, but also by the analytical method they advocated for resolving philosophical problems.

1. Method

Philosophy as precise, crystalline and pure

In the twentieth century, the term 'analysis', as it applies to philosophy, refers to the analysis of language and, in the modern era, the philosopher widely (though not universally) acknowledged to have inaugurated this approach to the subject was Frege.[10] The agenda is set in his first major work, *Begriffsschrift*, published in 1879.[11] The German word 'Begriffsschrift' means 'concept-writing' or 'ideography', and the purpose of using such a script is to free ourselves of the unclarities and misunderstandings that our use of imprecise, ordinary languages fosters. In the preface to the book, Frege writes:

> I believe that I can best make the relation of my ideography to ordinary language [Sprache des Lebens] clear if I compare it to that which the microscope has to the eye. Because of the range of its possible uses and the versatility with which it can adapt to the most diverse circumstances, the eye is far superior to the microscope. Considered as an optical instrument, to be sure, it exhibits many imperfections, which ordinarily remain unnoticed only on account of its intimate connection with our mental life. But, as soon as scientific goals demand great sharpness of resolution, the eye proves to be insufficient. The microscope, on the other hand, is perfectly suited to precisely such goals, but that is just why it is useless for all others.
>
> This ideography, likewise, is a device invented for certain scientific purposes, and one must not condemn it because it is not suited to others .... If it is one of the tasks of philosophy to break the domination of the word over the human spirit by laying bare the misconceptions that through the use of language often almost unavoidably arise concerning the relations between concepts and by freeing thought from that with which only the means of expression of ordinary language, constituted as they are, saddle it, then my ideography, further developed for these purposes, can become a useful tool for the philosopher. (van Heijenoort, 1967, pp. 6-7)

Frege's idea (recapitulating Leibniz) is that, with a perspicuous notation, we shall be able to lay bare the structure of clear thinking, by employing an artificial language the sentences of which reflect the way in which their counterpart thoughts decompose into constituent concepts. Frege argued that since many people can have the same thought, thoughts (and their constituent concepts) do not belong to any individual's psychological processes, nor, of course, are they objects that are found in the outside world. They occupy a third realm; they are timeless and immutable. Just as (on one plausible view) mathematical relations are independent of the human mind and await discovery by mathematicians, so the logical relations between thoughts (or propositions, as we should now call them) are mind-independent. A formal language is a useful 'tool' (to use Frege's word) to help us gain access to the realm of thoughts, and hence to acquire a true understanding of what (propositions) can be deduced from what. So, if one regards philosophy as largely a matter of deductive argumentation, one can appreciate the utility that Frege saw for his 'formula language, modelled upon that of arithmetic, for pure thought' – by using it, we are enabled to reason more perceptively.[12]

Russell, unaware of Frege's work, arrived at a similar conclusion concerning the utility of a mathematical approach to philosophy. The turning point for him was observing the performance of the Italian mathematician Giuseppe Peano at an International Congress of Philosophy held in Paris in July 1900. Peano read a paper of his own and contributed to the discussions of other papers. Russell was stimulated, and thought that he could put his finger on Peano's secret weapon. He writes, in his *Autobiography*: 'In discussions at the Congress I observed that he was always more precise than anyone else, and that he invariably got the better of any argument upon which he embarked. As the days went by, I decided that this must be owing to his mathematical logic.' Russell promptly learned Peano's notation and techniques, and started applying them to concerns of his own, with spectacular success, solving problem after problem that had hitherto seemed intractable. 'Intellectually, the month of September 1900 was the highest point of my life. I went about saying to myself that now at last I had done something worth doing, and I had the feeling that I must be careful not to be run over in the street before I had written it down' (Russell, 1975, pp. 147-8). When finally Russell made contact with Frege and stunned him with a paradox (see Chapter 4), he wrote out the reasoning in Peano's notation. *The Principles of Mathematics*, published in 1903, is littered with praise for his new hero who, so it seemed to Russell, offered definitive solutions to long-standing philosophical problems, including that of mathematical equality: 'This relation [equality] had puzzled those who endeavoured to philosophize about Arithmetic, until it was explained by Professor Peano' (Russell, 1903, p. 341). Russell held that mathematical logic – a perspicuous symbolic notation (a formal language) together with transparent deductive procedures – was the powerful agent needed to disperse philosophical fog.

It would be useful to have before us an example in which the devices of a formal language are brought to bear on a philosophical problem so that we can see how the problem is disposed of in the advertised manner. Perhaps the most famous, from the early years of Cambridge analysis, is Russell's Theory of Definite Descriptions, contained in his paper 'On Denoting' (Russell, 1905), a theory for which Wittgenstein had the highest praise.[13] The theory provides answers to a number of puzzles, which Russell sets out; these arise, surprisingly, from apparently plausible assumptions about how an ordinary language can serve as a communication device. Puzzles like these may seem to be trivial conundrums, so it is worth emphasizing that, as Russell noted, what is at stake are big issues such as the nature of language and the epistemological question of what can be known by acquaintance and what only by description. He recommends the devising of such conundrums because, as he says, '[a] logical theory may be tested by its capacity for dealing with puzzles ... since these serve much the same purpose as is served by experiments in physical science' (Russell, 1905, p. 485; 1956, p. 47). Unresolved puzzles provide the impetus, and serve as the testing ground, for new philosophical theories.

Definite descriptions function syntactically very much like proper names: in grammatically correct sentences in which the name 'Charles Darwin' occurs, we could, with no damage to the syntax, replace that name with the definite description 'the discoverer of evolutionary theory'. It seems reasonable to assume that definite descriptions serve the same semantic function as proper names, namely that of picking out or identifying the thing named. It therefore seems also reasonable to assume that, if a name and a definite description stand for the same object, then a sentence containing that name/definite description will retain its truth value after substitution of the corresponding definite description/name. For example, 'Charles Darwin was born in 1848' is false, and likewise, so is 'The discoverer of evolutionary theory was born in 1848'.

It is easy to show that at least one of the aforementioned assumptions, though plausible, is wrong. For consider the sentence 'My daughter wanted to know whether Charles Darwin was the discoverer of evolutionary theory'. That sentence is true. But substitute a name in place of the definite description in that sentence, and we get 'My daughter wanted to know whether Charles Darwin was Charles Darwin', a sentence which is false. Here, then, is a conundrum, simple to expound but irritatingly defiant of resolution.

Russell believed that we were wrong to assume that sentences containing definite descriptions have the same logic (enjoy the same deductive relationships) as sentences containing proper names. He writes: 'The difficulties concerning denoting are, I believe, all the result of a wrong analysis of propositions whose verbal expressions contain denoting phrases.'[14] Russell says that phrases containing *the* (i.e. definite descriptions) 'are by far the most interesting and difficult of denoting phrases'. The 'proper analysis' he offers of these runs as follows:

> Take as an instance 'the father of Charles II was executed'. This asserts that there was an x who was the father of Charles II and was executed. Now *the*, when it is strictly used, involves uniqueness .... Thus when we say 'x was the father of Charles II' we not only assert that x had a certain relation to Charles II, but also that nothing else had this relation. The relation in question, without the assumption of uniqueness, and without any denoting phrases, is expressed by 'x begat Charles II'. To get an equivalent of 'x was the father of Charles II', we must add, 'If y is other than x, y did not beget Charles II', or, what is equivalent, 'If y begat Charles II, y is identical with x.' Hence 'x is the father of Charles II' becomes: 'x begat Charles II; and "if y begat Charles II, y is identical with x" is always true of y.' Thus 'the father of Charles II was executed' becomes: 'It is not always false of x that x begat Charles II and that x was executed and that "if y begat Charles II, y is identical with x" is always true of y.'

With this analysis to hand, it is easy to solve the Charles Darwin puzzle (it's the Sir Walter Scott puzzle in Russell's original) together with several others. (Simplifying things a bit, it turns out, on analysis, that what my daughter really wanted to know was an answer to the question of whether it is the case that there is someone who discovered evolutionary theory and, if so, whether whoever that was, was one and the same person as Charles Darwin.) Note that the definite description 'the discoverer of evolutionary theory' has disappeared in this paraphrase.

To the modern student, the above quoted passage would seem tedious, archaic, fussy and trifling. Only if we imaginatively position ourselves in the philosophical milieu of the beginning of the twentieth century can we understand what a bombshell exploded in *Mind* in 1905 with the publication of 'On Denoting', and why the editor, darkly hinting that Russell was mad, invited him to withdraw the piece. Oxford and Cambridge were, at that time, at the centre of the philosophical world, where philosophers typically wrote in an obscure, verbose and florid prose; Hegelianism and Bradleian Idealism reigned supreme, and modern developments in logic were disdainfully ignored in favour of variations on Aristotelian syllogistic.[15] Russell, wielding his mathematical tools and the precision techniques of modern logic, cutting a swathe through the tradition, would have been as unwelcome as the industrial machinery when it first appeared in the factories of England a hundred and fifty years before.

For his part, Russell wanted to spread the gospel; he needed disciples. In a letter to Lady Ottoline Morrell, he says

> I believe a certain sort of mathematicians have far more philosophical capacity than most people who take up philosophy. Hitherto the people attracted to philosophy have been mostly those who loved the big generalizations, which were all wrong, so that few people with exact minds have taken up the subject. It has long been one of my dreams to found a great school of mathematically-minded philosophers, but I don't know whether I shall ever get it accomplished. I had hopes of Norton, but he has not the physique. Broad is all right, but has no fundamental originality. Wittgenstein of course is exactly my dream.[16]

Wittgenstein had the right physique and showed plenty of originality in repudiating key doctrines in Frege and Russell, and in constructing a comprehensive system of his own. But he shared their general analytical approach to philosophy and accepted much of their analytical apparatus. Like both Frege and Russell, the dream boy believed that the proper way to resolve philosophical problems was by spurning ordinary language and working with a logically perspicuous language, one free of ambiguity and amphiboly. The following two passages from the *Tractatus* (3.323-3.325) and (4.002-4.0031) stake out his methodology:

> 3.323 In everyday language it very frequently happens that the same word has different modes of signification – and so belongs to different symbols – or that two words that have different modes of signification are employed in propositions in what is superficially the same way.
>
> Thus the word 'is' figures as the copula, as a sign for identity, and as an expression for existence; 'exist' figures as an intransitive verb like 'go' and 'identical' as an adjective; we speak of *something*, but also of *something's* happening.
>
> (In the proposition, 'Green is green' – where the first word is the proper name of a person and the last an adjective – these words do not merely have different meanings: they are *different symbols*.)

3.324 In this way the most fundamental confusions are easily produced (the whole of philosophy is full of them).

3.325 In order to avoid such errors we must make use of a sign-language that excludes them by not using the same sign for different symbols and by not using in a superficially similar way signs that have different modes of signification: that is to say, a sign-language that is governed by logical grammar – by logical syntax.

(The conceptual notation of Frege and Russell is such a language, though, it is true, it fails to exclude all mistakes.)

4.002 Man possesses the ability to construct languages capable of expressing every sense, without having any idea how each word has meaning or what its meaning is – just as people speak without knowing how the individual sounds are produced

Everyday language is a part of the human organism and is no less complicated than it.

It is not humanly possible to gather immediately from it what the logic of language is.

Language disguises thought. So much so, that from the outward form of the clothing it is impossible to infer the form of the thought beneath it, because the outward form of the clothing is not designed to reveal the form of the body, but for entirely different purposes.

The tacit conventions on which the understanding of everyday language depends are enormously complicated.

4.003 Most of the propositions and questions to be found in philosophical works are not false but nonsensical. Consequently we cannot give any answer to questions of this kind, but can only establish that they are nonsensical. Most of the propositions and questions of philosophers arise from our failure to understand the logic of our language.

(They belong to the same class as the question whether the good is more or less identical than the beautiful.)

And it is not surprising that the deepest problems are in fact *not* problems at all.

4.0031 All philosophy is a 'critique of language' (though not in Mauthner's sense). It was Russell who performed the service of showing that the apparent logical form of a proposition need not be its real one.

In 1929, after returning to philosophy and at the beginning of his so-called 'transitional' period, Wittgenstein wrote a paper 'Some Remarks on Logical Form' in which he continues to embrace this approach. His characterisation of the proper method of pursuing philosophy is clear and succinct:

> The idea is to express in an appropriate symbolism what in ordinary language leads to endless misunderstandings. That is to say, where ordinary langauge disguises logical structure, where it allows the formation of pseudo-propositions, where it uses one term in an infinity of different meanings, we must replace it by a symbolism which gives a clear picture of the logical structure, excludes pseudo-propositions, and uses its terms unambiguously. (*RLF*, p. 163)

These remarks, especially *T* 4.002, express exactly the same sentiments as those expressed by Frege in the passage from *Begriffsschrift* cited earlier. As we shall now see, Wittgenstein adopts not just Frege's rationale, but also some of the particular tools that Frege brought to the job.

A brief outline of the *Tractatus* theory

It is a fact that we succeed in conversing with each other about how things are in the world. A person can say how things stand. The *Tractatus* addresses the question: What must be true of ourselves and of the world for this to be possible? Wittgenstein undertakes to establish *a priori* the conditions underwriting our ability to talk about the world. This is a project very much in the spirit of Kant.[17] Whereas scientific investigation reveals the empirical, or contingent, facts about the nature of the world, deducing the general *necessary* features the world and of language is the business of metaphysics. So, in the light of what has already been said about logic as a tool of philosophical analysis, it is clear why Wittgenstein claimed (in September, 1913) that '[p]hilosophy ... can neither confirm nor confute scientific investigations. It consists of logic and metaphysics, the former its basis' (*N*, p. 93). This conception of philosophy as purely descriptive and independent of the natural sciences is one that Wittgenstein retained throughout his life (see, e.g., *T* 4.111 (*PI* §109).

We make *statements* about the world; the statement (Satz) is the basic unit of information-giving.[18] In traditional grammar, a Satz (or the sentence used for making it) is divided into subject and predicate. For logical purposes, this is not a particularly illuminating method of division. To see why, consider the sentence 'Joel has just come into the room'. Here the subject expression 'Joel' plays the logical rôle of naming an individual. Compare, now, the sentence 'Nobody has just come into the room'. 'Nobody' is the grammatical subject, but we should hardly want to say that 'Nobody' plays the logical rôle of naming somebody! For logical purposes, so Frege thought, it is best to forget the traditional subject/predicate division and to use instead the function/argument division familiar from mathematics. (Those completely *unfamiliar* with mathematics should skim the next two paragraphs.)

A mathematical *function* delivers *values* when *arguments* are input. Thus, the value of the function '$3x + y^2$', when the arguments 5, 1 are slotted in for x, y respectively, is 16; for arguments <1, 2>, the value of the function is 3.25. We could say that the 'x' and 'y' mark gaps which need to be filled by arguments if the function is to have a value; a function is gappy or, as Frege put it, 'unsaturated'. It is easy to adapt this function/argument diagnostic for the analysis of Sätze. Take an unsaturated expression such as 'X returned Y to Z'. The result of filling the gaps with the expressions 'Britain', 'Hong Kong' and 'China' respectively is a Satz which has the value 'true'. Similarly, the expression 'X is short', when supplied with the singular term 'The Empire State Building' as argument, is a Satz which takes the value 'false'; substitute 'Dopey' for 'X' and the resulting Satz is true. This way of looking at Sätze is logically perspicuous because there is a categorical difference between singular terms – names and definite descriptions – which refer to complete, self-standing *objects* and functional expressions which stand for unsaturated or incomplete *concepts*.[19]

This theory of Frege's runs into a ticklish difficulty, as Frege himself came to realize. For consider the claim

H. The concept *horse* is a concept.

The italicization here serves as a quoting device, and Frege takes the quotation expression to be a name in apposition (Geach and Black, 1952, p. 46; Frege, 1979, p. 177). So, on his theory, both it and the singular term 'The concept *horse*' stand for *objects*, and that would mean that claim H is false since, as we noted, objects are categorically not concepts. In other words, on Frege's theory, H would be false, when quite clearly it is not: H is about as true as anything can be! At first, Frege tends to play down the difficulty, ascribing it to an 'awkwardness of language', 'a peculiar obstacle in the way of an understanding' which can be overcome by relying on a charitable reader meeting him halfway, not begrudging a 'pinch of salt' (Geach and Black, 1952, p. 54). Later, however, he comes to treat the difficulty more seriously: 'If I want to speak of a concept, language, with an almost irresistible force, compels me to use an inappropriate expression which obscures – I might almost say falsifies – the thought' (Frege, 1979, pp. 119, 177).

One way to deal with the problem – it would not be a very satisfactory way – is to abandon the Fregean machinery just because it leads us into this difficulty. This is not Wittgenstein's way. He says: 'Like Frege and Russell I construe a statement as a function of the expressions contained in it' (*T* 3.318). How, then, does Wittgenstein avoid the Frege problem? Well, consider 'Beavis, Butthead' and 'Is a dog is a leopard'. These are not proper sentences; they do not make sense in the way that sentences do. There is no way to explain *why* they don't make sense. You might attempt such an explanation: 'A singular term such as "Butthead" has to be inserted into the argument place in a function in order to produce a complete sentence.' But it is immediately clear that, far from *explaining* anything, this merely records our practice. We can *see* that a Satz like 'Dobbin is a horse' makes sense – the Satz, if you will, *shows* or manifests its sense – but there can be no *saying* why. The Satz 'Christopher is sombre' shows that the object Christopher features in what is stated. Two Sätze 'Christopher is sombre' and 'Christopher is sullen' show that the same object is mentioned in both of them (see *T* 4.1211). 'What expresses *itself* in language, *we* cannot express by means of language' (*T* 4.121) Thus, the famous thesis 'What *can* be shown, *cannot* be said' (*T* 4.1212). This is Wittgenstein's doctrine of *showing*.

'A name shows that it signifies an object, a sign for a number that it signifies a number etc.' (*T* 4.126). When you see '1 + 3 = 4' you know we are talking numbers. So a sentence like '1 is a number' is redundant, or useless. Now, Wittgenstein holds that '[i]f a sign is *useless* it is meaningless. That is the point of Occam's maxim' (*T* 3.328). So the sentence '1 is a number' is meaningless (bedeutungslos) or nonsensical (unsinnig) – see *T* 4.1272. Generalising, Wittgenstein's view is that we cannot make meaningful predications with words such as 'number', 'concept', 'object', 'fact' and 'function'. Such words represent what he calls 'formal concepts', and using them as if they were genuine predicates results only in pseudo-Sätze (*T* 4.1272).[20] So, for example, 'Christopher is an object' is a pseudo-Satz. And claim H., above, is a pseudo-Satz; it is neither true nor false. The way around Frege's difficulty is thus simple: stick to saying what is sayable.

19

The idea that there are things that can't be said but can only be shown is an intoxicating one, and it surfaces in various guises throughout the *Tractatus*.[21] Wittgenstein worked out the theory during his first extended visit to Norway in 1913-14, and he begins the dictation to Moore with the announcement that tautologies do not *say* anything: 'Logical so-called propositions *shew* [the] logical properties of language and therefore of [the] Universe, but *say* nothing' (*N*, p. 107; cf. *T* 6.12). It is clear why Wittgenstein calls tautologies 'so-called propositions'. A genuine proposition (Satz) says something, it says how things stand (*T* 4.5), so, if a tautology says nothing, it is no proposition; and the same is true of a contradiction – more about this in Chapter 4. This is a radical idea. Logic is traditionally conceived of as the repository of fundamental and highly general *truths*. So to claim, as Wittgenstein does, that all sentences in logic are tautologies (*T* 6.1) which say nothing (are empty, do not aim at truth) is iconoclastic.

The Satz 'Zlatko lives in Slovenia' says something about Zlatko, something that will be true or false, depending on where Zlatko lives, whereas the tautology 'It's not the case that Zlatko both lives in Slovenia and does not live in Slovenia' conveys no information at all; from it we learn nothing about Zlatko. A slightly more complicated tautology:

Z 'If it is the case both that Zlatko lives in Slovenia and, that, if he does so, he lives in Europe, then Zlatko lives in Europe'.

Here, again, no information.

It may seem that tautologies are entirely useless. But that is not Wittgenstein's position. He says that, while tautologies are senseless (sinnlos), they are not nonsensical (unsinnig) (*T* 4.461, 4.4611). For consider: as can be seen from the above two examples, tautologies are 'constructed' out of genuine propositions by performing logical operations, such as *negating* a proposition, *conjoining* two propositions, *disjoining* two propositions (p *or* q) and forming a *conditional* (*if* p *then* q), where for 'p' and 'q' we can substitute any propositions. The operators 'not', 'and', 'or' etc. (Wittgenstein calls them 'logical constants') do not represent anything. This is Wittgenstein's 'fundamental idea' (*T* 4.0312) – though he was by no means the first to hold it. So, contrary to what Russell once thought, we do not have to posit negative facts as being what propositions of the form 'Not-p' represent.[22] The office of the logical constants is simply to facilitate the construction of complex propositions (and of complex non-propositions – the tautologies and contradictions). Now, just as the fact that, under certain interference conditions, waves can cancel each other out (zero amplitude) tells us something interesting about the nature of waves, so the fact that certain combinations of logical operations on sense-ful (sinnvoll) propositions produce sinnlos (zero sense) tautologies shows us something about the logical properties of language (see *T* 6.121). This is particularly important for the theory of inference. For example, our second 'Zlatko' tautology Z shows that

B 'Zlatko lives in Europe.'

may be validly inferred from

A 'Zlatko lives in Slovenia, and if Zlatko lives in Slovenia then he lives in Europe.'

To see this, draw up the *truth-table* (another Wittgensteinian invention – see *T* 4.27-4.442) for an 'If ... then ...' proposition. (The truth table is just one way of writing out the complex proposition (*T* 4.442)):

p	q	
T	T	T
F	T	T
T	F	F
F	F	T

Each row indicates, on the right, the truth-value of the proposition 'If p then q' when the truth-values of the constituent propositions are as indicated in that row. We can see, from the third row, that the only circumstances under which an 'If ... then ...' proposition is false is when the antecedent 'p' is true and the consequent 'q' is false. Now, Z is an 'If ... then ...' sentence – it can be written 'If A then B'. And it is a tautology, which means that it cannot take the truth-value F[alse] no matter what the truth-values of its component propositions are. In other words (look at the third row of our truth-table) its antecedent 'A' cannot be true when its consequent 'B' is false, for otherwise Z would be false. But the criterion of a valid argument[23] (of a conclusion logically following from premises) is that its conclusion can't be false when the premises are true.[24] So the conditions for B logically following from A are just the same as the conditions for 'If A then B' being a tautology. Generalising, given any set of premises P_1, P_2, P_3, ... P_n and any conclusion C, we can tell whether those premises entail that conclusion simply by checking whether the corresponding conditional 'If (P_1 & P_2 & $_3$ & ... & $_n$) then C' is a tautology. The premises and the conclusion can be as complex as

21

you like, although the more distinct propositions there are in the argument, the more rows there are in the truth-table – for k propositions, 2^k rows.

There are two major rewards of this truth-table procedure. First, we now know how to tell, just by inspecting whether the corresponding conditional is a tautology, whether an argument is valid. 'The nature of the inference can be gathered only from the [component] propositions. They themselves are the only possible justification of the inference. "Laws of inference", which are supposed to justify inferences, as in the works of Frege and Russell, have no sense, and would be superfluous' (*T* 5.132).[25] Second, in the logic of propositions (nowadays called the propositional calculus), we do not need to show that a conclusion follows from axioms or premises by performing a proof (as did Russell and Whitehead in *Principia Mathematica* – some of their proofs are lengthy and demand ingenuity). The truth-table method is purely mechanical; it can be implemented in a simple computer program, and many such programs have now been written. The long *Tractatus* discussion on what tautologies show about inference runs from 6.1 to 6.1271. Here, and in those sections giving details of the logical system (5.2-5.5352), there are several technical criticisms of Frege and Russell.

The doctrine of what cannot be said applies also to ethics. In Wittgenstein's view, propositions can express nothing that is 'higher', so there are no propositions of ethics – ethics cannot be put into words; and the same is true of aesthetics (*T* 6.4-6.421) and of 'the mystical'. It is therefore understandable that, when giving Russell an overview of the *Tractatus*, Wittgenstein says

> The main point is the theory of what can be expressed (gesagt) by propositions – i.e. by language – (and, which comes to the same, what can be *thought*) and what can not be expressed by propositions, but only shown (gezeigt); which, I believe, is the cardinal problem of philosophy. (*LRKM*, letter dated 19.8.1919)

Once this point is grasped, more or less the whole of the rest of the *Tractatus* falls into place. The *Tractatus* enterprise consists of trying to spell out what is involved in making a statement, in saying how things are. (It is worth noting that, before adopting G.E. Moore's suggested title *Tractatus Logico-Philosophicus*, Wittgenstein had titled his work *Der Satz* (Bartley, 1973, p. 28). By thus sketching the bounds of the sayable we see, for free, what is unsayable (*T* 4.113-4.115), and it turns out that much of philosophy falls into that category. Small wonder, then, that the *Tractatus* had so instant an appeal for the logical positivists of the 1920s and 30s, who wanted to show that ethics, metaphysics and religious discourse were all so much mumbo-jumbo.[26]

Factual statements of ordinary language may be complex, either overtly or covertly. Consider, for example, 'The car is on top of the man and either nobody saw the accident or, if they did, then they are not coming forward as witnesses.' This is overtly complex in that it consists of several simpler sentences joined together with the logical constants 'and', 'or' and 'if ... then ...'. But, if we accept Russell's Theory of Definite Descriptions, it is covertly complex too, since the first conjunct 'The car is on top of the man' contains a definite description and, as we saw with the example of 'The father of Charles II was executed', such sentences, on analysis, turn out to be highly complex. Wittgenstein holds that an ordinary statement has a *complete* and *unique* analysis, the analysans containing only simple or *elementary* Sätze that can be analysed no further (*T* 5, 3.25, 3.26). Such elementary Sätze, in a way to be explained in Chapter 2, *picture* reality in virtue of having a structure in common with what they picture (*T* 2.1-2.225). So if 'Angus is on top of Brett' were an elementary statement (it's not, but never mind) it would correspond to a (possible) elementary state of affairs (Sachverhalt), that of Angus being on top of Brett.

When we acquire beliefs about the world, our beliefs are expressed not as strings of names or descriptions, e.g. 'Angus, the man Angus loves' but as *statements*. We don't have a belief 'Angus' (see *T* 3.142). That is why the (supposedly) elementary belief 'Angus is on top of Brett' must picture not an object or string of objects, but an elementary state of affairs (an 'atomic fact', in the Ogden translation). Hence the ontological claim, right at the beginning of the *Tractatus*, 'The world is the totality of facts, not of things' (*T* 1.1).[27]

An elementary Satz employs Names (I use a capital 'N' since these Wittgensteinian Names are not like ordinary proper names) but it is not, as we mentioned, just a string of Names, a mere medley of words, but Names standing in a determinate relation to one another (*T* 3.14, 3.141). Wittgenstein calls the perceptible sign of a Satz (the physical entity, be it written marks or spoken sounds) the 'propositional sign' (*T* 3.1-3.12). He then explains how Names-in-determinate-relations can be used to say something, to express a sense:

The essence of a propositional sign is very clearly seen if we imagine one composed of spatial objects (such as tables, chairs and books) instead of written signs.

Then the spatial arrangement of these things will express the sense of the proposition. (*T* 3.1431)

23

Clear and Queer Thinking

We often do this sort of thing at the dinner table, using salt cellars, cutlery etc. to recreate a real- or possible-world situation. There we use objects to stand for objects, whereas in an elementary Satz it is Names that stand for Objects (note the capital 'O'). In contrast to Frege and Russell, although a Satz is a function of the expressions contained in it, for Wittgenstein, a logically perspicuous propositional sign need not contain any words for functions. In our pretend elementary Satz 'Angus is on top of Brett', the expression 'is on top of' is not a symbol, it doesn't stand for any Object; what symbolises is *that* the expression 'is on top of' is between the names 'Angus' and 'Brett' (*N*, p. 108; *T* 3.1432).²⁸ So, in principle, we could dispense with the function words and simply place the names 'Angus' and 'Brett' in a particular relation to each other. If (following *T* 3.1431) we used a table and a chair to depict the same situation, we might place the chair on top of the table – we wouldn't need some extra item, an 'on top of'.²⁹

So, in summary, a *bona fide* Satz has sense, that is, it pictures some possible situation in the world (*T* 4.031) and is true if reality is as the Satz depicts it to be, false otherwise (*T* 2.21-2.225). Sätze can be analysed until we reach the level of elementary Sätze, and an elementary Satz contains only simple signs called Names (*T* 3.201, 3.202) articulated in a definite way. In a Satz (and only in a Satz) these Names stand for Objects (*T* 3.22, 3.3). Elementary states of affairs consist of configurations of Objects, that is, Objects linked together in a determinate way (*T* 2.0272-2.032) and the configuration of objects corresponds to the configuration of Names in the propositional sign (*T* 3.21). It is in virtue of this structural similarity, this logico-pictorial form, that we can use propositional signs to depict states of affairs (*T* 2.16-2.171; 2.18-2.203).

I have been rather enigmatic about the nature of Names and Objects. Wittgenstein gives no examples of either, and indicates that this is not something that 'we' can do (*N* entry 17.6.15, p. 62), though he does not say who 'we' are, and who, if anyone, can do it. It is an interpreter's nightmare trying to make sense of the conflicting indications in the texts. One might think, for example, that Wittgensteinian Names stand for particular, discrete entities. But Wittgenstein indicates that relations and properties are also Objects (*N*, p. 61). Again, the text lends support to the view that Objects are real, objective, unchanging entities that make up the substance of the world (*T* 2.021). Yet, if the world is *my* world (*T* 5.62) then one might think that its constituent Objects are subjective or private entities, such as sense-data. Or perhaps they are somehow neutral between the private and the public, between the 'inner' and the 'outer' (*DL*, p. 109; see Cook, 1994, p. 15). There are

24

various other interpretations that have been attempted, but I see no way of resolving the matter. On the available evidence, the question of what exactly Wittgenstein took Names and Objects to be is, I should say, undecidable.

Rejection of all that

The first criticism one could make of the *Tractatus* is that *even by its own lights* it fails. For, as we have seen, Wittgenstein argues that 'statements' involving formal concepts like 'function', 'concept', 'number' are, strictly speaking nonsense; they are non-statements, pseudo-Sätze. Yet the *Tractatus* is full of such words, and full of metaphysical pronouncements about language and the world when, according to the *Tractatus*, all that stuff is unsayable. It is only the statements of natural science that are sayable (*T* 6.53). 'The totality of true statements is the whole of natural science' (*T* 4.11) and '[p]hilosophy is not one of the natural sciences' (*T* 4.111). Wittgenstein tries to get out of this difficulty by claiming that there really are no 'philosophical statements', since philosophy is not a body of doctrine, but an activity consisting of elucidation and clarification (*T* 4.112). Yet it is hard to see how elucidation or clarification can be achieved *without saying anything*! At the end of the book he comes clean, or cleanish: he acknowledges that his own propositions are nonsensical, but still wants to say that they have some use.

> My propositions serve as elucidations in the following way: anyone who understands me eventually recognizes them as nonsensical, when he has used them – as steps – to climb up beyond them. (He must, so to speak, throw away the ladder after he has climbed up it.)
> He must transcend these propositions, and then he will see the world aright. (*T* 6.54)

It's a nice simile (which comes from Schopenhauer), but the idea is really just pie in the sky. We should be no more ready to accept it than to grant Frege the 'pinch of salt' he requests. Also, there are technical problems with the *Tractatus* which, by 1929, Wittgenstein had come to recognise. For example, tautologies and contradictions are said to arise from particular patterns of logical operation on Sätze. To take the simplest case, if we get any Satz, negate it, then conjoin that with the original unnegated Satz, we produce a contradiction: 'p & not-p'. Here 'p' can be any proposition you like; whatever the proposition, whatever

25

its sense, a contradiction is produced by this combination of operations. The criterion for contradictoriness or tautologousness is purely syntactical – the *senses* of the Sätze being operated on is irrelevant. By contrast, the single operation '&' produces neither tautology nor contradiction: if 'p' and 'q' are *bona fide* Sätze, then so is 'p & q'. But now consider the two Sätze 'Spot S at position X at time t is red' and 'Spot S at position X at time t is blue'. These cannot be meaningfully conjoined, or, at least, the conjunction says as little as 'She is 1.7 m tall and she is not'; it is impossible for a given spot to be both red and blue simultaneously. And the reason, this time, has to do with the *senses* of the Sätze, particularly with the 'inner connection' between 'red' and 'blue'. This is something not accommodated within the *Tractatus* theory. 'What was wrong with my conception', Wittgenstein says, 'was that I believed that the syntax of logical constants could be laid down without paying attention to the inner connection of Sätze. That is not how things actually are. I cannot, for example, say that red and blue are simultaneously at one and the same point' (*WVC*, p. 74).

There are several other defects and inconsistencies in the *Tractatus* theory. These need not detain us. For, after fretting over such details in his 'transitional' period, Wittgenstein subsequently came to see that his whole early approach was wrong. His solutions, in the *Tractatus*, to the problems posed by Frege and Russell, whatever their fascination and novelty, adopt the framework within which those problems themselves were posed. That is to say, it is a work of logical atomism, it accepts that the solutions to philosophical problems are to be had through logical analysis, adopts Frege's function/argument apparatus and operates with the tools of formal logic. This tradition is full of theories – the theory of sense and reference, the theory of definite descriptions, the theory of judgment etc. – so *in that tradition* a theory is required to solve its outstanding problems, and Wittgenstein accordingly constructs such theories, including a theory about the logical structure of the world, a theory of number and the picture theory of meaning. In his late writings he jettisons that tradition.

The *Philosophical Investigations*, published two years after Wittgenstein's death, is not an easy read. First, the style. There are plenty of short arguments, but no sustained stretch of argument of the kind we are used to in philosophical works. Wittgenstein seems to meander or, perhaps more charitably, to come at his problems again and again from different angles, although his initial ambition had been that 'the thoughts should proceed from one subject to another in a natural order and without breaks' (*PI*, p. vii). Second, the reasoning is frequently dialectical. Much of the text consists of questions rather than assertions, and Wittgenstein often addresses an imaginary interlocutor (sometimes it's not quite clear who is who). Third, Wittgenstein regularly fails to state the point of what he is saying and the reader has to work hard to discern the thrust of his argument. Fourth, it has been claimed by von Wright that Wittgenstein's later work does not belong in any philosophical tradition. This has been disputed (Garver, 1994), yet it does seem true that it is difficult to view much of Wittgenstein's later writing as a direct response to any well-established debates in philosophy, and careful work is needed to establish the impact of his contribution on traditional philosophical concerns.

In the Preface to the *Philosophical Investigations*, Wittgenstein writes

> Four years ago I had occasion to re-read my first book (the *Tractatus Logico-Philosophicus*) and to explain its ideas to someone. It suddenly seemed to me that I should publish those old thoughts and the new ones together: that the latter could be seen in the right light only by contrast with and against the background of my old way of thinking. (*PI*, p. viii)

He mentioned to Basil Reeve that he wanted to publish a refutation (Monk, 1990, p. 457). It is not some old thoughts, but his whole 'old way of thinking' that he wants to refute. On reflection, this 'way of thinking' contains some highly questionable presuppositions. In his early writings and through his transitional period, Wittgenstein had a certain conception of the nature of language. He says 'Language is a calculus. Thinking is playing the game, using the calculus …. Thought is the actual use of the linguistic calculus' (*DL*, p. 117). It is intensely irritating to observe commentator after commentator talking about the 'calculus conception of language' without bothering to make clear, either to themselves or to the reader, what they are talking about. Obviously the word 'calculus', in this context, does not refer to a branch of mathematics but has something to do with calculating, yet it is by no means obvious how speaking a language can be construed as performing a calculation (other than for generating syntactically correct sentences – but Wittgenstein is not talking about syntax). So what could a 'calculus conception of language' possibly be? What Wittgenstein calls a calculus is 'an abacus, a calculator, a calculating machine; it works by means of strokes, numerals etc.' (*WVC*, p. 106). 'In a calculus, we always use signs, though the calculus is quite independent of the particular scratches or other signs we use …. A calculus is never in itself right or wrong, but it may be rightly or wrongly used' (*DL*, p. 58). So a calculus is a device for manipulating signs in a mechanical way, i.e. in accordance with a set of rules. It is worth quoting in full the section of the *Philosophical Investigations* in which this notion of a calculus first makes an appearance:

> F.P. Ramsey once emphasized in conversation with me that logic was a 'normative science'. I do not know exactly what he had in mind, but it was doubtless closely related to what only dawned on me later: namely, that in philosophy we often *compare* the use of words with games and calculi which have fixed rules, but cannot say that someone who is using language *must* be playing such a game. – But if you say that our languages only *approximate* to such calculi you are standing on the very brink of a misunderstanding. For then it may look as if what we were talking about were an *ideal* language. As if our logic were, so to speak, a logic for a vacuum. – Whereas logic does not treat of language – or of thought – in the sense in which a natural science treats of a natural phenomenon, and the most that can be said is that we *construct* ideal languages. But here the word 'ideal' is liable to mislead, for it sounds as if these languages were better, more perfect, than our everyday language; and as if it took the logician to shew people at last what a proper sentence looked like.
>
> All this, however, can appear in the right light when one has attained greater clarity about the concepts of understanding, meaning, and thinking. For it will then also become clear what can lead us (and did lead me) to think that if anyone utters a sentence and *means* or *understands* it he is operating a calculus according to definite rules.[30]

From where did we get this idea that language is logically perspicuous, the manipulation of signs ('pieces' with fixed meaning) according to fixed rules? The 'crystalline purity of logic' was something we (i.e., he) demanded; it was not the result of any investigation we conducted (see *PI* §107); and the demand was unfounded. Frege believed that the logical analysis of statements gave us a glimpse into the realm of thought. But thoughts, in his sense, are curious atemporal mind-independent creatures. If one doesn't accept this Platonistic conception, the alternative seems to be that the analysis of statements reveals the structure of our concrete thinking. Yet is it really believable that, underlying our prosaic utterances are hugely complex combinations of elementary thoughts of which the ordinary thinker has no knowledge? And what about the idea that our statements, at least in their fully analysed form, consist just of names? Do numerals name objects ... what about prepositions. ...? Are these parts of speech dispensable; do they vanish in the analysis? Can they be reduced to names? Right at the beginning of *Philosophical Investigations*, this latter idea comes under attack.[31]

In the *Tractatus*, Wittgenstein had followed Frege and Russell in accepting the idea that enlightenment was to be gained from the logical analysis of language: he had gone so far as to claim that this method was revealing of the very structure of the world. But is it really the case, for example, that language can be 'analysed' in the manner of a chemical analysis? A bread roll can be broken into parts, but a knight's move in chess can't (*PG*, Appendix IV). Who is to say that language is like a bread roll in this respect? Certainly, a sentence – a group of words – can be split up in various ways, but it was one of Wittgenstein's great insights (which we shall discuss further in the next chapter) that linguistic transactions occur through the *uses* of sentences. A sentence can be used, for example, to raise a question, to issue and order.... Is it the case that a question or an order can be split up, analysed, in any revealing way? At *PI* §60, Wittgenstein says 'True, the broom is taken to pieces when one separates broomstick and brush; but does it follow that the order to bring the broom also consists of corresponding parts?' In other words, suppose that a sentence is used to give an order: can that order be analysed into component parts? Wittgenstein's answer is 'No'.

First, there is no saying what the simple parts consist of. You might be inclined to say that the simpler parts are the smaller ones. But that will not do. The net effect of two almost equal and opposite large forces (the *composition* of these forces, calculated via the 'parallelogram of forces') is a comparatively smaller force – in other words, the small net force is *analysed* into two *large* components. Again, a line can be divided (*analysed*) into two parts, but the parts may be *larger* than the original line if the dividing point lies beyond either end of the line (a notion used, for example, in the proof of Menelaus' Theorem). (See *PI* §48, where Wittgenstein says all this more briefly.) Second, certain wholes cannot be analysed into their parts because the whole is greater than the sum of its parts: the 'analysis' of the French Tricolor into three separated monochrome strips destroys the character of the flag; it is the juxtaposition, the particular arrangement of those strips that gives the flag its special character (*PI* §64). So the idea that language can be analysed – absolutely central to the Frege-Russell-*Tractatus* project – is scrutinized and abandoned.

Another Tractarian requirement (again, following Frege) is that sense be determinate, that there be no vagueness in statements (*T*

29

3.23). In his later writings, Wittgenstein perceives that this was just another stipulation without warrant. A 1936 manuscript records his *Tractatus* position and his subsequent rejection of it:

> I had of course formerly struggled against the idea that there isn't a perfect order in logic. 'Every sentence has a *precise* sense'; 'In logic there can't be unclarity, for otherwise there would be no clarity (and thus also no unclarity)': 'A logically unclear sentence is (would be) one which has no precise sense, thus *no* sense' – Here always lurked the idea of the ethereal sense (sense of a proposition), of that which one *meant, of mental processes* [dessen was man *meint, des geistigen Prozesses*]. (MS 152, p. 93)

These shadowy inner processes became a prime target of criticism in the late period writings. Does a speaker who says 'Stand roughly there' (see *PI* §71) or 'I want to buy some red trousers' really have something definite in mind? He may, if, for example, there is a particular pair of trousers he has long coveted; but he may just be on the lookout for any red or reddish trousers to complement his black shirt.

Is it even the philosopher's business to construct theories and give explanations? Already, at the end of the *Tractatus*, there is a preview of Wittgenstein's later answer – 'No'. He says there that the correct method in philosophy is to demonstrate to someone who wanted to say something metaphysical that he had failed to give a meaning to some of the expressions he had used (see *T* 6.53).[32] In the 'Big Typescript' of 1933, he writes:

> Unrest in philosophy comes from philosophers looking at, seeing, philosophy all wrong ... (Instead of turbulent conjectures and explanations, we want to give quiet demonstrations//statements//of linguistic facts//about linguistic facts//.)//we want the quiet noting of linguistic facts.// (TS 213, §92; also *Z* §447)

A long section of the *Philosophical Investigations* (§§89-133) is devoted to advocating Wittgenstein's new approach. Language bewitches us, leading us into deep confusions; the knots in our thinking arise from misappropriating language and the task of philosophy is to help untie these. He says 'We must do away with all *explanation*, and description alone must take its place' (*PI* §109). That proposition continues:

> And this description gets its light, that is to say its purpose, from the philosophical problems. These are, of course, not empirical

problems; they are solved, rather, by looking into the workings of our language, and that in such a way as to make us recognize those workings: *in despite of* an urge to misunderstand them. The problems are solved, not by giving new information, but by arranging what we have always known. Philosophy is a battle against the bewitchment of our intelligence by means of language.

This is probably the definitive, canonical statement of Wittgenstein's methodology. It is both a diagnosis of how we become trapped and a prescription for releasing ourselves from the fly-bottle (*PI* §309).

Like many of the remarks in this part of the *Philosophical Investigations*, §109 is beautifully written, and is almost spell-binding. But we should should not let ourselves be seduced, and should coldly ask whether Wittgenstein really has located the source of our philosophical ills. A critic might say 'Language is the product of evolution; evolution would not deliver us a system of communication that is inefficient, that leads us astray.' This criticism is wide of the mark. Wittgenstein himself insists that, for the ordinary purposes of communication, every sentence in our language 'is in order as it is' (*PI* §98; see also *BB* p. 28, *T* 5.5563). Similarly our bodies are very well adapted to the ordinary demands of the environment; evolution has seen to that. But some humans feel impelled to subject their bodies to extraordinary examinations – to climbing mountains, surviving in the freezing cold, running 26 miles, 385 yards – some crazy people even jump off cliffs wildly flapping their arms. Under such circumstances, bodies frequently fail, for they are asked to do what they are not equipped for doing, and the results are calamitous. This is physical self-abuse. Philosophy is intellectual self-abuse. We take what is perfectly serviceable – our language – and subject it to uses for which it was never intended. And end up with crazy conclusions: 'When we do philosophy we are like savages, primitive people, who hear the expressions of civilized men, put a false interpretation on them, and then draw the queerest conclusions from it' (*PI* §194). The results of *his* style of philosophy, Wittgenstein claims, 'are the uncovering of one or another piece of plain nonsense and of bumps that the understanding has got by running its head up against the limits of language. These bumps make us see the value of the discovery' (*PI* §119).

Wittgenstein describes his own investigation as a 'grammatical' one. He says: 'Such an investigation sheds light on our problem by clearing misunderstandings away. Misunderstandings concerning the use of words, caused, among other things, by certain analogies between the forms of expression in different regions of language' (*PI* §90). He talks of 'grammatical illusions' (*PI* §110). Obviously, by 'grammar', he does not mean syntax, or school grammar (*DL*, pp. 97-8). The 'grammatical illusions' he is talking about are conceptual confusions. He writes:

> The problems arising through a misinterpretation of our forms of language have the character of *depth*. They are deep disquietudes; their roots are as deep in us as the forms of our language and their significance is as great as the importance of our language.— Let us ask ourselves: why do we feel a grammatical joke to be *deep*? (And that is what the depth of philosophy is.) (*PI* §111)

It may seem weird that someone (especially Wittgenstein) should say that philosophy has the depth of a joke, but remember that we are talking about a *grammatical* joke, in the sense of 'grammar' I just mentioned. Perhaps this sense can be further explained by looking at a real-life example of a grammatical joke: One of my students who is Chinese and for whom English is a second language that she speaks reasonably well, went to pursue further studies at the University of Hawaii. She found the first few weeks rather tough and at one point in a lecture she put up her hand and said to the instructor, 'Please would you speak a bit slower.' He replied, 'No, you listen a bit faster.' The instructor was clearly a real swine, but the joke is a good one. It illustrates the 'grammatical' difference between 'speak' and 'listen', and hence indicates something interesting about the difference between the activities of speaking and listening. We can listen hard, but not fast. An example that Wittgenstein gives: 'Grammar allows us to talk of a higher degree of sweetness, but not of a higher degree of identity' (*DL* p. 49). To say of identical triplets Anita, Belle and Carmen that Anita is more identical to Belle than she is to Carmen would be a joke (sort of).

As 'grammatical' investigations go, the one just conducted on 'speaking' and 'listening' is, of course, an abundantly trivial example not representative of the careful explorations found in *Philosophical Investigations*. By understanding grammar, understanding the rôles of different words, we resolve philosophical paradoxes, and may reach substantive conclusions – for example that thinking is not generally an activity (see Chapter 3), that *understanding* itself is not a mental state (*PI* §182, 150 and the unnumbered text on *PI*, p. 59).[33] So, if the latter is right, a psychologist will get nowhere in trying to explain the *phenomenon* of understanding if he assumes, from the start, that he is dealing with mental states. Similarly, if Wittgenstein is right, we will get nowhere in trying to explain the phenomenon of reading, if we simply assume that, when reading, we feel the influence of the letters on us (*PI* §§168-70) We discover that this assumption is mistaken not by staring at the phrase 'feel the influence' – that is not what a 'grammatical' investigation is – but by considering circumstances under which we would, or would not use the phrase, comparing the experience of reading some sentences in a familiar language and looking at arbitrary doodles and flourishes, of reading ordinary print and words which are printed in capital letters, of reading English right to left instead of left to right.

It is sometimes said that Wittgenstein became an anti-scientific philosopher, because he investigated only the language used for talking about phenomena, rather than dealing with the phenomena themselves. This charge is unfair; what is true is that he was insistent that empirical enquiry be undertaken by those qualified to do it, and that philosophers should not play at being scientists. Suppose that we are interested in some real phenomena such as hope or grief. The first thing to note is that hope and grief could not be other than what we are talking about when we speak of people hoping or suffering from grief. And when we talk about hope and grief – when we use the words 'hope', 'grief' and their various morphological paradigms – what do we mean by them? That can only be determined by observing how such words are used. For example, although we can say: 'For a second, he felt a violent pain', we don't say 'For a second he felt deep grief' (*PI*, p. 174). Such facts are so obvious that it is easy to overlook them. We need to be reminded of them if we are, for example, about to succumb to the temptation to contrive a theory lumping pain and grief together as sensations. That's where philosophy comes in – assembling reminders (*PI* §§89, 127, 253). Philosophical investigation of hoping, believing and so on does not consist of examining underlying structures (that is someone else's business – at least in the case of those phenomena where it is legitimate business) but of helping to get a clear view of the concepts of *hope, belief* etc. as these are revealed in our unpolluted ways of speaking.

In his later, post-transitional period, represented quintessentially by *Philosophical Investigations* Part I, Wittgenstein seeks not to provide different answers to those questions which animated the *Tractatus*, but to undermine the tradition which nourished them. His very fundamental move is to show that, if it is reasonable to jettison the preconceptions on which the old tradition was founded – such preconceptions as that all words stand for things or that the function of language is to describe the world (and we can do that by looking at how words are actually used rather than engaging in fantasies inspired by unfounded visions of the workings of language as crystalline pure and simple) – then the whole house of cards collapses and the only task remaining for us is to take measures to avoid the temptation to build another one. These measures would involve returning the cards to the deck, where they can be used in the ordinary way, for playing honest games, rather than for making outlandish unstable constructions.

Commentators tend to have enormous difficulty in refraining from foisting theories on Wittgenstein despite his explicit disavowal of philosophical theorizing in his later writings.[34] Warren Goldfarb, rightly, it seems to me, sees Wittgenstein as trying to talk us (and himself) back from the precipice, just as we are about to make the fatal plunge into the abyss of theorizing. He writes

[Wittgenstein] wants to locate a stage that we might call pre-philosophical: a juncture at which one begins the search for a philosophical theory of this or that, not the place at which one becomes a Fregean, rather than a Russellian (or a Gricean or ...). In short, Wittgenstein is trying to depict the philosopher on his way into philosophy. At stake is some notion that significant moves are made at the moment when the idea of a *general account* is broached. (Goldfarb, 1983)

As soon as we ask for a general account, some conception or theory, we are in trouble. I shall not make the mistake of trying to give a general account of what is wrong, in general, with general accounts. As we proceed, we shall see, in particular cases, why Wittgenstein is more interested in showing us differences than in contriving generalizations.

The *Tractatus* is a general account of language *par excellence*. But that Wittgenstein came to reject that account does not mean that we should neglect it. Many ideas in the book, e.g., that statements must represent how things are in the world, that they have, or can be given a precise sense, that thoughts must have a language-like structure, still prove attractive to modern thinkers.[35] Those ideas and their consequences need to be understood if we are to be in a position properly to assess whether they can withstand, or must succumb, to the sort of pressure that Wittgenstein exerted on them in his later writings.

2

Meaning

The problem

There are computer programs for generating syntactically correct sentences of a language. Set such a program running and it will continue to spew out sentences until you shut it down. But the computer, when running that program, does not *mean* anything by what it says; it doesn't understand its own verbal outpourings. Neither does a parrot which has been trained to utter sentences under appropriate circumstances. By contrast, when I say something to a person, that person will typically understand what I mean. So humans have these remarkable twin abilities – to mean and to understand – which set us apart from machines and from all (or most) animals. The problem of meaning is to say what we have got that they have not. We speak; the computer spews. What is the difference between the speaking and the spewing?

This is, perhaps, an idiosyncratic way of setting out the problem, but I have wanted to frame it in broad terms and to leave open the question of whether the solution is to be found in philosophy or linguistics or psychology or brain science or in something else or by several of these disciplines in harness.

The early picture

What must language be that it be the vehicle of communication between humans? Can we identify *a priori* the conditions presupposed by our ability to make statements? What is the relation between language and reality? How can a statement – a bunch of words strung together – convey information about the world? The *Tractatus* answer to the last of these questions is easy to state: Language *pictures* the world; and the answers to the other questions follow from that. This picturing idea first occurred to Wittgenstein on 29 September 1914 while he was on active duty in the First World War. It was inspired by his reading a magazine report of a lawsuit in Paris concerning a car accident, where the aftermath was 'represented by means of dolls etc.' (*N*, p. 7). He was suddenly struck with the thought that, like a model, a statement can depict a situation. How? In the *Notebooks 1914-16* he sketches an answer which is probably clearer than the *Tractatus* account:

> Let us think of hieroglyphic writing in which each word is a representation of what it stands for. Let us think also of the fact that *actual* pictures of situations can be *right* and *wrong*.

> If the right-hand figure in this picture represents the man A, and the left-hand one stands for the man B, then the whole might assert, e.g.: 'A is fencing with B'. The statement in picture-writing can be true and false. It has a sense independent of its truth or falsehood ... It can be said that, while we are not certain of being able to turn all situations into pictures on paper, still we are certain that we can portray all *logical* properties of situations in a two-dimensional script.

If dolls and toy cars are not available for modelling an accident in which, as a witness reported it, a car landed up on top of a man, a pen-and-ink drawing could be used:

2. Meaning

Note that this is a picture of a *possible* situation; if the witness were lying, or if he misremembered, the picture would be false; only if the situation was as depicted is the picture true.

In the absence of an artist, another way of depicting the situation would be to use the *word* 'car' instead of the picture of a car, the word 'man' instead of the picture man. In so doing, we still succeed in capturing the essential features (the 'logical properties' as Wittgenstein calls them) of the situation. The word-sketch might look like this:

man
car

I have (perversely) put the word 'man' on top of the word 'car', although the situation being depicted is one in which the car is on top of the man. The point is that, so long as there is a fixed convention for representing relations between objects in the situation by means of a relation between the words for those objects (e.g. one name written above another represents that the object named by the lower name is on top of the other named object), then the sense of the picture will be understood. So, for example, if we want to represent the situation 'the man bought the car', then we might adopt the convention of placing the name of the thing bought at a distance of 3 cm and at an angle of 79° from the name of the buyer. In other words, this kind of picture-portrayal does not restrict us to depicting only those situations in which the relations between the objects depicted are purely spatial.

A situation that we want to describe can be 'translated' into a word-picture, just as we can construct music from a score. Though score and sound are physically different, they are structurally (or 'logically') similar:

A gramophone record, the musical idea, the written notes, and the sound-waves, all stand to one another in the same internal relation of depicting that holds between language and the world.

They are all constructed according to a common logical pattern.

(Like the two youths in the fairy-tale, their two horses, and their lilies. They are all in a certain sense one.) (*T* 4.014)

There is a translation key, a 'rule' for obtaining the symphony from the score, and one for deriving the symphony from the groove on the gramophone record or from the magnetic trace on the tape. The rule, in each case, is a law of projection (see *T* 4.0141). Similarly, when we depict a situation, either verbally or in thought, we project the situation (*T*

3.11-3.13); we model reality (*T* 2.12). The things in the situation are correlated with elements in the picture (*T* 2.13, 2.1514, 2.1515), the latter represent the former (*T* 2.131). 'The fact that the elements of a picture are related to one another in a determinate way represents that things are related to one another in the same way' (*T* 2.15). A picture represents its sense (*T* 2.221), that is to say it represents a possible situation (*T* 2.202).

As we saw, in the previous chapter, in a perspicuous notation as envisaged in the *Tractatus*, a situation can be pictured in language just by employing Names in configurations which are conventionally related to the configuration of the Objects in the situation. Predicates and relational expressions are not really needed.[1] For practical purposes, though, in the sentences of everyday language, it is typographically convenient to have a linear script rather than a two-dimensional juxtaposition of names. (And a non-linear language would be hell to speak.) So we employ predicates and relational expressions as auxiliary devices, for converting a two-dimensional relation of names into a linear script. It's ingenious: If we want to say that Angus loves Brett, then we could position the names 'Angus' and 'Brett' in that spatial relationship which, according to the conventions of this two-dimensional written language corresponds to the relation of love. But, very much more neatly and simply, we could place the relational expression 'loves' between the words 'Angus' and 'Brett' in a linear string, thus creating a new, unique one-dimensional relationship: 'Brett' is to the right of the sign 'love' to which 'Angus' is to the left. We can use this one-dimensional configuration to say that Angus loves Brett. So, where 'a' and 'b' are any names, and 'R' is a relational expression,

> Instead of, 'The complex sign "*aRb*" says that *a* stands to *b* in the relation R', we ought to put 'That "*a*" stands to "*b*" in a certain relation says *that aRb*'. (*T* 3.1432)[2]

The predicates and relational expressions serve no function other than to bring it about that the Names in the sentence are related in particular ways to one another. It would be easy to read this as advocating a nominalistic ontology which countenanced no relations or properties, in opposition to the view that Wittgenstein took in his *Notebooks 1914-16* (*N*, p. 61).

2. Meaning

The picture abandoned

The rationale behind the picture theory is that, since we use language to talk about the world, language must be connected to the world in some particularly intimate way, that language must represent reality. Indeed, at one point, Wittgenstein says that a picture 'reaches right out' to reality (T 2.1511), the elements of the picture acting as 'feelers' (T 2.1515). Now, this is a charming metaphor, but we shouldn't be fooled into thinking that it actually helps us to understand how language works, particularly when we remember that these feelers are those Wittgensteinian Names to which (in the *Tractatus* fairytale) ordinary people, though competent speakers, have no access. When reporting an incident to you, such as some trouble down at the mill, it is surely implausible to suppose (at least, when we remove the blinkers of theory) that there is some significant similarity, structural or otherwise, between the *sentence* 'There was some trouble down at t'mill' and the trouble.

The idea that language is connected to the world goes hand in hand with the *Tractatus* view that a logically perspicuous language consists exclusively of Names. For ordinary proper names can be regarded as labels that are fixed to objects by a process of ostensive definition. These labels can then be used as representatives – in a 'Lucky Draw', one does not need to put people into an urn; it is possible to use their names instead. At T 3.221, Wittgenstein says that Names are representatives of Objects. However, once the superstitious notion that ordinary statements can be analysed into these extraordinary minutiae (the Names) loses its stranglehold, a more realistic assessment of language comes into view. First, names no longer seem to be the dominant or most prominent features of speech. Second, correlatively, defining ostensively comes to be seen as just one among the many ways in which we engage linguistically with the world. Third, stating – saying how things stand (T 4.5) – which involves picking out items by means of their names and characterising them in some way, no longer appears to be the primary or paradigm function of language; there are many more acts that one can perform with words. Fourth, speakers do not typically provide mechanical translations of situations into descriptions of those situations (the 'calculus conception', discussed in the previous chapter); rather, they engage in a variety of activities in which the use of language plays an integral part. These criticisms of Wittgenstein's old way of thinking occupy the early sections of *Philosophical Investigations*.

In two drafts of the *Philosophical Investigations*, Wittgenstein began with a discussion of *meaning* and *understanding*. But, in the final version, he begins with a quotation from the *Confessions*, where St. Augustine is reminiscing about how he learned to talk. (Whether St. Augustine or anyone can truly claim to *recall* learning their mother tongue is difficult to say.) A probable reason why Wittgenstein ended up starting off with a sketch of the 'Augustinian' picture of language is that he wanted to highlight, right from the outset, a whole constellation of views enshrining a conception of language that he wished to undermine. St. Augustine is a convenient scapegoat. The misconception of language that Wittgenstein is attacking bears little relation to any theory that St. Augustine ever defended. If there is one theory which embodies most of the characteristics he here mentions, it is his own *Tractatus* theory. Presumably Wittgenstein is anxious to show that, in making those early errors, he was in good company.[3] The idea of using St. Augustine as a foil occurred to him quite early on. In MS 111 ('Bemerkungen zur Philosophie') dating from early August 1931, he inserts the note 'Augustine on the learning of language'.

Here is St. Augustine:

When they (my elders) named some object, and accordingly moved towards something, I saw this and I grasped that the thing was called by the sound they uttered when they meant to point it out. Their intention was shown by their bodily movements, as it were the natural language of all peoples: the expression of the face, the play of the eyes, the movement of other parts of the body, and the tone of voice which expresses our state of mind in seeking, having, rejecting or avoiding something. Thus, as I heard words repeatedly used in their proper places in various sentences, I gradually learnt to understand what objects they signified; and after I had trained my mouth to form these signs, I used them to express my own desires. (St. Augustine, *Confessions*, trans H. Chadwick, 1991, p. 10)

Wittgenstein comments: 'These words, it seems to me, give us a particular picture of the essence of human language. It is this: the individual words in language name objects – sentences are combinations of such names. In this picture of language we find the roots of the following idea: Every word has a meaning. This meaning is correlated with the word. It is the object for which the word stands' (*PI* §1).

The view that Wittgenstein is criticizing is that every word on its own (i.e., not in context, not in the mouth of a speaker) has a meaning or signification (Bedeutung) and that this meaning is an object for which the word stands.[4] In the Cambridge lectures he gave soon after his return to philosophy, he says: 'We confuse the meaning of a word and the bearer of a name' (*DL*, p. 62, Easter 1931). It is obviously true that words such as 'if ', 'nothing', 'superfluous' don't stand for any objects, but Wittgenstein says that, even in the case of proper names, we should not confuse their meanings and what they stand for. The point is elaborated in *PI* §§40-2: 'If Mr. N.N. dies, one says that the bearer of the name dies, not that the meaning [Bedeutung] dies' (*PI* §40). We can sometimes *explain* the meaning of a name by pointing to its bearer (*PI* §43), but, of course, that is a far cry from saying that the meaning of a name *is* its bearer. Even though some words can be used to stand for objects, standing for objects is not *typical* of what words are used for, but is what occurs only in a 'narrowly circumscribed region' of language (*PI* §3). Immediately after the above quoted remarks from §1, Wittgenstein writes:

Augustine does not speak of there being any difference between kinds of word. If you describe the learning of language in this way you are, I believe, thinking primarily of nouns like 'table', 'chair', 'bread', and of people's names, and only secondarily of the names of certain actions and properties; and of the remaining kinds of word as something that will take care of itself. (*PI* §1)

Words, like tools, are various in their functions but this variety of function is not reflected in the appearance of words when spoken or in script or in print; likewise, the handles in the cabin of a locomotive look rather similar but are used in many different ways and for very different purposes, such as for braking, for blowing a whistle, for shutting a valve (see *PI* §§11, 12). Just as it would be stupid to try to assimilate the various functions of tools ('They all modify something.' Well, a saw and a hammer might, but what about a ruler, a nail, a pot of glue? – see *PI* §14) so it is equally pointless to try to assimilate the functions of words (*PI* §10). If we say 'Every word in a language signifies something' then, as Wittgenstein puts it, 'we have so far said *nothing whatever*' (*PI* §13) (unless we're just trying to say, for example, that 'brillig', 'slithey', 'pilk' etc. are not words).

In order to illustrate the different sorts of function that different sorts of words play, Wittgenstein uses the pleasant example of someone (a child, perhaps) being sent to the grocer's shop with a slip of paper on which is written 'Five red apples'. After being presented with this slip, the shopkeeper (a figure of a more leisurely bygone age) goes through a variety of doddery procedures in order to comply with the request. On seeing the word 'apples', he opens a drawer marked 'apples'. For 'red', he looks up that word in a chart which contains samples of colours opposite their names. Finally, for 'five', he says the series of numbers (which he knows by heart) up to the word 'five' and, for each number, he takes an apple out of a drawer. This may seem like a pretty dull routine, until we glimpse its complexity. Consider what is involved in being able to use and understand a number word like 'five'. As a child, the shop-keeper learned to recite a series of sounds. This series was special in that each sound was different and they were invariably recited in a fixed order. If, in his own recitations, he varied that order, he was corrected by a caregiver. Later, the incipient shopkeeper learned to use those sounds for *numbering off* objects. If he numbered off an object but, instead of putting that object aside, he left it and assigned a new sound to it, he was corrected. Likewise, he was corrected if, upon uttering one sound, he put aside more than one object. Feedback from the caregiver taught him much else about the numerals. For each new collection, one had to restart the count from the beginning; only the last numeral in a particular count could be used to talk about the whole collection; if there were a collection of (say) five red apples, then 'red', but not 'five' could be said of *each* of the apples, and so on. Learning numerals involves participation in a complex suite of activities – you have mastered the word when you can engage in those activities – and, as Wittgenstein points out, there are many different *kinds* of words and correlatively many different sets of activity involved in their mastery.

It will be noted that, in the above discussion of the shopkeeper's actions, no mention of meanings was made. 'But what is the meaning (Bedeutung) of the word "five"?' asks Wittgenstein, and he replies 'No such thing was in question here, only how the word "five" is used.' The word 'five' does not stand for (bedeuten) an abstract object, and if you want to know what the word 'five' means, you simply observe how the word is used. The meaning of a word is not a certain something, and we can avoid the philosophical confusion of supposing that it must be by noting that, when we ask what a word means, we are asking how competent speakers *use* that word. If someone asks me for a clean spatula, I give him some object; if he asks me for the *meaning* of the word 'spatula', I give him not any object, concrete or abstract, but an *explanation*. Wittgenstein expresses the point rather stylishly: 'Meaning is what an explanation of meaning explains' (*PG*, p. 69).

As will be observed, the concept of *use* has crept into our discussion. Only recently has this concept been given its due respect in language studies. The advent of the discipline of applied linguistics coincides with the recognition of the importance of studying language as it is used in

2. Meaning

context. In philosophy too, the notion of *use* was badly neglected. But, in Wittgenstein's later writings, it is placed at the centre of the stage.

Meaning = use

The question 'What is the meaning of a word?' produces in us, so Wittgenstein claims, 'a mental cramp' (*BB*, p. 1; see also Austin, 1961). We say things like 'What is the meaning of the Turkish word "iki"?', 'She explained to me the meaning of the black cross on the road sign', but what we don't say in ordinary, non-philosophical discourse, is 'What is the meaning of a word?' The reason for the cramp is that '[w]e are up against one of the great sources of philosophical bewilderment: a substantive makes us look for something that corresponds to it'.[5] We make the misguided philosophical move of lifting the word 'meaning' out of its normal surroundings and, observing that it is a substantive, assume that therefore it must stand for some thing, and we ask 'What is that thing – what is the meaning of a word?' This assumption is made not just by philosophers but by all manner of people who theorize about meaning. Thus the linguist Ray Jackendoff (in the course of proposing a computational theory of meaning) writes: 'meanings are mentally represented ... meanings must be finitely representable and stored in a brain' (Jackendoff, 1987, p. 126). Likewise, the child developmentalist Paula Menyuk claims that lexical items must be represented semantically (as well as phonologically, orthographically and syntactically). She characterizes 'the big question' as 'How are word meanings encoded and stored in memory over time?' (Menyuk, 1988, pp. 139-40). Wittgenstein's point is that a meaning is not a something – not an object, not an image (*BB*, p. 5; *PI* §§6, 395-7), not a set of rules – not anything that can be stored. Linguists talk of 'mapping of meanings to forms'; but, if there are no such things as meanings, there cannot be any of that either. Yet meaning is not nothing either; in fact Wittgenstein is prepared to roughly characterise the meaning as 'that which is of importance about the sign' (*BB*, p. 5). A Satz from which, so to speak, its meaning had been drained would be, in Wittgenstein's phrase, 'an utterly dead and trivial thing'. 'But', he says 'if we had to name anything which is the life of the sign, we should have to say that it was its use' (*BB*, p. 4). 'In use it is *alive*' (*PI* §432). 'Look at the Satz as an instrument, and at its sense (Sinn) as its employment' (*PI* §421)

Clearly Wittgenstein regarded this insight as important and groundbreaking. At the beginning of a lecture delivered in 1938, he remarks 'If I had to say what is the main mistake made by philosophers of the

43

present generation, including Moore, I would say that it is that when language is looked at, what is looked at is a form of words and not the use made of the form of words.'[6] The interpretation of almost everything Wittgenstein said in his late period writings is controversial, but if there's one view that he states simply and unequivocally it is that meaning is use. At *PI* §43, he writes: 'For a large class of cases – though not for all – in which we employ the word "meaning" it can be defined thus: the meaning of a word is its use in the language'.

Curiosity compels us to wonder what exceptions Wittgenstein was alluding to. It is natural to read him as suggesting that, for some words, attention to their use does *not* reveal their meaning, and it is easy enough to envisage the kind of exceptions that he might have had in mind. Consider the lovely phrase 'my huckleberry friend', from Johnny Mercer's song 'Moon River'. Did it have a meaning on the first occasion of its use? No. Since there was no regularity of usage, there is no question of the first person who used those words using them correctly. The phrase had a lot of colour, but no literal meaning; perhaps it still does not.

Gordon Baker and Peter Hacker say that this is the wrong way to take Wittgenstein's exception clause. Their view is that by 'a large class of cases in which we employ the word "meaning" ', Wittgenstein is referring to phrases in which the word 'meaning' occurs, e.g. 'know the meaning of ', 'grasp the meaning', 'the word "sanction" has two almost opposite meanings'. In such cases, it is clear that we are talking about use. (Baker and Hacker, 1983a, pp. 99-100; also Hallett, 1977, p. 121). In the last example, for example, we could equally say 'the word "sanction" can be *used* in two almost opposite ways'. But obviously there are cases where no such paraphrase is available, e.g. 'Those spots mean measles', 'Your promise means a lot to me'. If this were the sort of exception that Wittgenstein had in mind, his claim (or at least the exception clause) would be uncontroversially true.

However, the Baker and Hacker interpretation, though interesting, is not obviously correct. For the very next sentence of *PI* §43 reads 'And the meaning of a name is sometimes explained by pointing to its bearer'. This does seem to indicate, *contra* Baker and Hacker, that *PI* §43 is about the meaning of words in general, not about the meaning of 'meaning'. But another possibility would be that, in line with Baker and Hacker's position, Wittgenstein is saying that the word 'meaning' as it occurs in the phrase 'the meaning of a name' has a different meaning from what it has in a sentence such as 'Tell me the meaning of the English idiom "Up yours" '. Thus when, at *PI* §79, Wittgenstein talks about 'the meaning of the name "N" ', he seems to mean 'what a certain individual means by "N" ' – what would nowadays be called 'speaker's meaning'.[7] It is true too that Wittgenstein accepts a Jamesian sense of 'meaning' – a characteristic feeling that accompanies the utterance or hearing of a word (TS 213, p. 33) and it is quite clear (and explicitly acknowledged by Wittgenstein in MS 180b (composed 1941), pp. 6-8) that 'meaning' in this sense cannot be identified with use – see next chapter.

Let us not allow ourselves to get bogged down (more than we have done already) in these exegetical niceties concerning what Wittgenstein wanted to exclude from his generalization. We know that, in his late period, he holds that, by and large, one should answer the question about the meaning of a word or a sentence by citing how that word or sentence is used. And the point seems an obvious one. Suppose that there is a builder A, and his assistant B, and that they speak a language consisting just of the four words 'block', 'pillar', 'slab' and 'beam' (see *PI* §2). When A calls out one of these words, B brings the stone which he has learnt to bring at such a call. The only way to answer the question of what A and B *mean* by their words, or whether they mean by them the same as we do, is to observe how they use those words. The labourers' four words may look and sound the same as ones that we sophisticated speakers use. But that hardly establishes that the words mean the same in their language and ours. For one thing, they use the word 'beam' in a way that would translate into our language as 'fetch a beam', and we rarely use the word that way. Second, if the labourers do not have concepts such as 'material' and 'solid', let alone 'horizontal', then it is hard to see how they *could* mean by 'beam' what we do. Note also that, since they do not have the word 'fetch', while it may be natural for *us* to interpret the builder's utterances of 'beam' as 'fetch a beam', there is nothing corresponding to 'fetch' in the mind of the builder.[8] Yet he and his assistant get on with their job very well using their primitive language. Their activity, consisting of language and the actions into which it is woven, is what Wittgenstein calls a *language-game* (*PI* §7). He gives numerous examples of such games in his later writings.[9]

It is not, then, words *qua* signs or sounds that have meaning but words-in-use. Words are used in a great variety of activities, and language-games are these word-*cum*-action activities. Unfortunately, some of Wittgenstein's characterisations of the notion of a language-game are not too clear, and many commentators have chased wild geese. Perhaps the best explanation he gives is this:

They are more or less akin to what in ordinary language we call games. Children are taught their native language by means of such games, and here they even have the entertaining character of games. We are not, however, regarding the language-games which we describe as incomplete parts of a language, but as languages complete in themselves, as complete systems of human communication. (*BB*, p. 81)

In contrast to the *Tractatus*, which offered an account of the essence of all language, Wittgenstein is now, in his later period, drawing attention to the *multiplicity* of very different kinds of systems of human communication.

And this multiplicity is not something fixed, given once for all; but new types of language, new language-games, as we may say, come into existence, and others become obsolete and get forgotten. (We can get a *rough picture* of this from the changes in mathematics.)
    Here the term 'language-*game*' is meant to bring into prominence the fact that the *speaking* of language is part of an activity, or of a form of life.

Review the multiplicity of language-games in the following examples, and in others:

    Giving orders, and obeying them —
    Describing the appearance of an object, or giving its measurement —
    Constructing an object from a description (a drawing) —
    Reporting an event —
    Speculating about an event —
    Forming and testing a hypothesis —
    Presenting the results of an experiment in tables and diagrams —
    Making up a story; and reading it —
    Play-acting —
    Singing catches —
    Guessing riddles —
    Making a joke; telling it —
    Solving a problem in practical arithmetic —
    Translating from one language into another —
    Asking, thanking, cursing, greeting, praying.

– It is interesting to compare the multiplicity of the tools in language and of the ways they are used, the multiplicity of kinds of word and sentence, with what logicians have said about the structure of language. (Including the author of the *Tractatus Logico-Philosophicus*.) (*PI* §23)

So language-games are activities in which speech is intimately involved. Perhaps it is impossible to give a *definition* of 'language-game', but the above list of samples clearly indicates what Wittgenstein had in mind. Notice, in this passage, the mention of a 'form of life'. Note too that praying, speculating about an event, telling riddles etc. are distinctively *human* activities; they are not forms of life that snakes or lions enjoy.

As we have seen, Wittgenstein regards the identification of meaning with use as an important insight, and the notion of *use* he invokes is related to other key notions in his later writings, such as *language-game* and *form of life*. It is also true, as we dicussed in the previous chapter, that the later Wittgenstein did not regard it as the philosopher's station to put forward theories:

Philosophy simply puts everything before us, and neither explains nor deduces anything. – Since everything lies open to view there is nothing to explain. For what is hidden, for example, is of no interest to us ...

The work of the philosopher consists in assembling reminders for a particular purpose.

If one tried to advance *theses* in philosophy, it would never be posible to debate them, because everyone would agree to them. (*PI* §§126-8)

Paul Horwich poses a nice dilemma: how can we read Wittgenstein's views on meaning in such a way as to accommodate 'two somewhat conflicting constraints: first, that his identification of meaning with use be genuinely illuminating; and second, that it not be a controversial theory – that it conform with his therapeutic, anti-theoretical metaphilosophical outlook'.[10] Horwich himself thinks that we can satisfy both constraints. He defends, against Kripke (1982), the idea that meaning is use and, in so doing, vindicates a minimalist account of *truth* to which both he (Horwich, 1990) and Wittgenstein subscribe.[11] So, if Horwich's defence is sound, the innocuous claim that meaning is use does have a substantial payoff in that it helps clarify an important philosophical concept, that of *truth*. But I shall take a different tack. By using a rather

47

extended example in applied linguistics, I shall attempt to show how the apparently flimsy idea that meaning is use can be genuinely illuminating – it provides, so I hope to establish, a plausible and superior alternative to current accounts of first-language acquisition. This example will both illustrate the point of Wittgenstein's linking of language-games to first-language *learning* (e.g., *BB*, p. 17; *PI* §§1, 5, 6)[12] and will facilitate an accurate (and simple) interpretation of other Wittgensteinian claims about meaning that have provoked a vast, dense literature.

Meaning-acquisition

In the *Lectures and Conversations on Aesthetics, Psychology and Religious Belief*, just before the remark already cited on the neglect by contemporary philosophers of *language in use*, Wittgenstein says:

> One thing we always do when discussing a word is to ask how we were taught it. Doing this on the one hand destroys a variety of misconceptions, on the other hand gives you a primitive language in which the word is used. Although this language is not what you talk when you are twenty, you get a rough approximation to what kind of language game is going to be played ... One thing that is immensely important in teaching is exaggerated gestures and facial expressions. The word is taught as a substitute for a facial expression or a gesture. The gestures, tones of voice, etc., in this case [the sort of words in whose mastery Wittgenstein is interested in this passage are what he calls 'aesthetic adjectives', such as 'good', 'fine' and 'lovely'] are expressions of approval. What *makes* the word an interjection of approval? It is the game it appears in, not the form of words. (*LA*, pp. 1-2)

In the light of subsequent research in language development and psycholinguistics beginning in the 1960s, one is bound to say that these remarks, with their emphasis on gesture and tone, are astonishingly farsighted – as a very quick pass through the empirical literature will reveal.

A view once widely held among linguists was that an infant's utterances had to have some syntactic structure before that child could properly be credited with language – with the capacity to mean anything by its words. Since, obviously, one-word utterances have no such structure, this view entails that semantic ability begins at roughly the age of 18 months, when a child starts to use two-word utterances. But the dictum *no semantic ability without syntactic complexity* was never

48

2. Meaning

given any decent rationale. The workmen in *PI* §2 used single-word utterances in their language-game but, if you think that example far-fetched, just think of the early single-word utterances of infants. It would be perverse *not* to see at least some of these as having a meaning, e.g. an indication of pleasure or of fear, of the rejection of something offered. Drop this unfounded requirement for syntactic complexity and there is no bar to extending investigation of possible semantic ability right back to the early months of the child's life, when it is struggling with its first single-word utterances. Such considerations have led modern developmental theorists to study the child's prelinguistic cognitive abilities, in particular, what Piaget called sensori-motor intelligence, in order to discover how these abilities bear upon the emergence of linguistic skills (Lock, 1976, pp. 10-11).

We do things with words, such as asking questions, making promises, giving orders. Such doings are known as *speech acts*.[13] An intriguing question is whether we can do any of these things *without* words, i.e. whether, prelinguistically, we can perform comparable actions. Such speechless speech acts are called *performatives*.[14] Bates, Camaioni and Volterra investigated the acquisition of performatives prior to speech. They concluded: 'There was no single moment when the performative structures could be said to "sprout" propositions. Instead, words as symbolic vehicles with corresponding referents emerged gradually out of the action schemes of sensorimotor communication' Bates et al. 1979, 125).[15]

There appears to be a phase of prosodic development prior to the acquisition of words. Before the development of any lexis, the infant of about 10 months begins to use specific types of gesture to indicate intent.[16] Further, using feedback from the caregiver, the infant comes to associate the different intonation patterns it produces with different speech acts (Menyuk, 1988, p. 116).[17] This is a process of considerable complexity. In Paul Ziff's words, 'humans constantly attend to their own behavior, thoughts and feelings; they attend and react to the effects they have on others. Still more, they are apt to react to their own reactions, and then, perhaps, react again' (Ziff, 1988, p. 15).

Theories of meaning in the Gricean tradition *define* meaning in terms of such a complex relationship between speaker and hearer. Roughly speaking, to mean something by an utterance is, on this view, to intend your utterance to produce a certain effect on an audience by getting your audience to recognize that that is your intention.[18] Intending someone to recognize your intention may seem a somewhat recondite business until one understands its developmental precursors. At an early age, grasping the significance of gestures and intonation

49

patterns (its own and those of its caregivers) is achieved in virtue of the highly interactive relationship between infant and guardian. Jerome Bruner explains how there is an easy transition from here to the recognition of the intentions which infuse the speech acts of adults:

> Paradoxically, the learning of speech acts may be easier and less mysterious than the learning either of syntax or semantics. For the child's syntactic errors are rarely followed by corrective feedback, and semantic feedback is often lax. But speech acts, on the contrary, get not only immediate feedback but also correction. Not surprising, then, that prelinguistic communicative acts precede lexico-grammatical speech in their appearance. Not surprising, then, that such primitive 'speech act' patterns may serve as a kind of matrix in which lexico-grammatical achievements can be substituted for earlier gestural or vocal procedures.[19]

What one would like to know, in the greatest possible detail, is what is involved in this process, this transition from the prelinguistic to the linguistic. Here is one idiotic suggestion: the infant, at the age of about 6 months, is waving its limbs around and making a variety of sounds – communicating, in a primitive kind of way. Then, over the next few months, its head starts getting filled with semantic representations – representations which are either of, or which have, the meaning of 'mama', the meaning of 'me', of 'give', 'big', etc. Once a semantic representation latches onto an appropriate sound (or onto an appropriate 'phonological representation') PRESTO!, the infant can use words instead of gestures; it can make meaningful utterances, it can produce locutionary acts. As I said, an idiotic fable. Yet, if you start to probe what linguists can possibly mean by 'the mapping of meanings to forms', it turns out to be precisely the unbelievable process I have just depicted. And what encourages such a fantastic theory is a conception of meanings as entities that are possessed, represented, matched to other entities, mismatched, and so on.

It is quite common to tell someone the meaning of a particular word: we do so by delivering a phrase or sentence couched in words which (we hope) are familiar to the enquirer. But from this common and true observation, it is all too easy to infer that *there is a meaning* which each word has, that meanings are things which can exist independently of sounds, and need to be matched to them. This is just armchair theorizing of the worst sort; it is prompted not by any empirical observation but by the assumption that, since the substantive 'meaning' occurs in phrases like 'tell someone the meaning of ...' there must be meanings.

2. Meaning

Yet, by a similar token, would we say that since 'nothing' is a substantive, there must be nothings – the somethings for which the substantive 'nothing' stands? We would, of course, say nothing of the sort, so we don't yet have a reason for saying that there must be meanings.

Is there any theoretical need for postulating semantic representations? What could such things be in their physical, neurological realization? What cluster of neurons, or what complex pattern of interneuronal events could *be* the semantical representation of 'dog'? A neuronal coding of some definition, like 'a four-legged flesh-eating animal of the genus *canis*'? (It would take a smart infant, just learning the meaning of the word 'dog', to have *that* in his head!) Could the neuronal pattern be a picture? Even if it were and even if, by some miracle, it resembled a dog, it would not be *seen* by anyone (we do not look inside our own heads). And if we need some neuronal sketch to invest the word 'dog' with meaning, and that neuronal sketch is a pattern of neurons firing, wouldn't we need to invest that physical pattern with meaning? To do that would require, by this line of thinking, a new neuronal sketch of *it* ... and so on, ad infinitum. Further, what image or picture could be the representation of the meaning of a word such as 'night' or 'weather' or 'whether' or 'by'?

If, as I have argued, there are no such things as meanings, then *a fortiori*, there are no representations of meanings. The contrary suggestion leads to all the unanswerable questions of the previous paragraph. 'But', someone might protest, 'how could a child learn what the word 'dog" means *without* forming a mental representation of the meaning of "dog"? ' Before we get down to the nitty-gritty of discussing actual cases of acquisition, a quick response to this query is in order: Consider a steam-governor in which the pressure of steam in an inlet pipe forces a spindle to rotate, spinning a pair of balls which rise, causing a lever to act on a valve which controls the pressure of steam in the original inlet pipe. This is a dynamic system which self-adjusts; it reacts to its own effects (cf. Ziff, 1988, above) and it does so without representations or computations (Van Gelder, 1995). Compare a 'system' consisting of an infant and its caregiver. The caregiver says 'dog' when both see a dog; the infant subsequently says 'dog' sometimes appropriately, sometimes not, but self-adjusts in the light of feedback from the caregiver, and their usage of 'dog' converges. There are, of course, interesting things happening in the infant's brain but nothing so far compels us to say that it forms the mental representation of the meaning of 'dog'.

Let us now take seriously Wittgenstein's dictum that meaning is use in order to see whether it points in the direction of a more realistic account of how first language is acquired. As we shall shortly see, an

51

infant uses words differently at different points in its linguistic development, so the Wittgensteinian line would be that meaning-acquisition is gradual, in the sense that there is a semantical progression from the baby production of gestures and sounds to the young child's ability to speak much the same way as we adults do. The view is, then, that adult meaning may be partially grasped and gradually acquired.[20] This is obviously quite different from the view that *meanings* are things that must be either present or absent, all or nothing, either attached or unattached to one's words. It will suffice, for present purposes, to look in detail at the acquisition process for just one word, 'mama'. This is a good word to choose, first, because it is common to languages from disparate language groups, second, because it is learned very early, uncontaminated, so to speak, by much concurrent linguistic development that would obscure our study of it.

That the words for the female parent are strikingly similar to each other in so many different languages was the phenomenon that Roman Jakobson sought to explain in a paper (Jakobson, 1962, 538-45) that provides us with a useful starting point. The story begins with the child sucking contentedly at its mother's breast or on its feeding bottle.

> Often the sucking activities of a child are accompanied by a slight nasal murmur, the only phonation which can be produced when the lips are pressed to the mother's breast or to the feeding bottle and the mouth is full. Later, this phonatory reaction to nursing is reproduced as an anticipatory signal at the mere sight of food and finally as the manifestation of a desire to eat, or more generally, as an expression of discontent and impatient longing for missing food or absent nurser, and any ungranted wish. When the mouth is free from nutrition, the nasal murmur may be supplied with an oral, particularly labial release. (Jakobson, 1962, p. 542)

So, when junior does not get what junior wants? Murmuring 'mmmmm' doesn't do much good as a way of expressing impatient dissatisfaction; this is the time to bring in the high energy vowels:

> The compact vowel displays the maximal energy output, while the diffuse consonant with an oral occlusion represents the maximal reduction in the energy output. Thus nursery names for mother and father, like the earliest meaningful units emerging in infant speech, are based on the polarity between the optimal consonant and the optimal vowel. (Jakobson, 1962, pp. 540-1)

2. Meaning

In other words, if you want attention, terminate the mmmmurmuring with the blasting of an '/a/' – '/ma/'. It is important that the *same* noisy syllable '/ma/' be repeated, for otherwise the sounds might be construed just as babbling, not as demands: 'In contradistinction to the "wild sounds" of babbling exercises, the phonemes are to be recognizable, distinguishable, identifiable; and in accordance with these requirements, they must be deliberately repeatable' (Jakobson, 1962, p. 542). Hence 'mama', and a similar explanation holds for 'papa'.[21]

An objection that might be raised to this account is that it ignores the rôle of input – of the language being spoken around the child. Children *hear* a particular set of phonetic targets in the speech of people around them, and those uses help shape the children's uses too (De Boysson-Bardies and Vihman, 1991). This objection misunderstands the thrust of Jakobson's argument. Of course the child's early 'mama' utterances are rewarded and reinforced by the female adult caregiver. But how is it that all adults from the most diverse linguistic backgrounds have so similar a word for the female parent? An answer in terms of phonetic targets cannot, without circularity, account for this *commonality*. The objection can also be refuted empirically by observing the utterances of those infants who, for the first few months of their lives, are in the care of a silent adult.

It may be helpful to set out, in tabular form, some of the stages in the infant's development of the mastery of the word for its mother.[22] The 'MTYPE' referred to in the third column is the type of meaning that a speech sound has at a particular stage of its use: either natural meaning (meaning$_n$) as in 'those spots mean (are a natural sign of) measles' or non-natural meaning (meaning$_{nn}$) as in 'When Jacques said "Je suis fatigué" he meant that he was tired.' Meaning$_{nn}$ is intentional (the speaker intends to evoke some response in the hearer), whereas, obviously, those tell-tale spots on the skin don't have intentions (Grice, 1957).

STAGE	SOUND	SIGNIFIES	MTYPE	MEANS
I	/mm/	contentment	n	Yumm
II	/mm/	anticipation	n	Here we go
III	/mama/	impatience	?nn	Eat right now
IV	/mama/	specific wish	nn	I want mum

We are asking: What does the child *mean* by these noises at the different stages? As will become clear, the entries in the final column are a *bit* of a joke. On a Wittgensteinian view, the question of what a child means at some point when it utters a sound is identical with the question of

53

how the child is *using* the sounds, of how it 'weaves' the sound into its actions. The baby murmur of contentment is a natural response to something nice. When it makes that sound in anticipation of satisfaction, the baby is displaying a conditioned response, like Pavlov's dogs slavering at the sound of a bell which, as they have learned, heralds imminent satisfaction. Behaviour at this low level of sophistication is not action; it involves no intention; it has only natural meaning (meaning$_n$). However, probably by stage III, and certainly by stage IV, the child is selecting the sound 'mama' from a range of options open to it, and is using that particular noise to elicit a particular kind of response. When the child reaches the point of intending to elicit that response by getting the hearer to recognize that intention, then its utterance has meaning proper, non-natural meaning (meaning$_{nn}$).

The linguist M.A.K. Halliday claims that

> the child already has a linguistic system before he has any words or structures at all. He is capable of expressing a considerable range of meanings, meanings which at first seem difficult to pin down, because they do not translate easily into adult language, but which become transparent when interpreted functionally, in the light of the question 'What has the child learnt to do by means of language?' (Halliday, 1975, p. 6)

Obviously, the meanings ascribed, in the right-hand column of the above table, to the infant's sounds are 'translations' into the language of an adult. An infant may utter, and respond to some word 'X' without using that word our way; without having our concept of X.[23] Paula Menyuk writes:

> It has ... been observed that children comprehend words at about eight to nine months, but this comprehension appears to be limited to certain contexts. For example, the mother may say 'Daddy's coming' and the infant looks toward the door through which Daddy usually comes, or a favorite object such as 'teddy' is named, and the child looks toward the named object. In these instances, it is not even clear whether the child has learned to associate the name with an object in a certain context or if the mother has cued the child to look in a certain direction. (Menyuk, 1988, p. 143)

What we have here may not just be a matter of its being underdetermined by the evidence what the mother's words mean to the child, but a matter of incommensurability – there may be no way for us to say, in

2. Meaning

our adult language, what the words mean to the child[24] – and this may be true not just of comprehension, but of the production of words too. It is clear, I think, that there is no simple answer to the question 'What does a child mean by "mmmmm" or by "mama"?' Not only does it mean different things at different times during the acquisition period, but also (and here I disagree with Halliday) what it does mean may not be capturable within the conceptual scheme of adult speakers. Not until about the age of two years does an infant possess the category structure of its linguistic community (Choi and Bowerman, 1991). The 10-month-old baby starts screaming 'mama'. Does it mean, as *we* should say, that it wants a banana (bringing it a bottle of milk pacifies it, but what it *really* wants is a banana), that it wants a bit of banana-stuff (Quine, 1960, pp. 26-57), that it is feeling sick, that it has made a discovery, or does it mean some unholy mixture of all of these? Perhaps one claim that may be made with some definiteness is that the baby's early meaning for 'mama' is associated with satisfaction of hunger, and so is dependent on the possession of a sensorium. This provides a partial vindication of a conclusion drawn by Searle in his well known diatribe against 'Strong A.I.': What has *our* kind of meaning has to have something like *our* kind of brain (Searle, 1980; 1984), viz., a brain that delivers qualia (the phenomenological, felt quality of things), something that no existing microprocessor has achieved.[25]

Even during stage IV of the development depicted above, the child is not using the word 'mama' as a name for its mother. It is using the word as a means for summoning its mother, just as the builder in *PI* §2 uses 'slab' to summon a slab. The word 'mama' could not be said to be employed as a *name* until the child is able to say things *about* its mother (e.g. 'Mama come', 'Mama nice'), and more progress needs to be made before the child comes to use the word 'mama' or 'mother' as a common noun fitting any woman who stands in the same relation to someone else as the child's own mother stands to that child. This entails the child's distancing itself from the egocentric standpoint, a phenomenon discussed by Piaget.[26] Jakobson cites the Bulgarian nursery form 'mama' as being *intermediate* between proper and common noun, and it is unlikely that this intermediate mode of meaning is confined to Bulgarians. There are thus at least six stages in the mastery of 'mother', and, of course, to be a *real* master of a language a speaker has to progress beyond the literal.

I have paid special attention to the word for mother, since we have a highly plausible account of the development of its acquisition from the subjective, hunger-related sense to an objective, 'mother-related' sense. But empirical studies have also been done on changes in children's uses of other words that are acquired early on – words such as 'gone', 'no', 'more', 'there', 'uh-oh' and 'down'. Alison Gopnik has argued that infants use these words in ways different from the use of *any* lexical items or syntactic structures in adult English (Gopnik, 1984). That claim may be somewhat exaggerated, but it does seem clear that the infants' uses are (as one might expect) more general and more egocentric; they normally occur when certain sorts of movement are observed or induced by the child, when its plans are realized or thwarted. Clearly, what a child *can* mean is constrained by its level of cognitive development. If, for example, a very young infant does not possess our concept of an object, then the infant could hardly be expected to use the word 'gone' as we do. For, when we say that something is gone, we typically allow that the same object might move about and return. On the extreme Piagetian view – which, of course, has been brought into serious question (Donaldson, 1978) – for the very young infant, what is out of sight ceases to exist.

Our early uses of words are in rapid flux. They come to conform to the adult norm the more we become immersed in the complex world in which activities such as spoon-feeding, playing, pretending and delving into the nature of subatomic matter take place. It is hardly surprising that, in the animal world where the range of activities extends little beyond the four 'f's (feeding, fighting, fleeing and fooling around), a much more primitive understanding is all that is possible. Thus, one's dog might respond correctly to a request to fetch one's slippers, might even anticipate one's wanting one's slippers, but would be unlikely to regard slippers as artefacts or as objects of purchase or barter, and is even more unlikely to reflect on how *he* would look wearing them.[27]

An important category of concepts, the acquisition of which is early and gradualistic is that of the colour concepts. Children first learn to recognize white, black and the bright primary colours. But, as Michael Dummett points out,

[a]t this stage, they have an immense amount still to learn before they have acquired the colour-concepts possessed by adults. They do not know how to apply colour-words to transparent substances or to light sources, and, when they first extend the application of the words to these things, they will make mistakes, such as calling water 'white' ... They have so far been taught to apply colour words only to matt surfaces, and cannot allow for the gleams that characterise glossy ones, nor be aware of the change in the appearance of a reflecting surface such as that of water in a pond or coffee in a cup according to the depth of focus of the eyes. They have not yet appreciated how many intermediate and indeterminate shades

are to be seen ... A child who has mastered the first stage in learning the use of colour words thus has a great deal more to learn before he has attained to the adult use; but, still, what he has learned is an indispensable foundation for the rest, and it is therefore profitable to ask in what his grasp of the senses of colour-words, at that stage, consists. (Dummett, 1993, 90-1)

Like us, then, Dummett finds it convenient to talk of stages of development, and, if we make the Wittgensteinian identification of how a person uses a word with what that word, in that person's mouth, means, then we can see Dummett comparing infant and adult meaning in terms of the structure of their respective contrast sets: the infant contrasts a colour word with less other colour words, but also makes contrasts where mature speakers make none – when, for example, it withholds the attribution of 'red' to a red, shiny surface.

It is possible, then, to describe the child's evolving acquisition of a word in terms of changes in what the child identifies as the sets of expressions *contrasting* with that word. This idea is enshrined in a powerful and empirically resilient theory of language-development due to Eve Clark.[28] The rather vague concept of *how an individual uses an expression* can be given some flesh by comparing two individuals' uses of an expression (or one individual's diachronic uses) in terms of the range of expressions regarded by the individual as contrasting with the given expression. So, for example, I use 'white' differently from the way Dummett's child uses it: I *contrast* 'white' with 'colourless' – anything which is colourless I, unlike the child, don't call 'white'. Of course, this way of 'beefing up' Wittgenstein's dictum that meaning is use, though it may have merit, does not do justice to his idea that the use of an expression is its rôle in various *activities*.

The meaning-gradualism I have been sketching ties in rather beautifully with Steven Pinker's resolution of a puzzle (he calls it a 'paradox') about how children acquire the argument structures of verbs. The argument structure of a verb is the blueprint of the combinations with subject, object and oblique object that are permissible or obligatory for that verb. Thus 'devour' has a different argument structure from 'eat' in that the latter does not require an object; 'put' requires subject, object and oblique object – all are obligatory. (In this discussion of Pinker, I'll be using 'subject' and 'object' to mean 'grammatical subject', 'grammatical object'.) The paradox is that we do master the argument structures of certain verbs even though there does not seem to be any way in which we could do so. For example, many verbs dativize. The following pairs are all permissible:

57

John gave a painting to the museum.
John gave the museum a painting.

John threw the ball to Mary.
John threw Mary the ball.

John told a story to his son.
John told his son a story.

Since children are productive, we might therefore expect them to generalize from such cases and adopt a rule to the effect that any verb V which has the prepositional dative argument structure

$$NP_1 \; V \; NP_2 \; to \; NP_3$$

will also have the double object form

$$NP_1 \; V \; NP_3 \; NP_2$$

Now, as a matter of fact, not all verbs with the prepositional argument structure dativize:

John donated a painting to the museum.
*John donated the museum a painting.

John explained the story to his son.
*John explained his son the story.

but, given that children do not receive explicit correction of their grammatical errors, or, in the rare instances when they do, do not profit from the experience (Pinker, 1989, pp. 8-16), they seem to have no way of knowing about these exceptions to the generalization. Yet, of course, they do somehow get to know them eventually.

The nub of Pinker's solution to this problem is as follows. In natural languages, rules for well-formedness are semantically constrained. For example, all dativizable verbs share the semantic property that they must be capable of denoting prospective possession (either literal of metaphorical) of the referent of the second object (NP_2) by the referent of the first object (NP_3) (Pinker, 1989, p. 48). That is why 'drive' doesn't dativize:

John drove his car to Chicago.
*John drove Chicago his car.

2. Meaning

Pinker maintains that lexical rules are, at least in part, semantic operations. This is the reason why it is natural that they are sensitive to semantic conditions. The specific proposal is 'that part of what lexical rules do is change the semantic structures of verbs' lexical entries' and the '[s]yntactic argument structures of verbs are predictable from their semantic structures via the application of *linking rules*' (Pinker, 1989, p. 62). So, taking dativization as an example, a lexical rule converts a predicate meaning 'to cause X to go to Y' (where 'go' doesn't necessarily imply motion, e.g. 'He gave $500 to the museum' means 'He caused $500 to go to the museum') into a second predicate meaning 'to cause Y to have X'. There are cases where the application of the rule would change the meaning of the verb in such a way that the new 'meaning' just doesn't make sense – e.g. '*to cause Chicago to have his car'. These are the cases that we exempt from application of the rule. Paradox lost.

This explanation looks fine for the easy cases where the referent of the indirect object in the prepositional construction could not possess the referent of the direct object. But it does not explain why 'give' dativizes yet 'donate' does not when the two are so very nearly synonymous. Pinker speculates that a morphophonological constraint is operative here – dativizable verbs tend to have native (Germanic), not Latinate or Latinate-sounding stems (Pinker, 1989, pp. 45-7, 118-23). They do; but why the constraint? We argued that the childhood process of meaning-acquisition is one in which gradual meaning-change occurs. And Pinker's theory requires an agent's grasp of meaning-change as a precondition of grasping the rules for which verbs do and which verbs don't alternate between pairs of argument structures. Children up to the age of 6 have been reported as producing ungrammatical double object datives (Mazurkewich and White, 1984) – which means, on Pinker's theory, that they have not grasped the adult *meaning* of the relevant verbs. Other kinds of argument structure error, for example ungrammatical passives, are committed by children up to around the age of 9. Latinate verbs are generally more difficult, learnèd and abstract than their near-synonymous native counterparts, and tend to be acquired in late childhood/early adolescence,[29] i.e. *after* the period when meaning-changes occur. Hence, if the meaning-changes (better: meaning-switches) involved in Pinker's lexical rules occur only during the time when gradual meaning-change of the sort I have been discussing takes place (and this would be a topic for further empirical research) then we have an explanation of the different behaviour with respect to dativization of Latinate/non-Latinate pairs of verbs.

Clear and Queer Thinking

Gradualism versus Fodor's mad dog nativism

So much by way of advertisement for the merits of the theory of meaning-gradualism. Our contention has been that Wittgenstein's claim that the meaning of an expression is its use in the language (or in language-games) supports an empirical theory that satisfyingly explains a number of phenomena in first language acquisition. It is good to have this theory on the market, for an alternative proposed by Jerry Fodor and described by him as 'the only game in town' looks exceedingly shaky.

Fodor and his followers think that the development of semantic competence requires our possession of Mentalese – an innate language of thought (Fodor, 1975). In Fodor's view, this inner code is a fully fledged language – it contains a vast array of lexical items, a syntax and a semantics.[30] There are 'truth definitions' – biconditionals each of which matches a natural language predicate to the predicate in Mentalese which is true of exactly the same objects as those of which the natural language predicate is true (Fodor, 1975, pp. 80-1). The story of how an infant learns the word 'mother' would go something like this: The child hears the word 'mother' on a few occasions and thereby gains some clues about what that term applies to (the extension of the term). On the basis of this evidence, it begins to construct a hypothesis about which term or terms in its Mentalese the word 'mother' matches. Presumably, *prior* to successfully acquiring the right meaning for 'mother' the child's hypothesis about the meaning of 'mother' must be disjunctive (and, at first, *highly* disjunctive) in form, viz.

'y is a mother' is true if and only if M_1x or M_2x or M_3x or ...

where 'x' is the Mentalese counterpart of the singular term 'y' and each of the M_i is a Mentalese predicate with a fixed extension that includes prominent elements of the situations in which the child has, up to that point, encountered 'mother'-utterances (so 'M_1' could be the Mentalese word for 'cot', 'M_2' for 'face', 'M_3' for 'mother' etc.). Suppose the child settles, eventually, for 'M_3', and that subsequently all objects it hears referred to as 'mother' fall within the extension of 'M_3'. The hypothesis that 'mother' has the meaning of 'M_3' is confirmed, and the child now has fully fledged mastery of the term 'mother'. The concentrated frown on the face of the Fodorian baby indicates the mental effort of figuring out how to eliminate disjuncts.

Fodor's account of language-acquisition entails that Mentalese counterparts to all the primitive expressions of (say) atomic physics are available to a new-born baby (Fodor, 1975, pp. 80, 97) because all the predicates of a natural language that are not compounds of other expressions must be learned, on Fodor's theory, by being paired with predicates of an unlearned Mentalese. The account is therefore ludicrous, but not impossible, and Fodor is prepared to bite the bullet because he believes that our semantical abilities can have no other explanation.[31]

We would do well, I think, not to take Fodor as our guide. He goes astray right at the beginning – his underlying assumption is that semantical ability consists fundamentally of the ability to convey, in language, information about the world. For him, the paradigm case of language learning is learning truth-definitions which match statements of the form 'x is P' with statements in Mentalese (Fodor, 1975, p. 59). But, when you step back to consider it, *making statements* is the last thing on a child's mind. What benefits could an infant reap by issuing sentences of the form 'This is how things stand'?[32] As we have seen, in all but the final stages of the development of the word for 'mother', no statement-making is involved. Instead, we find the word 'mama' being used as an instrument – as a way of getting things done.[33]

In a nutshell, the difference between Fodor's account of meaning acquisition and the gradualism that I have been advocating can be expressed this way: For Fodor, learning new vocabulary in one's first natural language consists in matching words of that language with words of another language (Mentalese) the meanings of which we already know. To have mastered a new predicate 'P' is to have assembled sufficient evidence to warrant the belief that, for all y and corresponding x, statements of the form 'Py' are true if and only if 'Mx', where 'M' is the Mentalese predicate which matches the ordinary language predicate 'P'. In this respect, as he acknowledges, Fodor's description of the mastery of one's first public language, in terms of matching up pairs of expressions, perfectly describes what is involved in the old-fashioned way of learning one's *second* language (Fodor, 1975, pp. 58-9). By contrast, we have argued that one's first natural language is indeed the first *language* that one has. We have seen that, at least in the case of certain words, we can trace how the infant acquires them by observing how, from the earliest months, it produces sounds and gestures as a response to, and which elicit responses from, objects (particularly human objects) in its environment. By a complex process of feedback, the infant gradually modifies those sounds and gestures and comes to use them to get what it wants.[34] Some of the things it wants – for example, relief from hunger – and some of the abilities it has – for example, the ability to make sounds and to be particularly moved by particular

61

patterns of sound – may be innate. But our account of language development certainly does not call for an innate *language* nor do we require that the infant become a master of bilingual biconditionals.[35]

Fodor requires a Language of Thought which comes gift-wrapped at birth with a semantics – all the (thousands of) Mentalese words with which we are born have meaning, already locked inside our heads. On my account, meaning cannot be 'internal' and 'private' like that. I, by contrast, have sketched a naturalistic account of the language development of a baby. An infant's words have meaning only after that infant has become inducted into using words in the customary way, and this process requires at least one other person; wolf children don't and can't learn a language (at least while the wolves remain *in loco parentis*). This process is gradualistic – there is a transition from very early sounds and gestures which have only meaning$_n$ to a use of words which approaches and eventually reaches that of an adult. The diary studies of child developmentalists record this process, showing how children overextend and underextend the application of a word before arriving at the correct extension. I cannot see how, without further extravagant assumptions, Fodor can warp his theory to the empirical data. The real difference is that Fodor's is a lunatic fantasy, a fairytale; mine is the outline of a scientific account which squares with what is known about infant cognitive development in general.

The view just sketched embraces what Andy Clark has called a 'minimal rationalism' in which we posit not extensive innate knowledge but 'whatever minimal set of biases and structure will ensure the emergence, under realistic environmental conditions, of the basic knowledge necessary for early success and subsequent learning' (Clark, 1993b, p. 597). Clark provides a delightful demonstration that in a connectionist net, the initial state of knowledge will not generally be specifiable in statement form; nor, we may add, will the knowledge state be so specifiable in the initial training period when the weighting of connections between 'neurons' (nodes) is undergoing adjustment. In this respect, at least, a connectionist approach provides a model of the sort of incommensurability of infant and adult utterances that we were discussing earlier. It is interesting also that some aspects of language-learning exhibited by neural nets follow similar patterns of success and backsliding that is observed in infants. But this research itself is in the infant stage of its development, and we should not make a song and dance of it (yet).

2. Meaning

Questions about meaning – some answers

By looking at the evidence from empirical studies of children's linguistic development, we have shown that Fodor's account of semantic ability in terms of an innate language of thought is by no means the only game in town. A more plausible alternative emerges once we start asking how vocal sounds are used early on, and how the use of those sounds changes over time. It is no wonder that Wittgenstein paid particular attention to first language *learning*, since so many headaches about meaning are alleviated once we consider how meaning is acquired – how people develop the ability to use words for communicative (and ruminative) purposes. In his later writings, Wittgenstein looks at a number of interesting questions about meaning. I immodestly contend that we are now in a good position to give the right answers, briefly and simply.

What gives words their life?

'The signs of our language seem dead', muses Wittgenstein's imaginary interlocutor (*BB*, p. 3). Yet words play a vital rôle in our lives; they are not dead, they carry meaning. It is natural to suppose that it is our *processing* of words that makes all the difference, that transforms them from inert physical marks into these wonderful things that *mean*, that put us in touch with the world and with each other. So we get to thinking that there must be a marvellous, almost occult mechanism that does this processing:

It seems that there are *certain definite* mental processes bound up with the working of language, processes through which alone language can function. I mean the processes of understanding and meaning. The signs of our language seem dead without these mental processes; and it might seem that the only function of the signs is to induce such processes, and that these are the things we ought really to be interested in. Thus if you are asked what is the relation between a name and the thing it names, you will be inclined to answer that the relation is a psychological one, and perhaps when you say this you think in particular of the mechanism of association. We are tempted to think that the action of language consists of two parts; an inorganic part, the handling of signs, and an organic part, which we may call understanding these signs, meaning them, interpreting them, thinking. These latter activities seem to take place in a queer kind of medium, the mind; and the mechanism of the mind, the nature of which, it seems, we

63

don't quite understand, can bring about effects which no material mechanism could. Thus e.g. a thought (which is such a mental process) can agree or disagree with reality; I am able to think of a man who isn't present; I am able to imagine him, 'mean him' in a remark which I make about him, even if he is thousands of miles away or dead. 'What a queer mechanism,' one might say, 'the mechanism of wishing must be if I can wish that which will never happen'. (*BB*, pp. 3-4)

The temptation is to say that 'the mechanism of the mind must be of a most peculiar kind to do what the mind does' and our comparison here is with some physical process, say, that of an amoeba which takes food by extending 'arms', splits up into similar cells each of which grows and behaves like the original one, and we say 'of what a queer nature the protoplasm must be to act in such a way' (*BB*, p. 5).

But, in depicting the mind as a mechanism that invests 'dead' signs with meaning, we are presupposing that words are inert – that they are mere physical inscriptions or packets of sound – so that some process, perhaps an 'act of meaning', is required to imbue them with the intentional life they have when used by a speaker or writer. Our examination of the learning of words reveals that this is a topsy-turvy attitude. Words have semantical life not because of an *élan vitale* injected, in real time or off-line, into utterances of them but because of the way they are taught and learned. In the case of the words we learn first, the learner is not credited with a knowledge of them until he or she weaves them appropriately into context, action and interaction.

The expression 'the meaning of a word' might suggest that its meaning is something that a word has, something quite distinct from the word, so that the word itself is something meaning-less or dead. But this is just a product of that great source of philosophical bewilderment mentioned earlier: that of thinking that a substantive – in this case 'the meaning of ...'– must stand for some thing which is detachable from the word, and which actually is detached in the case of a meaningless expression. So, on this conception, the word is just an ink mark, or some other physical token, such as a burst of sound. That this is a *mistaken* conception can be seen by considering what happens when a new word gets introduced into a language. This involves a community coming to *use* what were hitherto just meaningless marks. Marks themselves are not words. What makes something a word, as opposed to just (say) a doodle in ink, is not its physical shape. A word, like a statement, is *suffused* with meaning (sinnvoll); the meaning is no more a detachable part than is the smile on the face of the Cheshire cat or the value from

2. Meaning

a valuable cow (see *PI* §120). Vygotsky reaches the same conclusion: 'meaning is an inalienable part of word as such .... A word without meaning is an empty sound, no longer a part of human speech' (Vygotsky, 1962, p. 5).

In mediaeval tracts on semantics, three forms of 'supposition' (*reference, standing for*) were identified: *personal* (where a word stands for a person or thing); *material* (where a word stands for the very mark used to write that word, e.g. ' "Man" contains three letters'); *simple* (where words stand for concepts). Note that, in all three cases, words are treated as fully fledged semantical entities. But by the time of Hobbes, a different conception seems to have gained ascendancy – that words are merely meaningless *marks* or *signs*. This view has it that words acquire meaning by being associated with something else, e.g. with 'ideas' (eighteenth-century British Empiricism) or with abstract objective 'senses' (Frege). One possible explanation for this shift away from the sound mediaeval conception is the invention of the printing press, which made possible the production of multiple copies of text with no authorial assistance (Ong, 1982, pp. 118-19). It is interesting to contrast the ancient Chinese view of language wherein words are conceived primarily as vehicles for intervening in the world (for example, for controlling people) thus automatically serving a semantical function. There would have been less temptation for the Chinese to take the Hobbesian route since, if ancient Chinese characters are ideographic, we cannot regard them as physical signs, 'marks chosen at pleasure' (i.e. as purely conventional); they are by nature semantical entities (Hansen, 1989).

Words are *identified functionally*, i.e. according to their use, so that, in contrast to formal model theory, meaning is not something superimposed upon an uninterpreted matrix. This should be quite clear if only from the fact that physical tokens as different as an inscription in ink and a moving pressure wave may be (manifestations of) the *same word*.[36] The notions of a word *qua* physical token or *qua* syntactical element can be construed as abstracted from this richer notion of a constituent of language-in-use.[37] There may seem to be no big gain in taking this 'top-down' approach – abstracting from the word to reach the sign – rather than the 'bottom-up' approach of pumping up the sign until we get a proper (sinnvoll) word. The gain is that, if we think of the pumping up as the *addition* of some things (meanings), then we have to postulate a meaning-processing mechanism, and theorists waste their time in attempting to explain how this mythical engine works. We want to account for all meaning-phenomena, including *meaning-acquisition*, without following such false leads. There are, to be sure, plenty

65

of scientific questions to be asked about *meaning* and *understanding*. We need to learn a great deal about the neurological structures that underpin our abilities to learn language and to engage in diverse kinds of linguistic practice. But we want to avoid *specious* questions that arise out of grammatical confusion.

A paradox about meaning

Wittgenstein begins a famous section of the *Philosophical Investigations* with the remark: 'This was our paradox: no course of action could be determined by a rule, because every course of action can be made out to accord with the rule' (*PI* §201). He is not talking about traditional rules of school grammar or of spelling ('i' before 'e', except after 'c') but about semantical rules; rules of meaning. What are these rules, and where is the paradox?

Language is not wayward or unruly – well, only slightly so. Humpty Dumpty was wrong to think that one can use words and mean by them whatever one wishes, at least, if one wants to be understood. It can be argued – though this is controversial – that words are elastic in that one can create metaphors that stretch the normal or literal meanings of certain words. But even the creation of metaphor is not a free-for-all. I can talk about the face of the deep or the unacceptable face of capitalism or the dark face of evil, but if I start talking about the face of my pencil, or the face of the number 7, my hearers will merely be bemused. When we say that language has semantical rules, all that means is that words can be used correctly and incorrectly; or, if you prefer jargon, that meaning is normative.

Adult speakers use words in a regular way, with a certain meaning – and deviating from this way would, except under special circumstances, be regarded as breaking a rule of language. But what are these rules? We have already encountered one example in the very first proposition of the *Philosophical Investigations*. Recall that there the shopkeeper who is given a slip of paper with 'Five red apples' written on it, gets a table (a colour chart), looks up 'red' and then looks at the colour sample opposite it. Such a table is the expression of a rule in the language-game (*PI* §53) for it tells the shopkeeper how to use the colour words correctly, for example, it shows him the colour *correctly* signified by 'red'. There are games which are played with definite, precise rules (*PI* §54) but there are also games in which there is some vagueness in the rules – not that this prevents them being perfectly playable games. For example, when *we* use the word 'red', we don't use a colour chart matching that word with a certain definite shade of colour. Red shades off, in one direction into pink; in another direction into orange. There are no precise boundaries in this territory. That's how it is with the colour words; they are by nature vague. By contrast, the builders' language with 'slab', 'beam' etc. (*PI* §2) is completely precise and apparently unproblematic.

Except that it's not unproblematic. Wittgenstein invites us to consider a variant of the builders' language-game, one in which, instead of calling out the names of the stones he wants, the builder (A) gives his assistant (B) written signs:

> Imagine a language-game like [the one in *PI* §2] played with the help of a table. The signs given to B by A are now written ones. B has a table; in the first column are the signs used in the game, in the second pictures of building stones. A shows B such a written sign; B looks it up in the table, looks at the picture opposite, and so on. So the table is a rule which he follows in executing an order. – One learns to look the picture up in the table by receiving a training, and part of this training consists perhaps in the pupil's learning to pass with his finger horizontally from left to right; and so, as it were, to draw a series of horizontal lines on the table.
>
> Suppose different ways of reading a table were now introduced; one time, as above according to the schema:

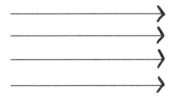

> another time like this:

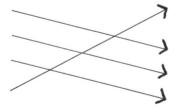

> or in some other way. – Such a schema is supplied with the table as the rule for its use.
>
> Can we not now imagine further rules to explain *this* one? And, on the other hand, was that first table incomplete without the

67

schema of arrows? And are other tables incomplete without their schemata? (*PI* §86)

The first of these schemata looks the more 'natural', but, without explicit instructions, we are not sure how to read it. The schema is not self-interpreting. On the left of the table is a column of words – 'block', 'pillar', 'slab', 'beam' – on the right is a column of pictures of the four types of building stone. Now, how do we read the first schema? Here is one way: use the sign on the left of an arrow to refer to the object depicted *one below* the object depicted to the right of that arrow, or, where there is no object below, to refer to the object depicted at the top. When I said that the schema is not self-interpreting, I meant that there is nothing to rule out its being interpreted in the way I've just suggested, or in any other way. So, do we need a rule for interpreting that schema? But if so, then, by the same line of reasoning, that new rule is open to multiple interpretations; it is not self-interpreting. So it looks as if we shall need *another* rule telling us how to interpret *it*, and so on *ad infinitum*. We have already encountered the very same type of infinite regress argument when we considered not schema which need to be interpreted, but 'neuronal sketches'.

This, then, is the paradox alluded to in §201: we can understand the written signs and spoken sounds of our language with no trouble at all, yet, if the argument given above is correct, we should have *infinite* trouble, because we must interpret the signs, interpret that interpretation, interpret that one, and so on *ad infinitum*. The paradox *and its solution* are given in the passage (*PI* §§198-202), which I quote, omitting §200.

'But how can a rule show me what I have to do at *this* point? Whatever I do is, on some interpretation, in accord with the rule.'– That is not what we ought to say, but rather: any interpretation still hangs in the air along with what it interprets, and cannot give it any support. Interpretations by themselves do not determine meaning.

'Then can whatever I do be brought into accord with the rule?'– Let me ask this: what has the expression of a rule – say a sign post – got to do with my actions? What sort of connection is there here? – Well, perhaps this one: I have been trained to react to this sign in a particular way, and now I do so react to it.

But that is only to give a causal connection; to tell how it has come about that we now go by the sign-post; not what this going-by-the-sign really consists in. On the contrary; I have further indicated that a person goes by a sign-post only in so far as there exists a regular use of sign-posts, a custom (*PI* §198).

Is what we call 'obeying a rule' something that it would be possible for only *one* man to do only *once* in his life? – This is of course a note on the grammar of the expression 'to obey a rule'.
It is not possible that there should have been only one occasion on which someone obeyed a rule. It is not possible that there should have been only one occasion on which a report was made, an order given or understood; and so on. – To obey a rule, to make a report, to give an order, to play a game of chess, are *customs* (uses, institutions). (*PI* §199)

This was our paradox: no course of action could be determined by a rule, because every course of action can be made out to accord with the rule. The answer was: if everything can be made out to accord with the rule, then it can also be made out to conflict with it. And so there would be neither accord nor conflict here.
It can be seen that there is a misunderstanding here from the mere fact that in the course of our argument we give one interpretation after another; as if each one contented us at least for a moment, until we thought of yet another standing behind it. What this shews is that there is a way of grasping a rule which is *not* an *interpretation*, but which is exhibited in what we call 'obeying the rule' and 'going against it' in actual cases.
Hence there is an inclination to say: every action according to the rule is an interpretation. But we ought to restrict the term 'interpretation' to the substitution of one expression of the rule for another. (*PI* §201)

And hence also 'obeying a rule' is a practice. And to *think* one is obeying a rule is not to obey a rule. Hence it is not possible to obey a rule 'privately': otherwise thinking one was obeying a rule would be the same thing as obeying it. (*PI* §202)

In short, to understand what a sign means is *not* to *interpret* that sign. The infant learner does not grasp the meaning of a sign – something spoken to it or written down – by *interpreting* (and in particular, not by interpreting a sign as meaning one of the words of its Mentalese). No, *it is trained to react* in a certain way. In the very first months, this training presupposes certain fundamental abilities of the infant such as its being able to make certain sounds or gestures and to perceive certain changes in the audiovisual environment. At the early stage of training, an infant can be conditioned to react in a particular way to a particular sound, or to produce a certain sound to provoke a certain response. 'But that is only to give a causal connection' says the objector at (*PI* §198), and that is true; and at this early stage of the learning process, all the infant has is meaning$_n$. Only when the child has become inducted into the customs of the language and has become master of a technique (*PI* §199) can we say that it has acquired the meanings of words.

Custom and technique – what are these? First, custom (or institution). Owning a house is, in our society, an institution. If you move into a house, or even build a house for yourself, you do not (yet) own it. There are all sorts of formalities to be completed, for there are *rules* governing house ownership to which you have to comply. Similarly, there is more to speaking language than uttering right-sounding sounds – one must use words in conformity with and as conforming to certain rules. Of course, the semantical rules of language are boring, and breaking them can be fun. But you have to know at least what it is to break them before you can break them. This, as Wittgenstein might say, is a grammatical remark: Finnegan's infancy must precede Finnegans Wake.

Conforming to the rules does not mean that one has to be able to formulate the rules; all that is required is that one must have a conception of using words *correctly*. Correctness is not a matter of what seems right to me; it is an objective matter. So, as Davidson has pointed out, the language-learner needs the concept of *objectivity* or *intersubjectivity* (Davidson, 1975; 1992). In first-language learning, this sense of correctness is not normally inculcated by explicit correction of an infant's misuses. The understanding of correctness comes with the recognition that, when uttering a word while pointing at something, both learner and teacher are trying to fasten on to the *same* object. The infant learns to use the word 'table' not as a name for its private visual impression of the table, but as a name for the same object as the one for which its caregiver is using that name. This achievement requires the complex feats of reacting to reactions and recognizing the intentions of others. It requires a second person (Verheggen, 1997). Where some discrepancy between teacher use and learner use arises, the learner will defer to the teacher, for the teacher is the custodian of the custom. That's not quite how the infant would put matters; what is true, though, is that, for this brief stage in the child's development, it is happy to acknowledge that the adult is always right, and it will seek to conform to the adult usage. A mere conditioned response to a stimulus is no acknowledgment of such intersubjective agreement, and without intersubjectivity as the guiding light, there is no conception of correctness.

2. Meaning

Non-human animals, so far as we know, never have this normativity training, and this is one good reason for denying that their tweetings, gruntings or complex dancings amount to language. Whether some monkeys, camels, or other promising-looking animals can acquire language through training by humans is an open question. But bearing in mind that what is involved, is *inter alia*, getting the learner to intend to utter sounds in order to provoke a reaction in the hearer, and to intend that the reaction be a function of the hearer's recognition of that intention, we may reasonably doubt that those creatures have the necessary metarepresentational brain power to really get the hang of language-using.[38] As for computers, one could put a neural net through a training so that, through engagement with the actual world and correction of its initial errors, it learns to fit the right nouns to the right objects.[39] But, again, this is a far cry from true language-competence. For first, there is much more to language than the labelling of objects; second, though the 'normativity training' results in the net being able to apply nouns correctly to objects it never encountered during the training, the net doesn't thereby acquire the sense that there are constraints on correct usage (the training has merely subjected it to those constraints), nor is it equipped for meaning-change which, in natural languages, usually comes about under pressure of peculiarly human needs and interests. The net can, at best, mimic a thin time-slice of a small part of the linguistic behaviour of a community of speakers.

Even when, as in the case of words for our pains and other sensations, there is no external *object* which is the common focus of teacher and learner, there has to be at least perceptible external *behaviour* to guarantee the intersubjectivity of sense – for how could a teacher guide the learner to the correct words for sensations if the learner were using those words to refer to something inner and private to which the teacher had no access?[40] The same point could be made about the meaning of the word 'I' against someone who holds (with Frege) that each of us attaches a unique, private meaning to that word (Ellenbogen, 1997).

Another aspect of the acquisition of the meaning of words is alluded to in Wittgenstein's talk of *technique*. He says that understanding a language is mastery of a technique and he seems to be suggesting (extremely puzzlingly) that, before one can understand a sentence, one has to have mastered the whole language (*PI* §199). Well, that's not what he's suggesting. The point is simply that, for an infant to be credited with an understanding of the meaning of a word, it has to do more than to react to that single word in a fixed way: the infant must understand how that word is related to other words. (It has not learned the word 'cat' if it thinks that some cats are called 'dogs' or if it denies

71

that cats are animals; it must know something about that with which 'cat' contrasts.) Similarly, one does not understand or believe just one sentence in isolation. 'Light dawns gradually over the whole', as Wittgenstein charmingly puts it (Z §141).

We have been labouring to cast some light on Wittgenstein's claim that 'there is a way of grasping a rule which is *not* an *interpretation*' (*PI* §201). It turned out that the grasping is achieved by *learning*. 'You learned the *concept* "pain" when you learned language' (*PI* §384). 'How do I know that this colour is red? – It would be an answer to say: "I have learnt English"' (*PI* §381). Now that we have glimpsed something of the complexity of what happens in first language acquisition, we can appreciate that these are anything but casual, throwaway remarks.

Wittgenstein says that grasping a rule 'is exhibited in what we call "obeying the rule" and "going against it" in actual cases' (*PI* §201). One might agree that this is how the grasp of a rule is *exhibited*, but that doesn't tell us what grasping a rule *consists in*. It would be natural to suppose that when I have grasped the rule for the word 'dog', i.e., when I know how to use the word 'dog' correctly, then I have acquired a certain internal cognitive state; that seems a plausible theory. However, as we shall see in the next section, it is a view that Wittgenstein thinks we ought to resist – though the alternative he offers has seemed 'wholly mysterious' to some (Grayling, 1991, p. 67).

Kripkensteinian scepticism

An entertaining book by Saul Kripke (1982) has generated a lively debate in the philosophical literature.[41] Kripke discusses an apparently outlandish sceptical suggestion – that when you or I, under perfectly normal circumstances, use a perfectly ordinary word like 'dog', there is no fact about us which constitutes our meaning *dog* rather than something completely different. Kripke recognizes that, though he finds the problem canvassed in *Philosophical Investigations*, his formulation may not meet with Wittgenstein's approval, so he asks his reader to think of him as 'expounding neither "Wittgenstein's" argument nor "Kripke's": rather Wittgenstein's argument as it struck Kripke, as it presented a problem for him' (p. 5). Elsewhere, he portrays himself as 'almost like an attorney presenting a major philosophical argument as it struck me' (p. ix). There is, however, serious doubt as to whether the argument before the court was ever propounded by Wittgenstein and, since Kripke does not claim it as his own, authorship is sometimes credited to a fictional Kripkenstein.

2. Meaning

Anyway, here's the so-called 'Wittgensteinian Paradox' as set out by Kripke:

I, like almost all English speakers, use the word 'plus' and the symbol '+' to denote a well-known mathematical function, addition. The function is defined for all pairs of positive integers. By means of my external symbolic representation and my internal mental representation, I 'grasp' the rule for addition. One point is crucial to my 'grasp' of this rule. Although I myself have computed only finitely many sums in the past, the rule determines my answer for indefinitely many new sums that I have never previously considered. This is the whole point of the notion that in learning to add I grasp a rule: my past intentions regarding addition determine a unique answer for indefinitely many new cases in the future.

Let me suppose, for example, that '68 + 57' is a computation that I have never performed before. Since I have performed – even silently to myself, let alone in my publicly observable behavior – only finitely many computations in the past, such an example surely exists. In fact, the same finitude guarantees that there is an example exceeding, in both its arguments, all previous computations. I shall assume in what follows that '68 + 57' serves for this purpose as well.

I perform the computation, obtaining, of course, the answer '125'. I am confident, perhaps after checking my work, that '125' is the correct answer. It is correct both in the arithmetical sense that 125 is the sum of 68 and 57, and in the metalinguistic sense that 'plus', as I intended to use that word in the past, denoted a function which, when applied to the numbers I called '68' and '57', yields the value 125.

Now suppose I encounter a bizarre sceptic. This sceptic questions my certainty about my answer, in what I just called the 'metalinguistic' sense. Perhaps, he suggests, as I used the term 'plus' in the past, the answer I intended for '68 + 57' should have been '5'! Of course the sceptic's suggestion is obviously insane. My initial response to such a suggestion might be that the challenger should go back to school and learn to add. Let the challenger, however, continue. After all, he says, if I am now so confident that, as I used the symbol '+', my intention was that '68 + 57' should turn out to denote 125, this cannot be because I explicitly gave myself instructions that 125 is the result of performing the addition in this particular instance. By hypothesis, I did no such thing. But of

73

course the idea is that, in this new instance, I should apply the very same function or rule that I applied so many times in the past. But who is to say what function this was? In the past I gave myself only a finite number of examples instantiating this function. All, we have supposed, involved numbers smaller than 57. So perhaps in the past I used 'plus' and '+' to denote a function which I will call 'quus' and symbolize by '⊕'. It is defined by:

$$x \oplus y = x+y, \text{ if } x, y < 57$$
$$= 5 \text{ otherwise.}$$

Who is to say that this is not the function I previously meant by '+'?
The sceptic claims (or feigns to claim) that I am now misinterpreting my own previous usage. By 'plus', he says, I *always meant* quus; now, under the influence of some insane frenzy, or a bout of LSD, I have come to misinterpret my own previous usage. (Kripke, 1982, pp. 7-9)

As Kripke says, the references to LSD and insane frenzy are just for dramatic effect. The straight statement of the problem goes like this:

Ordinarily, I suppose that, in computing '68 + 57' as I do, I do not simply make an unjustified leap in the dark. I follow directions I previously gave myself that uniquely determine that in this new instance I should say '125'. What are these directions? By hypothesis, I never explicitly told myself that I should say '125' in this very instance. Nor can I say that I should simply 'do the same thing I always did,' if this means 'compute according to the rule exhibited by my previous examples.' That rule could just as well have been the rule for quaddition (the quus function) as for addition. (Kripke, 1982, pp. 10-11)

It's not a matter of my misremembering how I used a particular word in the past; the question is how *could* I have meant the word one way rather than another – what fact about my then state ensures that I meant the word then in the same way as (or in a different way from) the way I use it now? You may be inclined to reply: there are many numbers that I have never added before but, should I now add a pair of them, then, if I am sufficiently careful, I will get their sum, not their quum, and I am justified in saying that, because I know the rules for addition, which apply in every case, old and new. For example, in adding 57 to 68, I use the 'carry' rule: take the rightmost integer in each of the numbers to be added and add them: that's 15, so write down 5 and carry the 1 to the next column. At this point, however, the sceptic will say 'What justifies you in thinking that what you have in your head is the 'carry' rule, not the 'quarry' rule – that's the rule which is like the 'carry' rule, except that when the numbers to be added are ≥ 57, you just add the rightmost integers as before, but then write down the rightmost integer in their quum and then stop right there; calculation over? Or the even simpler rule: like the 'carry' rule, but if the numbers to be added are ≥ 57, write down the answer 5?

Although Kripke takes as his example a word from mathematics, any word would do. (When I used the word 'parrot' in the past, perhaps I really meant 'quarrot', a word which applies to the parrots I've seen in the past but to what you and other normal people will call 'carrots' in the future.) One good reason for choosing a mathematical example is that it is easy to get a graphical representation of this problem of anomalous continuation: given a finite number of points, we may be able to draw a nice smooth curve through them, and this curve may seem to have a 'natural' extension beyond those points that it joins. But, of course, there is an infinite number of ways of extending the curve beyond the finite segment drawn, and for each such continuation, there will be a mathematical function (a 'rule') which describes it. *Each* such function, of course, fits the original finite data.

The conclusion to which this argument appears to lead is very striking. If there is nothing about me – about my mind, brain or behaviour – which could indicate that I meant a particular word in a particular way, then I would not be able to say that when I use a word now, I mean by it just what I meant by it in the past. If Kripke is right about the sceptical conclusion, then 'there can be no such thing as meaning anything by any word' (p. 55) and this implies that all human conversation is just meaningless babble. We all know people whose conversation does fit that description, but the conclusion of the 'sceptical argument' retailed by Kripke is that *all* human discourse, from humdrum interchanges to learnèd papers in mathematics and physics, is meaningless.

Kripke shows that various ways of attempting to escape the sceptical conclusion do not work. Perhaps the most obvious escape route is to suggest that what it is about me that guarantees that I meant *plus* by plus, is not that I was in some suitable 'plus'-meaning state, but that I had the *disposition* to give the sum (not the quum) of x and y if asked what 'x + y' is. Had I been asked in the past for '68 + 57' (which I was not), I *would have* answered '125'. However, this response misses the real problem. So I would have been disposed to answer '125' – lucky me! The problem was not about what I would have said but about what fact about me would have *justified* my saying it rather than saying (say) '5' (pp. 11, 22-37). We are at a loss for an answer to *this* question.

Kripke himself advocates what he calls a 'sceptical solution' to this paradox which escapes the sceptical conclusion. He *accepts* the sceptical claim that there is no fact about a person that constitutes that person meaning something by a given word, but he thinks it possible that we may yet be entitled to say that the person does mean something by that word. Kripke's prescription is this: abandon the search for any fact F that will satisfy a condition such as 'Saul means *plus* when he says "plus" if and only if F ' and say instead 'Saul means *plus* by "plus" if and only if he is inclined to use the word "plus" as (most) members in his linguistic community do'.[42] One's first reaction to this suggestion might be – perhaps *all* of them are wrong; perhaps they all say 'plus' and really mean *quus*. But clearly this reply is question-begging; it presupposes just that conception of meaning that Kripke repudiates – the conception that there is some fact about Saul or his fellow speakers that constitutes their meaning something (*plus*, *quus* or whatever) by 'plus'.

Elizabeth Anscombe, in her review of Kripke's book, traces to Leibniz the claim that there is an indefinite number of rules consistent with a finite body of data (Anscombe, 1985). Kripke's quus example is a variation on this theme. Although Kripke is wrong to think that his 'Wittgensteinian Paradox' is the paradox referred to at *PI* §201 – the latter paradox (discussed in the previous section) concerns whether the understanding of what someone says requires that we interpret his words[43] – the interesting question is whether the Kripkenstein paradox occurs in Wittgenstein's late writings at all and, if it does, how Wittgenstein tackles it.

There is some, by no means uncontroversial, evidence for the presence of the Kripkenstein paradox in the Wittgenstein corpus (*PI* §§185ff., 213, 226; *RFM* I-3). Perhaps the closest Wittgenstein gets is at *PI* §§191, 197, where he has his interlocutor expostulate 'It is as if we could grasp the whole use of the word in a flash'. We do say things like this – we do suddenly (or not so suddenly) grasp the meaning of a word. But if the meaning of a word is its use – how the word is *and will be* used – then there is apparently something strange going on, for in grasping the meaning of a word, a person somehow reaches into the future. And Kripke will ask: just what fact about a person now justifies ascribing this grasp of meaning to him. For suppose that both you and I now grasp the meaning of the same word (or at least we think we do) but that, after a while our uses of this word diverge. Then, looking back from the future, one would have to say that either you or I or both of us have not grasped what the word means even though (let's suppose) our present agreement in the use of that word is total.

Wittgenstein's response to this problem is that the request for justification is misplaced. It arises from a false picture we have that, once we grasp the meaning of a word, its future use is, in some *queer* way, somehow already present in us (*PI* §§195, 197) just as its possibilities of future movement seem to be written into a machine (*PI* §§193, 194). We think that grasping a meaning puts us on the visible section of rails invisibly laid to infinity (*PI* §218). But these are misleading analogies.

I can use a word correctly (I use '+' correctly if I say '8 + 8 = 16') even though no future-oriented justification of the sort sought by the sceptic is available. 'To use a word without a justification (Rechtfertigung) is not to use it wrongly (zu Unrecht)' (*PI* §289; RFM VII-40). 'If I have exhausted the justifications I have reached bedrock, and my spade is turned. Then I am inclined to say "This is simply what I do" ' (*PI* §217). I use words blindly (*PI* §219), but that does not mean *wildly* – I just follow my natural inclination – it comes 'second nature' to me, it comes as a 'matter of course' (*PI* §238) to either apply a word (say 'blue') to a new case (e.g. a shade of colour I've never seen before) or to withhold the word. Of course, it comes as second nature to you too, because our (second-) natures are pretty much the same: this is agreement not in opinions but in 'form of life' (*PI* §241); we engage in similar language-games. It is indeed lucky that we humans are constituted rather similarly; we have similar basic needs, generally discriminate the same colours and sounds, have similar emotional reactions, and so on. Needless to say, there are interesting *differences* between us too, but without the massive agreement on fundamentals, no language or mutual understanding would be possible.

We might disagree about whether the man on the beach is a spy, but we could not have such a disagreement if we were built so differently that we were unable to agree in our judgment about what 'the', 'man', 'on' etc. mean. Take a simpler example: The anaconda is poised to strike. It has in the past successfully constricted deer and antelope, and so we, having observed all its past behaviour, might attribute to it the rule: If hungry, and if x is a nearby deer or antelope, strike at x. This anaconda has never encountered an elephant. So quoologists might ascribe to it the rule: If hungry and if x is a nearby deer, antelope or elephant, strike at x. However, we would not say that the quoologist was maintaining a healthy scepticism; we would say that he was *mad* for ignoring rather obvious evolutionary constraints.[44]

Of course, there is no guaranteeing that it will not happen that sometime in the future, through an evolutionary anomaly, a quanaconda is born which strikes at elephants. And, as we saw in the case of the development of infants, it is not always the case that future linguistic use will not differ from current use. To say that meaning is use is only to say that present meaning is present use. Meanings change. The word 'number' certainly means something different now to what it meant two thousand years ago; the extension of that word is not 'closed by a frontier' (*PI* §68). Again, consider the word 'fulsome', which means 'cloying', 'false' etc.; the word connotes something distinctly unpleasant. It is wearisome hearing people using the word to mean just the opposite, but that they do is understandable, since, in their ignorant way, they are thinking 'full', 'wholesome', 'handsome' ... Yet this 'ignorant' sense is now listed in *Webster's Dictionary*. Previous editions and other dictionaries do not list this sense,[45] but, now that it is sanctioned by Webster's, it will gain even greater currency, and future dictionaries will have to list it. This is real history, not armchair linguistics. Some prominent, though illiterate person, uses the word wrongly; a lexicographer now has an authoritative source for the new sense and includes it in a popular dictionary. After a while, a *statistically significant* proportion of people use the word in the new way, and that way then becomes the *right* way – there is no other criterion of correct usage. Peter Hacker says '*correct use* is not a statistical concept', and he backs this up by saying, 'If it were, then *inter alia*, there would be no deferring to experts to explain the use of technical and quasi-technical terms; appeal to socio-linguistic surveys would suffice' (Hacker, 1996a, pp. 208, 323). The example just given (and such examples could, of course, be multiplied) shows that Hacker is wrong about this. Expertise is frequently overridden or submerged by popular usage.

3

Mind

Wittgenstein and psychology

In this chapter, I shall trace the development of Wittgenstein's views on the mind – from the disturbed ravings of a melancholy soldier, through a taut and elegant theory of thought in the *Tractatus* to, in his late work, perceptive discussions of our mental lives and of the human condition. Wittgenstein himself did some work in experimental psychology both in his early years at Cambridge (when David Pinsent was one of his subjects) and in a clinical research unit during the Second World War.[1] He read contemporary psychologists such as William James and Wolfgang Köhler, but had a jaundiced view of psychology, thinking it to be riddled with conceptual confusion (*PI* Part II sect. xiv, p. 232; *RPP I* §1039).

Much of what Wittgenstein writes, in his later work in the philosophy of psychology, is in reaction to the empirical theories set out by William James in *The Principles of Psychology* (first published in 1890). It is, of course, hard to tell for sure, but the evidence seems to indicate that Wittgenstein spent more time studying James than he devoted to any other academic writer, with the possible exception of Frege. Wittgenstein thought James a decent human being and (not unconnectedly) a philosopher/psychologist worthy of study.[2] *The Principles* is written in a pleasingly straightforward style; whatever James had to say, he said clearly, and much of it sounds like the plain good sense that Wittgenstein shows it is not. Wittgenstein was generally disdainful of what little purely philosophical writings on the mind he read, reserving particular vitriol for the works of Russell (see Shanker, 1993). However, his writings on the philosophy of psychology do not read like skirmishes with contemporaries. Much of his thinking is of direct relevance to current psychological investigations, and a wider understanding of his views is overdue, given the recent welcome advent of serious collaboration between philosophers and psychologists.

If there is one thing that distinguishes Wittgenstein from all other philosphers it is his nose for what is philosophically puzzling (Kripke,

1982, p. 60). His philosophical development can be viewed, from one important perspective, in terms of an increasing appreciation and wonderment at various aspects of the human psyche. Much of his later writing is an attempt to show that contemporary psychologists did not get as far as describing the phenomena accurately, that their theories were inadequate, and that some of the puzzles are not even amenable to scientific explanation. There are various aspects of the philosophy of our mental make-up on which Wittgenstein wrote. I shall focus on three broad categories: thinking, belief and sensation.

Wartime musings

Prolonged isolation on the bank of a Norwegian fjord in the years 1913-14, an austere regime of sensuous deprivation and intense concentration when, as he put it, his 'mind was really on fire', produced striking results for Wittgenstein in the field of philosophical logic – the theory of the nature of the propositions and of tautologies and contradictions, the doctrine of ineffability, the semantic method for studying logical entailment and much more. But his views in general philosophy remained amazingly naive, perhaps not surprisingly, considering how little he had studied the subject. Some of his subsequent wartime jottings indicate that Wittgenstein was still wetting the bed, philosophically speaking.

In the autumn of 1916, after a period of bitter fighting on the Russian front, Wittgenstein, depressed and lonely while on leave in Vienna, passed through a phase which can perhaps best be described as Buddhistic. This is revealed by the following extracts from his wartime notebooks:

> The philosophical I is not the human being, not the human body or the human soul with the psychological properties, but the metaphysical subject, the boundary (not a part) of the world. The human body, however, my body in particular, is a part of the world among others, among animals, plants, stones etc., etc.
>
> Whoever realizes this will not want to procure a pre-eminent place for his own body or for the human body.
>
> He will regard humans and animals quite naively as things which are similar and which belong together. (*N* entry for 2.9.16, p. 82)

> But now at last the connexion of ethics with the world has to be made clear. (entry for 9.10.16, p. 84)

A stone, the body of a beast, the body of a man, my body, all stand on the same level. That is why what happens, whether it comes from a stone or from my body is neither good nor bad. (entry for 12.10.16, p. 84)

One conception: As I can infer my spirit (character, will) from my physiognomy, so I can infer the spirit (will) of each thing from *its* physiognomy.

But can I *infer* my spirit from my physiognomy?

Isn't this relationship purely empirical?

Does my body really express anything?

Is it itself an internal expression of something?

Is e.g., an angry face angry in itself or merely because it is empirically connected with bad temper?

But it is clear that the causal nexus is not a nexus at all.

Now is it true (following the psycho-physical conception) that my character is expressed only in the build of *my* body or brain and not equally in the build of the whole of the rest of the world?

This contains a salient point. This parallelism, then, really exists between my spirit, i.e. spirit, and the world.

Only remember that the spirit of the snake, of the lion, is *your* spirit. For it is only from yourself that you are acquainted with spirit at all.

Now of course the question is why I have given a snake just this spirit.

And the answer to this can only lie in the psycho-physical parallelism: If I were to look like the snake and to do what it does then I should be such-and-such.

The same with the elephant, with the fly, with the wasp.

But the question arises whether even here, my body is not on the same level with that of the wasp and of the snake (and surely it is so), so that I have neither inferred from that of the wasp to mine nor from mine to that of the wasp. Is this the solution of the puzzle why men have always believed that there was *one* spirit common to the whole world? And in that case it would, of course, also be common to lifeless things too. (entry for 15.10.16, pp. 84-5)

And in this sense I can also speak of a will that is common to the whole world.

But this will is in a higher sense *my* will.

As my idea is the world, in the same way my will is the world-will. (entry for 17.10.16, p. 85)

The experience one has when reading this part of Wittgenstein's diary is rather like that of reading Newton's manuscripts and discovering long tracts of alchemy along with what we should now count as *bona fide* physics; commentators tend to pass over it in embarrassed silence. Wittgenstein's work had just begun to broaden out 'from the foundations of logic to the essence of the world' (entry for 2.8.16, p. 79). We find here a wonderful amalgam of ideas, some half-formed – Wittgenstein confesses his 'crude mistakes' and the 'complete unclarity of all these sentences' (entries for 29.7.16 and 2.8.16, pp. 78, 79) – some banal, some extremely sharp, ranging across metaphysics, ethics, the philosophy of mind and mysticism. Some of these reflections are Schopenhauerian. That is, says Wittgenstein, the human will, not the world of Idea, that is the bearer of good and evil (entries for 21.7.16 and 2.8.16, pp.76, 79).[3] But to live happily involves, in some way, forsaking one's will, living 'in the present' (entry for 8.7.16, p. 74) and therefore free of hope and fear; free, *a fortiori* of the fear of death (see entries for 8.7.16 and 14.7.16, pp.74, 76). Wittgenstein seems to have really talked himself into this 'philosophy of life'. He readily exposed himself to danger in the heat of battle when under heavy artillery fire, and was decorated for his bravery.[4]

One month before this Buddhistic turn, and anticipating Henry Ford, Wittgenstein asked 'What has history to do with me?' He immediately replied to that question with an answer which very neatly captures the solipsism and idealism to which he subscribed at that time: History has nothing to do with him because 'mine is the first and only world' (entry for 2.9.16, p. 82). What is interesting is that, in the space of one month, Wittgenstein moved away from solipsism and Schopenhauerian idealism. He describes his journey thus: 'This is the way I have travelled: Idealism singles men out from the world as unique, solipsism singles me alone out, and at last I see that I too belong with the rest of the world, and so on the one side *nothing* is left over, and on the other side, as unique, *the world*. In this way idealism leads to realism if it is strictly thought out' (entry for 20.10.16, p. 85).

'Strictly thought out'?! That seems a rather generous description of these adolescent ramblings. At the beginning of the journey, Wittgenstein espouses Schopenhauer's idealism, a metaphysics in which there is no real world independent of human minds; there is, on one side (side A), human beings, on the other (side B), the world-as-perceived-by-humans. Now, some individual who is attracted to this doctrine might go a bit further, and reflect that perhaps all other people are just contrivances of his perception, the same as the rest of the world is. The solipsist is someone who really believes this is so; it's just me on side A, my world-as-perceived-by-me on side B. But then (the last stage in Wittgenstein's odyssey) realising that if everyone else has disappeared into this immaterial world of idea, so might I – *ping*! – the erstwhile solipsist jumps across the gap, leaving nothing on side A, and my world-as-perceived-by-and-including-me on side B. Except that, now that I have departed from side A, there is no 'my' and no 'me'; what is on side B cannot be the figment of an observer's mind, for there is now no observer. Hence on this side, it is no longer the world-perceived-by-X, for there is no X who stands apart from the world, so it must be the world *simpliciter*, the real world! So I am part of the real world, along with the rocks and the raccoons; I occupy no privileged place.[5] [See diagram on p. 84]

Whether Wittgenstein had any direct contact with oriental philosophy, or whether it was channelled via Schopenhauer, or whether he dreamed up, all on his own, the stuff about the spirits of lions and snakes and stones, and of humans belonging together with animals, is not clear.[6] What is, of course, striking, is the huge distance between these views and what he says in his later writings on the distinctiveness of human beings: 'We only say of a human being and what is like one that it thinks' (*PI* §360); 'only of a living human being and what resembles (behaves like) a living human being can one say: it has sensations; it sees; is blind; hears; is deaf; is conscious or unconscious' (*PI* §281).[7] 'What has a soul, or pain, to do with a stone? Only of what behaves like a human being can one say that it *has* pains' (*PI* §283). As for the lion, far from our enjoying a rapport with a fellow spirit, 'If a lion could talk, we could not understand him' (*PI* II xi, p. 223).

We know, from a beautiful letter (quoted in Chapter 5) written to him by some of the settlers in Skjolden after he had left to fight in the First World War, that Wittgenstein was careful to cause no suffering to any animals. His conception of bliss is bovine: 'we could say that the man is fulfilling the purpose of existence who no longer needs to have any purpose except to live. That is to say, who is content' (*N* entry for 6.7.16, p. 73).

It may begin to seem as if Wittgenstein's only concern with the mind in his wartime notebooks is with *peace of mind*, but this is far from the case. He has some remarks on the Cartesian *res cogitans*, claiming that belief in such a 'thinking subject' is mere superstition, an illusion (entries for 4.8.16, 5.8.16, p. 80) and, although he acknowledges the existence of a 'willing subject' (a subject that acts, not one that merely wishes that things will happen) (entry for 5.8.16, p. 80; also 4.11.16, p. 88), he denies that there are interior acts of will which cause action: 'The

84

act of the will is not the cause of the action but is the action itself' (entry for 4.11.16, p. 87). He spends some time elaborating this position.

At one point in the course of the discussion on will, Wittgenstein raises the question 'Can I try to will something?' In a philosophical quiz show, most philosophers, when asked to name the date when this question first appeared in the literature, would be at least thirty years off the mark. The same is true of the question 'Is seeing an activity?' which drops out of the blue on 29.7.16 (N, p. 77). One associates the discussion of such issues with 'Oxford' philosophy of the late 1940s, with Gilbert Ryle's *Concept of Mind* and, of course, with the *Philosophical Investigations*. The will, for example, receives extended discussion in *PI* and in Wittgenstein's last lectures *LPP*. At *PI* §615, Wittgenstein quotes the thesis that willing must be the action itself, and he answers in the negative his question of twenty years earlier about whether one can try to will something (*PI* §§618, 619). It is fascinating to see questions raised in these First World War notebooks that were put on the back burner for so many years; fascinating also that the early babblings about our oneness with the beasts should be so thoroughly repudiated in Wittgenstein's late writings on what it is to be human.

Thinking

The early mechanistic conception of the mind

Most of Wittgenstein's wartime notebooks were destroyed, on his orders. One gets the impression that he had thought a lot about thinking, but there is little written record of this. In the *Notebooks 1914-16* he says: 'Now it is becoming clear why I thought that thinking and language were the same. For thinking is a kind of language. For a thought too is, of course, a logical picture of the proposition, and therefore it just is a kind of proposition'[8] (*N* entry for 12.9.16, p. 82). This foreshadows the conception of thinking that is set out in the *Tractatus*.

In the *Tractatus*, Wittgenstein has very little to say about the mind or our mental lives. There is a very brief discussion of the nature of thoughts and there is a short and highly opaque section (5.54-5.5423) dealing with the notion of *belief*. When pressed by Russell on the question of what the constituents of thoughts are, Wittgenstein says that he doesn't know (*N*, p. 130); but this doesn't seem to bother him at all – he knows, he says, that a thought *must* have psychic constituents; it is 'irrelevant' to him how these are related to what in the world the thought is about – 'It would be a matter of psychology to find out' (*N*, p. 129). As for what many people take to be the central question in the philosophy of mind: does a human being consist of two categorically distinct parts, a mind and a body?, Wittgenstein has an amazingly dismissive answer: there is nothing special about any particular number, 'there are no privileged numbers in logic, and hence (*sic*) there is no philosophical monism or dualism, etc.' (*T* 4.128).[9]

That the *Tractatus* is so thin on the subject does not indicate that, early on, Wittgenstein was not interested in questions about the human mind, or was ignorant of the issues. Indeed, as we shall see, some of what he has to say is interesting and important, and many of his early views, which he later repudiated, are now warmly embraced by leading philosophers and cognitive scientists.

We must distinguish the *a priori*, philosophical investigation of what we and the world must be like for it to be possible for us to present to ourselves and others states of the world, from the empirical question of what is going on in our heads when such presentations are made. Wittgenstein says that there is a risk (presumably one to be avoided) of confusing the study of sign-language[10] with 'unessential psychological investigations' of thought processes (*T* 4.1121).[11]

A picture, in the technical sense of the *Tractatus*, is a model of reality (*T* 2.12); it presents a possible situation (*T* 2.11). There are various kinds of picture. A statement (Satz), for example, is one kind (*T* 4.01, 4.011). If someone says to me, 'Your daughter is in love with a serial killer', then he is presenting a possible situation, one which I hope to hell is not actual. A *thought* is another type of picture: 'A logical picture of facts is a thought' (*T* 3). We examined, in Chapter 2, the *Tractatus* theory, which occupies 2.1-2.221, of how pictures depict reality.

If I have the thought that 'my daughter is in love with a priest' then (if this makes sense) I present a possible situation to myself. If I want to make that thought available to others, I must express it, for example in speaking or in writing. A statement is a perceptible expression of a thought (*T* 3.1), although, when we are using ordinary, colloquial language, it may not be clear *which* thought is being expressed, for such language disguises thought (*Tractatus* 4.002). In the *Tractatus* theory, a thought is an inner presentation; it presents a possible situation in exactly the same way as does a statement; the elements of this presentation, the Names, signify the objects in the presented situation (*T* 2.131, 3.203). To have a thought is to picture (in the *Tractatus* sense) a state of affairs (see *T* 3.001). The relation between a thought and a statement could be put like this: to make a statement is just to think out loud. 'Der Gedanke ist der sinnvolle Satz' (*T* 4). The phrase 'sinnvolle Satz' ('sense-full statement') is, strictly speaking, pleonastic, since every Satz must have a Sinn (*T* 3.144, 4.064). A thought, then, is a (silent) statement.[12]

3. Mind

A written sentence is a group of physical marks, of signs; it is what Wittgenstein calls a 'Satzzeichen' (*T* 3.12ff.). Similarly, the stuff of a thought is a Satzzeichen (*T* 3.5), in this case, a bundle of physical, *psychical* elements, the physical nature of which is not a subject for the *logical* investigation conducted in the *Tractatus*. (This distinction between a thought *qua* physical entity inside the head and a thought as identified by logical criteria – what it implies and what implies it – has become prominent in modern debates on the doctrine of *externalism*.) The relation between the stuff of a thought and a thought is the same as the relation between a Satzzeichen and a Satz: when we *apply* (employ) a Satzzeichen to depict a situation, the result is a Satz. A Satz is a Satzzeichen in its application (Anwendung) (*T* 3.262). Likewise, a Satzzeichen *applied* but unvoiced – merely thought (gedachte) – is a thought (see *T* 3.5).

Wittgenstein distinguishes between a sign (Zeichen) and a symbol (Symbol; also 'Ausdruck', 'expression'). In the statement 'Green is green' about the person Green, the first and third words are different symbols since each contributes differently to the sense of the statement (*T* 3.323); the word 'green' and any other element of a statement does not signify anything when it appears on its own, outside of a statement (*T* 3.3). A Satz itself is a symbol (*T* 3.31); and 'In order to recognize a symbol by its sign we must observe how it is used ...' (*T* 3.326). A sign is inert – a blob of ink, a burst of sound etc. – people express themselves by *using* signs; we figure out what they are expressing by observing their use of signs. The point is most clearly made at *T* 3.262, although Pears and McGuinness make a mess of the translation. They misleadingly suggest that the signs themselves express a sense, but that sometimes they don't do so clearly – a near miss – and that we have to look at their application to clear things up. But there is nothing corresponding to 'clear' or 'clearly' in the German original. The best translation I can come up with (to which the Ogden rendering is a much closer approximation) is: 'What does not get expressed in the sign is shown by its application. What is swallowed up in the signs, their application brings out.' That itself is none too clear, but the point can be illustrated easily enough: if freak desert winds blow sand into a pattern that looks like this: *Elle me suit*, we would not say that here was a sign that expressed anything.[13] But a Frenchman might use a sign similar in appearance to that one to express his paranoia, or an Englishman (Tarzan) might use one to express his attraction towards the Australian actress Elle McPherson. The distinction being made here between sign and application is none other than (a generalized version of) the distinction between sentence and statement later made famous by Strawson (1950)

87

Clear and Queer Thinking

in his assault on Russell's theory of denoting: a statement is the *use* of a sentence on a given occasion – see also Austin (1950).

Many writers have maintained that the connection between language and the world is made in thought. That a thought is a kind of direct, natural representation of a situation, with sentences of different languages having not natural, but conventional relations to that thought. The following passage from Russell's essay 'On Propositions: what they are and how they mean' vents such a view:

> The first question to be asked is: Can the relation called 'meaning' be a direct relation between the word as a physical occurrence and the object itself, or must the relation pass through a 'mental' intermediary which could be called the idea of the object? (Russell, 1956, p. 290)

Russell's answer is that there are indeed such mental middlemen; there are what he calls 'image propositions' which image in the mind states of affairs. And an ordinary spoken or written sentence means (Russell's word) this mentalistic counterpart.[14]

Various commentators argue that, in the *Tractatus*, Wittgenstein holds this view too. But they've got him wrong. Unlike Russell and other empiricists who think that states of affairs stamp representations or impressions on the mind, Wittgenstein takes a thought – a 'logical picture' (*T* 3) – to be not an inert copy, but an active presentation to the thinker (*T* 3.001) of a possible state of affairs (*T* 2.202, 2.221). Similarly, when we make a statement, we project a possible situation (*T* 3.11), usually for the consideration of a hearer. Of course, this does not mean that we project the state of affairs in the same way as we project a projectile such as a stone. So a statement about (say) a mountain does not literally contain a mountain (*T* 3.13) – in contrast to the view that Russell once held that propositions contain as constituents real-world objects. No, a state of affairs is projected in the sense in which a photographic slide is projected, or in which one shape is projected into another in projective geometry. This accounts for the fact that, in the *Tractatus* theory, there is a structural similarity, an isomorphism, between a possible situation and the corresponding thought or statement which depicts it.

This Wittgensteinian notion of a thought as an active presentation will ring bells for Kant scholars. In Richard Aquila's words, cognitive faculties are regarded by Kant 'as the means by which the mind "represents" various objects to itself'. 'Cognitive states, in the sense that was new with Kant, are not cognitive relations with objects, nor

88

are they themselves peculiar objects supposed to mediate the occurrence of cognitive relations. They are simply the perceiver's awareness of possible objects';[15] in Wittgenstein's terms, a thinker's presenting a possible state of affairs to himself.

As I have tried to show, for Wittgenstein in his early period, thought is just one type of speech (the silent type). The conception of thought as silent speech has a distinguished ancestry. A lot of mediaeval discussion centred on the lexis and grammar of this 'mental language'. Fodor's 'Language of Thought' hypothesis, discussed in the previous chapter, belongs in this tradition, though it is arguably less sophisticated than (say) William of Occam's version.[16] The so-called 'symbolic paradigm' in A.I. (Artificial Intelligence) is built on just this conception of thinking.

As late as 1930-31, Wittgenstein was still advocating the kind of pictorial account of thinking that he had propounded in the *Tractatus*. In MS 108, p. 217, he writes 'Thinking is forming pictures of various kinds and in various ways'. 'Thinking is the use of symbols' (MS 108, p. 201).[17] It would be appropriate to label the conception of thinking advanced in the *Tractatus* 'mechanistic'. The mechanism is one which projects a situation into words. One could think of a robot scanning the scene in front of it, translating (projecting) the situation into a batch of fine-grained descriptions (which would be its thoughts if (only) it had access to them), then translating that, via a fuzzy algorithm, into some sentences of an everyday language, which it might utter – in a suitably flat, robotic tone.

This mechanistic conception of the mind and what Wittgenstein termed the 'calculus' conception of language (discussed in Chapter 1) are two sides of the same coin. To operate a calculus according to definite rules implies that there is a set of rules for depicting a situation we want to think about or describe, and that thinking – the manipulation of psychical signs – can be treated 'from the point of view that it could also be performed by a machine' (MS 110, p. 2). With his increasing awareness of the distinctiveness of human beings and of the rich tapestry which is our complicated form of life (*PI*, p. 174) Wittgenstein dropped this wholly artificial picture of thinking as a mechanical activity, and began to investigate the reality of our mental lives in its subtlety, complexity and diversity.[18]

Thinking in the later works

Turn to the later writings on thinking, and one notices a fantastic difference between the type of investigation that Wittgenstein is now conducting and the treatment of thinking in his early work. In the

Tractatus, he did not get much beyond viewing thinking as making pictures, in mental language, of situations, and performing inferences in conformity to the rules of logic. His rejection of this view is explicit:

It isn't true that thinking is a kind of speaking, as I once said. The concept 'thinking' is *categorially* different from the concept 'speaking'. (Z §7)

As Hacker puts it: 'We conceive of thinking as an invisible stream. And so we assimilate the grammar of 'thinking' to that of 'speaking', and this comparison plays havoc with our attempt to get a clear picture of thinking' (Hacker, 1990, p. 151). In the later writings, Wittgenstein does not go in for *a priori* theorizing about what thinking must be like. It is the empirical phenomenon (or phenomena) of thinking in which he is interested.[19] In his early work, he had been content to regard a thought just as an inner statement (*T* 3.1) but, in his later work, he comes to see that there are many types of thinking to which that characterization completely fails to do justice. 'Thinking', he says, 'is a widely ramified concept. A concept that comprises many manifestations of life. The *phenomena* of thinking are widely scattered' (*Z* §110; *RPP II* §§216, 218, 220) – as too are the phenomena of intending (*Z* §49; *RPP I* §830).

The questions of whether thinking requires language, and of whether animals can be credited with thinking, are raised in the restlessly inquisitive fashion typical of Wittgenstein's late, late style of enquiry:

He says 'I want to go out now', then suddenly says 'No', and does something else. As he said 'No', it suddenly occurred to him that he wanted first of all to ... – He said 'No', but did he also think 'No'? Didn't he just think about that other thing? One can say he was thinking about it. But to do that he didn't have to pronounce a thought, either silently or out loud. To be sure, he could later clothe the intention in a sentence. When his intentions changed maybe a picture was in his mind, or he didn't just say 'No', but some one word, the equivalent of a picture. For example, if he wanted to wash his hands he might have looked at them and made a face. 'But is that thinking?' – I don't know. Don't we say in such cases that someone has 'thought something over', has 'changed his mind'?

But is it absolutely necessary that he gain the command of a language for this kind of thinking? Couldn't an 'intelligent' beast act this way? It has been trained to fetch an object from one place and take it to another. Now it starts walking toward the goal without the object, suddenly turns around (as if it said 'Oh, I forgot ...!') and fetches the object, etc. If we were to see something like this we would say that at that time something had happened within it, in its mind. What then has happened within me when I act this way? 'Not much at all,' I would like to say. And what happens inside is no more important than what can happen outside, through speaking, drawing etc. (From which you can learn how the word 'thinking' is used.) (*RPP II* §6)

Armchair theorists, as well as psychologists and computer scientists, tend to think of thinking as an activity that takes place in the head. This is, perhaps, a natural assumption to make; where else, after all, could thinking take place? Deep Blue (the computer that first defeated Gary Kasparov at chess) is surely (they say) thinking of its next move, and if that thinking goes on in the microprocessor, then isn't Kasparov's going on (somewhat less rapidly) in his brain? We say to someone who has done something silly: 'Use your head' and we mean 'In future, think about what you are doing'; in other words: 'Use your head for thinking.'

There are several things wrong with the 'natural assumption'. The brain is, no doubt, intimately involved in our thinking, but that does not show that thinking takes place in the brain. Our legs are closely involved with our running – but we don't say that running takes place in our legs. Damage a leg and one's running may be impaired; damage the brain and one's thinking may be impaired. True, yet these observations do not make us conclude that running really is in the legs, nor should they lead us to conclude that thinking is really in the head. Hacker points out that 'it is I, not my brain, that thinks. And when I think, I can say what it is that I think. It would be absurd to say "My brain is thinking it over, but I don't yet know what conclusion it has reached!" ' (Hacker, 1990, p. 152).

I rack my brains trying to remember something ... and eventually succeed. But likewise, it doesn't follow that remembering is an activity or a process that takes place in the brain. The computer 'brain' can retrieve data from a particular location in memory, or can compare an input pattern with resident patters ('searching'). But we do not call those kinds of processes 'remembering', and 'racking one's brain', or one's memory, is nothing like that. Whatever processes occur *in the brain* when we think or remember, we do not use the words 'thinking' or 'remembering' to stand for *those* kinds of processes. Nor, we might add, do they stand for processes occurring in some gaseous mind-stuff or in some yet unexplored medium (*PI* §§305-8, 339).

Even if we suppose that, when thinking, word-like signs pass through our brains, it still does not follow that thinking is a brain process. The signs 'I'll * buy * my * daughter * a * horse * for * her * next * birthday' (or a coding of them) may pass through my brain; they may even be accompanied by images of a horse and of my daughter. Or (if you prefer minds to brains) the signs and images may dance on an inner Cartesian stage. But there is a great difference between this inner drama and my actually *thinking that* I shall buy my daughter a horse for her next birthday. For those selfsame signs and images may perform their ghostly dance in the mind/brain of a parrot or of a computer, but we would not credit either of these with thinking the thought. Neither parrot nor computer has the concept *horse*, neither know the significance of birthdays. To have the concept *horse* is to have *learned* that concept. It is through the process of learning (see previous chapter) that we come to see that a word like 'horse' is used to refer to those things cavorting in the field, and to know that words have a normative dimension, that is, that they may be applied rightly and wrongly. Possession of the concept *horse* requires at least that much. A book or a movie contains words and/or images. But it is an obvious error (obvious when it has been pointed out) to suppose that the book or movie *itself* consists of thoughts, has concepts, or understands the significance of anything. It makes no difference whether the words and images appear on a page, on a screen, in a microprocessor or in the brain of a parrot. The procession of word-signs through any medium is not yet enough to count as thinking.

A parade of inner signs, then, is not sufficient for thinking; but is it even *necessary*? A distinguished tradition, of which Plato is an early representative, regards thinking as inner *dialogue* (*RPP I* §180). Thinking is equated with the having of thoughts where the latter are conceived of as entities having a linguistic structure. But this conception is rooted in a confusion of two senses of the word 'thought'. A thought, in one sense of the word, is simply an act of speech from which the sound has been abstracted – a theoretical entity created by ignoring a certain feature of the speech act.[20] Thoughts thus conceived clearly are quasi-linguistic creatures. It is a serious mistake, however, to assimilate thoughts in this sense with elements or constituents of thinking.

There is no disputing that sometimes, instead of saying something out loud, we keep to ourselves, i.e. 'think', what we could have made available to an audience. From this, it is all too easy to infer that thinking generally is just unvoiced *speech*. To make this inference, however, is to assimilate the logical grammar of 'I was thinking that p, but then I came right out and said it' to 'I was hiding my key, but then I took it out of my pocket and gave it to her'. This similarity of grammar may tempt us to regard thoughts as objects which are hidden – particular kinds of objects: those that can be said out loud. So thoughts come to be regarded rather like sentences written in invisible ink, and, like sentences, to be composed of words – of mental words. One problem with this assimilation is that sentences are identified by their intrinsic features, but the same is not true of thoughts. Consider this: Dirk, who doesn't believe that Elvis Presley is dead, sees a man walking in Memphis whom he takes to be Elvis, and he starts having thoughts about that guy (whom we, but not he, know to be not Elvis, but Ernest Pratt). Dirk thinks that that guy has a strange walk. It would be quite proper for me to report Dirk's thought to you by saying that Dirk thinks that that guy Ernest Pratt has a strange way of walking, even though Dirk himself doesn't know the name 'Ernest Pratt'. There's no 'Ernest Pratt' in Dirk's mind; no sentence in his mind which contains that name; yet he is having a *thought* about Ernest Pratt in virtue of thinking about that guy whom he mistakes for Elvis.

Thinking that p is not thinking 'p' (Churchland, 1986, pp. 386-99). A brief Wittgensteinian argument makes the point: 'If thought were a language, it would make sense for a person to raise the question of what he meant by what he thought or by a constituent of his thought; but it makes no sense to think that N.N. is in New York, and to wonder what one means thereby, or to wonder who one means by "N.N." ' (Hacker, 1996a, p. 333). What we have to do is to refuse to construe 'I was thinking that p' as 'I had the thought "p" '. An alternative construal is 'I had a thought expressible thus: p'. The latter analysis, which simply makes thoughts what are *expressed by* the use of sentences and not themselves essentially sentence-involving, allows scope for us to say that we often think before we speak, without committing ourselves to the view that thinking, in general, is just silent saying, or that it is approximately replicated by speech, or indeed that thinking has anything like a linguistic structure.

When we report the products of our thinking or of someone else's, we perforce use language to do so. The thinking is undoubtedly *expressed* linguistically, because language is the vehicle for making manifest, amongst other things, what a person has thought or is thinking. But to conclude that the thinking itself – either the process or the immediate product – is linguistic or sentential is to transfer properties of the vehicle of expression onto what it is that is being expressed – an unwarranted move.[21]

We have the word 'think'; it is a verb, so naturally (but mistakenly) we suppose that it stands for some particular activity, that there is something that thinking is, something that constitutes the essence of thinking. But *thinking* is a 'ragged' notion (*RPP I* §554). Wittgenstein gives this useful reminder:

> Remember that our language might possess a variety of different words: one for 'thinking out loud'; one for thinking as one talks to oneself in the imagination; one for a pause during which something or other floats before the mind, after which, however, we are able to give a confident answer.
>
> One word for a thought expressed in a sentence; one for the lightning thought which I may later 'clothe in words'; one for wordless thinking as one works. (*Z* §122; also *RPP II* §215)

Thus, in answer to the question of whether or not we think in language, Wittgenstein would say that this is a false dichotomy. He accepts that there is some thinking in language where, as he puts it, 'language is itself the vehicle of thought' (*PI* §329) but he also cites examples of wordless thought. For example, consider someone (let's call him MacGyver) doing work that involves comparison, trial, choice – perhaps constructing an appliance out of various bits of stuff with a given set of tools. MacGyver (like Einstein) does not think in language, but could later put his thoughts into words, 'and in such a fashion that we, who might see the work in progress, could accept this account' (*Z* §100).

By contrast, Wittgenstein doubts that we should accept the testimony of the deaf mute Mr. Ballard (a case discussed by William James (1890, pp. 256-9)) as evidence that *in this case* there is wordless thinking:

> William James, in order to show that thought is possible without speech, quotes the recollection of a deaf-mute, Mr. Ballard, who wrote that in his early youth, even before he could speak, he had thoughts about God and the world. – What can he have meant? – Ballard writes: 'It was during those delightful rides, some two or three years before my initiation into the rudiments of written language, that I began to ask myself the question: how came the world into being?' – Are you sure – one would like to ask – that this is the correct translation of your wordless thought into words? And why does this question – which otherwise seems not to exist – raise its head here? Do I want to say that the writer's memory deceives him? – I don't even know if I should say that. These recollections are a queer memory phenomenon, – and I do not know what conclusions one can draw from them about the past of the man who recounts them. (*PI* §342; also *RPP II* §214)

James takes the view that this case illustrates that 'a deaf and dumb man can weave his tactile and visual images into a system of thought quite as effective and rational as that of a word-user' (James, 1890, p. 256). But that view is just blind optimism. What you get from weaving tactile and visual images are just colour-feely images, and it is completely unclear whether any succession of such images (a silent but tactile movie) could *without any reliance on language* be an examination of the question of how the world came into being.[22]

Would it be correct to say that some thinking requires language but other thinking does not? Wittgenstein says: 'We will not say he can be angry only if he has words. But can you wonder whether it will rain the day after tomorrow without words; or wonder whether there are 100 or 101 people in the room without numerals?' (*LPP*, p. 180) If I am asked to play football one afternoon next week, I have to consider that each of my Tuesdays and Fridays is already fully committed. Could I think this unless there were some counterpart to the words 'Tuesday' and 'Friday' in my thinking? It is hard to see how. This is an illustration that there is a kind of 'thinking in language', as indicated at *PI* §329. An even stronger claim is that some species of thinking are *facilitated* or *made possible* only by our prior possession of certain parts of language (Clark, 1997, pp. 207-8). If, in the course of a discussion, a methodical person says: 'There are five things wrong with your argument', and proceeds to document them, has he rehearsed these criticisms in his head? Does he stack some 'key words'? Here may be a case where a particularly sophisticated kind of thinking is supported only by leaning on language.

Belief

The topic of *belief* makes a brief, obscure, and, so most commentators seem to think, tangential appearance in the *Tractatus*. In the *Philosophical Investigations* and other late works, the topic is discussed more thoroughly but, as Peter Winch notes, 'even amongst those who do take a serious interest in Wittgenstein's work, his treatment of belief is seldom given a central place'. Yet, Winch continues, 'I myself think that what he writes about this is both of great importance in itself and also absolutely central to the main thrust of his philosophizing' (Winch, 1996, pp. 7-8). I concur with Winch's assessment, and I am indebted to him for the illumination he has thrown on the recalcitrant *Tractatus* passage.

Early beliefs

Here, in full, is Wittgenstein's discussion of *belief* in the *Tractatus*:

5.54   In the general form of a statement [Satz form], statements occur in other statements only as bases of truth-operations.

5.541   At first sight it looks as if it were also possible for one statement to occur in another in a different way.
Particularly with certain forms of statement in psychology, such as 'A believes that *p* is the case' and 'A has the thought *p*' etc.
For if these are considered superficially, it looks as if the statement *p* stood in some kind of relation to an object *A*.
(And in modern theory of knowledge (Russell, Moore, etc.) these statements have actually been construed in this way.)

5.542   It is clear, however, that 'A believes that *p*', 'A has the thought *p*' and 'A says *p*' are of the form ' "*p*" says *p*': and this does not involve a correlation of a fact with an object, but rather the correlation of facts by means of the correlation of their objects.

5.5421   This shows too that there is no such thing as the soul – the subject, etc. – as it is conceived in the superficial psychology of the present day.
Indeed a composite soul would no longer be a soul.

5.5422   The correct explanation of the form of the statement, 'A makes the judgement *p*', must show that it is impossible for a judgement to be a piece of nonsense.
(Russell's theory does not satisfy this requirement.)

5.5423   To perceive a complex means to perceive that its constituents are related to one another in such and such a way.
This no doubt also explains why there are two possible ways of seeing the figure [*opposite*] as a cube; and all similar phenomena. For we really see two different facts.
(If I look in the first place at the corners marked *a* and only glance at the *b*'s, then the *a*'s appear to be in front, and *vice versa*.)

An irate reader will protest 'What on earth is the relevance of the Necker Cube to this discussion of *belief* ?'; 'Whatever happened to A in the analysis given at *T* 5.542?'; How could ' "p" says p' be the analysis of

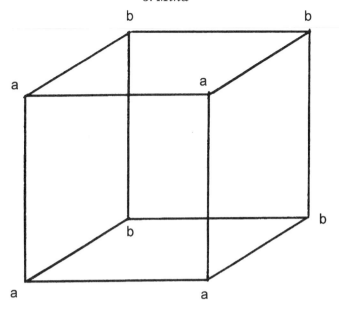

both 'A believes p' and 'B believes p'? One preliminary point that ought to be made is that ' "p" says p' is is *not* supposed to be the complete analysis of any attitude-ascribing statement. In the *Tractatus*, Wittgenstein simply gestures towards Russell's analysis of statements containing definite descriptions as a model of how the analysis of statements ought to be done, but he never gets down to doing one himself.

What Wittgenstein is discussing in the passage just cited is his thesis that all complex statements are truth-functions of simple ones – that the only way for a statement to occur in another is as a truth-functional component. If this were the case, then what can we make of attitude-ascriptions of the form 'A believes p', 'A hopes that p' etc.? Such ascriptions seem to be counterexamples to that thesis since in these a contained statement 'p' seems to be not conjoined, disjoined or in any other way truth-functionally related to any other statement, but to be related, somehow, to A.[23]

Wittgenstein is trying to show that, surface appearances to the contrary, in 'A believes that p', the proposition 'p' is not related to an object A (*T* 5.541).[24] The temptation is to think that, since it's not related to a physical object – A's *body* doesn't believe – that the relatum must be a Cartesian ego, or psychological subject. But it is worth recalling the doubts cast, in the *Notebooks 1914-16*, on the notion of a pure thinking thing, and, in the *Tractatus* too, Wittgenstein insists that '[t]here is no such thing as the subject that thinks or entertains ideas' (*Tractatus* 5.631).

The first point to remember, when trying to unravel this passage, is that the sorts of thing that may be substituted for 'p' in the schema ' "p" says p' are Sätze, and these are not abstract entities but are, as we have seen, the *uses* of sentences on occasions; and a sentence is used by *someone*. The 'p' that is mentioned in ' "p" says p' (the first one) is *A's* Satz (which may be a silent one if A keeps his beliefs to himself), so there is no need for further reference to A. The second 'p' is the speaker's (i.e. the person who is ascribing an attitude to A). That person is saying that an aspect of A's behaviour (in the simplest case, the utterance by A of 'p') *bespeaks* A's belief that p. A's behaviour may be totally strange, but it cannot literally be nonsensical – we can describe it. Hence there is no question of his behaviour bespeaking, or giving expression to, a *nonsensical* belief or judgment (see *T* 5.5422).[25]

There is a logical connection between behaving (or being disposed to behave) in a certain way and believing that p. A person who believes that p will be disposed to act in a way consistent with his holding that belief. Wittgenstein, then, is espousing a version of logical behaviourism; the soul (the 'ghost in the machine') does not figure in his analysis. Suppose that A has a belief that he never expresses, nor has ever been disposed to express, for example, the belief that he will not die within the next two and a half seconds (I'll ignore the interesting question of whether we actually do have beliefs that we are never inclined to express). In such cases, the first 'p' in ' "p" says p', is to be replaced by a description of facets of A's behaviour and dispositions which, in the eye of the ascriber, constitute evidence for ascribing to A the belief that p. We mention A and his complex dispositions to behave; there is no mention of a proposition related to A's simple soul.

Wittgenstein seems to have anticipated one of the now standard objections to logical behaviourism: there is no neat, unique relationship between a given mental state and a specific kind of behaviour. For example, take A's assertion 'My wife might come home early tonight'. This piece of verbal behaviour may bespeak a hope or a fear or some other mental state; we can see it in a variety of different ways (hence the allusion to the Necker Cube (*T* 5.5423), which may be seen now one way, now another). Under normal circumstances, an agent's behaviour will be the product not of a single mental state, such as a belief that p or a desire for B, but on a whole bundle of concurrent states. In practice, one can usually correctly interpret what a speaker means in a given context by virtue of those 'stillschweigenden Abmachungen' (*T* 4.002), the tacit conventions or unspoken cues on which detection of agents' mental conditions and the understanding of everyday conversation depend.

Later belief

Belief, hope and expectation are all dispositions, whereas thinking is occurrent, in that it happens on occasion. Wittgenstein calls the difference between believing and thinking a 'grammatical' one (*PI* §574). This is easy enough to illustrate: 'I was thinking about weakness of will, then felt thirsty, stopped thinking about that conundrum and went to have a beer'. Substituting 'believe' for 'think' in that last sentence results in nonsense.

There is a certain nonsensicality or absurdity involved in an utterance such as 'It isn't raining, but I believe that it is' or 'Vivian is my friend, but I don't believe that is so'[26] even though, paradoxically, the utterances are syntactically unimpeachable and could apparently even be true. Although G.E. Moore was not the first to discuss such utterances, it is he who gives his name to the paradox and it was his reading a paper on the subject to the Moral Sciences Club at Cambridge in October 1944 that first sparked Wittgenstein's interest in the problem. Wittgenstein devotes Section X of Part II of the *Philosophical Investigations* to it, and there is a lengthier discussion in *RPP I* §§460-504, with additional remarks scattered elsewhere.

The paradox is that a Mooronic utterance appears to consist in a conjunction of two statements, both of which could be true (see Wittgenstein's interlocutor at *RPP II* §418) – yet the speaker cannot himself believe the conjunction. Or, in a statement of the problem offered by Bas van Fraassen (1995, p. 27): 'How could I agree that I could not coherently believe something which I can clearly see *could* be true?' Substitute 'suppose' for 'see' and we have a formulation quite close to Wittgenstein's (*PI*, p. 190). He takes a Mooronic utterance to be senseless, so his problem is how to account for the fact that it makes no sense to say something like 'I believe that it's raining, but it isn't', whereas it makes good sense for someone to say such a thing of me (putting my name in place of the 'I'), or for me to say of me that I believe*d* it was raining when it wasn't (*PI*, p. 191).

As in the case of all paradoxes, the challenge is to explain how, starting from an apparently true premise and proceeding by apparently valid steps of argument, we arrive at a crazy conclusion. In the case of the Moore paradox, we begin with the reasonable assumption that if some proposition could be true and is intelligible to a speaker, then that speaker can intelligibly assert that proposition. Now, some proposition, for example, *that the Earth moves in an elliptical orbit yet that fact is not believed by me*, could be true, and I understand it perfectly well. So anyone, and, in particular, I myself, should be able, perfectly sensibly, to assert that proposition. And this is precisely the crazy, or unacceptable conclusion – for in fact it would be absurd for me to assert that proposition.

One would expect a satisfactory solution of this paradox to throw light on the concept of *belief*. Wittgenstein's first thoughts on the subject are contained in a letter he wrote to Moore on the day after the above-mentioned session at the Moral Sciences Club:

> Pointing out that 'absurdity' which is in fact something *similar* to a contradiction, though it isn't one, is so important that I *hope you'll publish* your paper. By the way, don't be shocked at my saying it's something 'similar' to a contradiction. This means roughly: it plays a similar rôle in logic. You have said something about the *logic* of assertion. Viz.: It makes sense to say 'Let's suppose: p is the case and I don't believe that p is the case', whereas it makes *no* sense to assert 'p is the case and I don't believe that p is the case'. This *assertion* has to be ruled out and *is* ruled out by 'common sense', just as a contradiction is. And this just shows that logic isn't as simple as logicians think it is. In particular: that contradiction isn't the *unique* thing people think it is. It isn't the *only* logically inadmissible form …. (*LRKM*, p. 177)

When I ascribe a belief that p to you, I do so on the basis of evidence, commonly the evidence of what you say. So my ascription is a result of an inference as to your disposition to think that p. When I ascribe to myself a belief that I once held, this may, again, be based on evidence, evidence of what I once wrote, or on my memory of views I once held. But when, here and now, I say 'I believe …' I am not usually drawing on evidence, nor inferring anything about my own dispositions, I am *expressing* a belief, not reporting one. 'My own relation to my words is wholly different from other people's' (*PI*, p. 192). In actual use, the first person singular present tense of the verb 'to believe' does work different from what it does in all other inflexions, and in some cases, none – e.g. 'I believe falsely that …'.[27] I can mistrust my own senses, but not my own belief, so, while it may be appropriate to say 'He seems to believe …', there is not normally the occasion to say 'I seem to believe …' (*PI*, pp. 191-2). If to say, 'I believe that it is raining' is to express the belief that it is raining, then, from a logical point of view, it cannot be so different from my assertion 'It is raining' with which I normally express that belief.[28] There will be a rhetorical difference: the prefix 'I believe' may indicate a certain hesitancy or guardedness on my part; in other conversational contexts it may indicate the opposite – complete confidence in my claim.

The 'grammar' or 'logic' of the verb 'believe' is different from that of, say, 'write' or 'chew' (*RPP I* §472). In saying 'I chew', I am describing the same sort of activity (or disposition, in the case of tobacco) that I describe by saying 'He chews'. The word 'wish' is more similar, in its first person present singular use, to 'believe' than to 'chew'. If I say 'I wish you'd go away', I'm not describing my inner state, but inviting you to disappear (*RPP I* §477). It is certainly possible for me to wish you to go away, while encouraging you to stay – maybe you're a pain in the neck, but I fear that, if I'm not nice to you, you'll go off and do serious damage to yourself or others – but that in no way detracts from the absurdity of my *saying* to you 'I wish that you'd go away, but please stay'; it is absurd *unless* special circumstances prevail, such as that I am trying to taunt an unlikeable deaf person for the amusement of my friends.

'I believe that p' is most frequently used as an expression of belief, not a description of one; someone who utters it is typically asserting that p. That is to say that the job done by my utterance of 'I believe that p' is roughly that done by my simple assertion 'p'. And a speaker who says 'I don't believe that p' is typically expressing his refusal to accept the proposition. Thus a speaker who says 'p, but I don't believe that p' is, or purports to be, simultaneously putting a proposition forward and taking it back. So what is absurd about a Mooronic utterance is just what is absurd about the utterance of a straight contradiction.[29]

The Mooronic utterance is not a formal contradiction in that it is not of the form 'p and not-p', but, in mouthing a Mooronic utterance, a speaker is contradicting (speaking against) himself and is thus acting absurdly. That is why Wittgenstein says, in his letter to Moore, that contradiction isn't the *unique* thing people think it is. What I take him to be saying is that contradiction manifests itself in many guises, related (perhaps in the family way) to 'straight' contradiction; the Moorean absurdity is '*similar* to a contradiction, though it isn't one'. When Wittgenstein talks about logic, he does not mean formal logic, such as first-order logic, which studies the entailment relations between sentence schemata – he condemns such logic as 'dull and useless'[30] and names Russell as one of its misguided exponents. In his later writings, Wittgenstein uses the word 'logic' to mean the logic of language, specifically, the logic of language-in-use, i.e., the study of real linguistic behaviour, not of 'some non-spatial, non-temporal phantasm'.[31] If we 'forget' that the Mooronic sentence 'It is raining, but I do not believe that it is raining' is being used by me, and comment on it as if it were a kind of free-floating sentence, then the circumstances described in it certainly could co-exist – me not believing that it's raining when in fact it is. But *under* those circumstances, in which I don't believe that it is raining, I certainly would not candidly assert that it is raining, I would not *use* the Mooronic sentence there-then, nor would any other sane person similarly situated. As we noted in Chapter 2, Wittgenstein argues that only in *use* (i.e. in language-games) do sentences have sense, and he calls the failure to see this 'the main mistake made by philosophers of the present generation' (*LA*, p. 2). Interestingly, when he said this (in 1938) he specifically included Moore in the generalization, so it is not surprising that he was so pleased to find Moore, in 1944, making a contribution to the logic of assertion, i.e. to the logic of language-in-use.

Wittgenstein holds that mostly (but not always) sentences of the form 'p and not-p' have no use and hence have no sense and *a fortiori* are not false. This is a view that he held throughout his philosophical life (see Chapter 4). If you say to me, in all seriousness 'Today is Tuesday and it isn't', I'll just shrug my shoulders sadly, and call the asylum. It is in the light of this position on contradiction that we should see what Wittgenstein is claiming when he says that a Mooronic utterance is 'similar to' a contradiction. It is a quasi-contradiction; it has no sense. Using the example 'I believe he'll come, but he certainly won't come', Wittgenstein remarks

If I say that to someone, it tells him that he won't come but that nevertheless I am convinced of the opposite and will act according to this belief. However, by the very fact that I am reporting to someone else that he won't come, I am not acting according to this belief. (*LW I* §142)

In other words, the speaker is *undermining* himself in a way that renders his behaviour unintelligible in that we cannot figure out what he could mean by his words. To perform the speech-act of reporting that a particular person will not come is not consistent with acting out a sincere conviction that he *will* come. To assert a straight contradiction (were that possible) would be to take back what you put forward. This is perhaps the most dramatic way of undermining oneself. Making a Mooronic assertion is another way. Uttering a Liar sentence is another, for when one asserts (or purports to assert)

S: S is false

one is asserting S and, in so doing, *denying* S (claiming it to be false). Someone who issues a Mooronic utterance does not make any sense to us, 'we should regard him as demented'; 'if he seemed to be serious, I would be stunned' I might say 'Run that by me again' and if he did so I should conclude that he had a linguistic disorder.[32] Similarly, we wouldn't know what to make of someone who, without intending to joke, said 'I am immensely modest' or 'I've forgotten that my best friend's name is Harry' (Foley, 1986, n. 33).

Wittgenstein's solution to the Moore paradox is simple and compelling. Consider the following dialogue:

A: I believe it's raining.
B: I don't believe so.

If each of these statements were about its utterer or his mind, then the speakers would not be contradicting each other; yet clearly they are (*RPP II* §420) – perhaps even more clearly were B to say 'I believe that it's not raining'. Of course, my statement 'I believe that it is raining' throws light on my state of mind, but so does my statement (i.e. my use of the sentence) 'It is raining' (*PI*, p. 191). It does not follow that either statement is a report or description of my inner state. We must distinguish between the expression of a belief or opinion by a speaker, and that speaker's describing the belief or opinion he holds. These are easy to confuse, because sometimes the same sentence can be used for both jobs.[33]

There are several objections that could be made to Wittgenstein's solution, and it will help clarify his position to see how these can be met. The first objection derives from the Frege-Geach point that 'a proposition may occur in discourse now asserted, now unasserted, and yet be recognizably the same proposition' (Geach, 1972, p. 254). If utterances of the form 'I believe that p' are expressions of belief – assertions – then we could not account for how they feature *unasserted* in, say, the antecedents of conditionals.

This objection rests on the 'phantasm' picture of language mentioned earlier. We really have to disabuse ourselves of the notion that a bit of language serves the same function in whatever context it occurs. As we have seen, 'believes' works differently in 'He believes' and in 'I believe'; and it works differently in 'I believe' and in 'If I believe'. In fact, it is in terms of the latter difference that Wittgenstein *sets up* the problem, both in his letter to Moore (already quoted), and in the *Philosophical Investigations*:

> Moore's paradox can be put like this: the expression 'I believe that this is the case' is used like the assertion 'This is the case'; and yet the *hypothesis* that I believe this is the case is not used like the hypothesis that this is the case.[34]

103

'If p ...' is about what p is about; 'If I believe p ...' is about me, about my dispositions.

Another objection, due to Jonathan Cohen is that, in some circumstances, saying something does not imply belief in that thing (Cohen, 1993, p. 69), so in such circumstances, there is nothing particularly untoward in saying that thing and adding that you don't believe it. Again, this objection would not worry Wittgenstein. Only a 'craving for generality' of the sort he disdains would lead one to hold that the behaviour of 'I believe' is the same in *all* circumstances. Cohen gives an example in which the use of 'I believe' implies acceptance and not belief. Wittgenstein himself gives several such examples; in one of them, the announcer at the train station announces that a train is on schedule, but – perhaps groundlessly – is convinced that it will not arrive on time, and therefore says 'Train No. ... will arrive at ... o'clock. Personally I don't believe it' (*RPP I* §486). In cases like this, Wittgenstein comments, '[It] is possible to think out a language-game in which these words would not strike us as absurd' (*RPP I* §495). Or a Mooronic utterance can be made because of some pathology, such as a split personality. In a case like that, Wittgenstein says that the speaker 'no longer play[s] the ordinary language-game, but some different one' (*RPP I* §820. There are these cases where Mooronic assertions are apt, just as there are instances where the utterance of a contradiction is intelligible. In such instances there is some story to be told, against which background an utterance which, when viewed 'cold' or context-less looks odd, makes perfectly good sense.

There are, as Wittgenstein acknowledges, surroundings in which a first-person-present use of 'believe' does serve to describe a belief. Robert Stalnaker hits upon one such circumstance.[35] He imagines someone reflecting about his own obligations: 'If I believe that it would be better for France if Jospin were to win, then I ought to give money to his campaign ... Tiens!, I do believe that it would be better for France if Jospin were to win, ergo ....' Here we have someone reflecting on his own belief state and using words to announce a discovery about himself. Again, if someone speaking about him says 'Robert believes that Balladur will win' but Robert, overhearing this, corrects him by saying 'No I don't; I think it will be Chirac' then Robert (Stalnaker) is contradicting the speaker and so is denying that he is in the state of mind that the speaker said he was in. This example is valuable because, while Wittgenstein gives the impression that first-person-present uses of 'believe' describe the person's state of mind only under strange, unusual circumstances, Stalnaker shows that the verb can be so used in perfectly ordinary situations. Now, given that 'I believe ...' can often be used by me to describe what is on my mind' then a Wittgensteinian solution, even if it is perfectly correct for the 'avowal' cases, is not going to apply to those Mooronic utterances where it *is* so used for describing my state of mind. For, in such cases, it is still absurd for a speaker to make an assertion of the form 'I believe p, but p is not so', and we still have the problem of explaining *why* it is absurd. Norman Malcolm considers (but not seriously enough) non-avowal Mooronisms and says that the speaker, is speaking *of* himself, but speaking *as if* he were another person (Malcolm, 1995, p. 204). Yet the examples of Stalnaker's that I have cited do not fall under this description.

The root problem, as Stalnaker points out, is not about speaking but 'about belief itself, and a person's relation to his own beliefs'. I think that, for the cases we are considering where an individual is describing his own belief, a solution is straightforward. If I say of someone 'p is not true, but he believes that it is', I am accusing him of misjudging: I judge p to be untrue, but he (perhaps because he does not have such good evidence as I do, perhaps because he is stupider etc.) judges that p is true; there is some difference between me and him which is responsible for the fact that we judge differently whether p is true. Now, obviously, the first-person analogue is absurd, because *I* cannot have less evidence than I, *I* cannot be stupider than I, there cannot be a difference between me and me. This is why we not only cannot assert Mooronically but also cannot believe Mooronically; why we cannot have a Mooronic attitude. To believe that p is to be disposed generally to act in a way consistent with p's being true. So, to believe: (p is not the case but I believe that p) is to be disposed to act as if it were true that not-p while *at the same time* being disposed to act in a way consistent with p's being true. Can't be done. The *fundamentum in re* is an incompatibility of *action*.[36]

It may be rational now to believe that my opinions or desires with regard to some event are going to be different at some time in the future. So it might be sensible for Ulysses to bind himself to the mast while he is still only mildly excited by the thought of the Sirens, knowing that he could be fatally overcome by lust when he hears them singing.[37] Future tense Mooronisms 'p, but I shall come to believe not-p' present difficult epistemological problems, but the present tense cases are easy. The present-tense cases, however, are sufficient to alert us to the point, crucial to Wittgenstein's later philosophy, that much of our mentalistic talk is *not* the reporting of private, inner processes. The difference between my arm going up involuntarily and my deliberately raising my arm is *not* that the latter involves an inner act of (say) anticipating the experience associated with that movement;[38] pains and other sensations are not (as we shall shortly see) 'inner objects' that I introspect.

Sensations

There is no mention of sensations in Wittgenstein's early writings. Many modern writers regard an understanding of qualia (the felt or phenomenal qualities associated with experiences, e.g. how a pain in the stomach feels to you, how a mountain looks to you) as being the key to the understanding of mind. In his late writings, Wittgenstein frequently uses the example of pain in his discussions of 'private language', but, in the last six years of his life (what I have been calling his 'late, late' period), he came to realize that the landscape of sensations is rich and variegated and worthy of study in its own right (Vendler, 1995). He undertook many exploratory expeditions.

A very private constipation

My grandma used to say that food didn't taste as good as it did in her youth. She attributed this to modern methods of food production. But another possibility is that the food itself hadn't changed much over the years, but that there had been a deterioration of her taste acuity. If her sense of taste had become less discriminating, it is no wonder that food had come to taste more bland to her. This is quite a plausible hypothesis; it is well known that, in old age, the eyes and ears become less discriminating, so why not also the tongue? Now imagine that, as a girl, my grandma had (don't ask me how) given the private name T to a certain taste sensation.[39] If, much later in life, she wanted to use the word T, how could she or anyone know that she was using it correctly? 'One would like to say: whatever is going to seem right to [her] is right. And that only means that here we can't talk about "right" ' (*PI* §258).

It's the same with constipation. When constipated on some occasion, let's suppose she felt a certain unpleasant sensation and named it 'C'. But now, unconstipated, she sees the word 'C' but does not call to mind the feeling – for calling that sensation to mind can only mean having it 'on demand', and that cannot be done: one can remember *that* one had a certain painful experience, but exactly what the experience was, what it felt like, can only be recalled by having it again. Yet unconstipated people can use the phrase 'feel constipated' perfectly well. The feeling, though (definitely) not a nothing is not a private object the contemplation of which is necessary for the correct use of the phrase;[40] likewise, the correct use of the word 'green' does not require the calling to mind of a private image. This is not to deny that the word 'green' may sometimes evoke certain images for you and sometimes different ones for me, nor that you may have a peculiar experience associated with the

3. Mind

word that I do not have (see next section). It is just to deny that what I *mean* by 'green' is determined by such private associations.

If I say of myself that it is only from my own case that I know what the word 'pain' means – must I not say the same of other people too? And how can I generalize the *one* case so irresponsibly?
Now someone tells me that he knows what pain is only from his own case! – Suppose everyone had a box with something in it: we call it a 'beetle'. No one can look into anyone else's box, and everyone says he knows what a beetle is only by looking at his beetle. – Here it would be quite possible for everyone to have something different in his box. One might even imagine such a thing constantly changing. – But suppose the word 'beetle' had a use in these people's language? – If so it would not be used as the name of a thing. The thing in the box has no place in the language-game at all; not even as a something: for the box might even be empty. – No, one can 'divide through' by the thing in the box; it cancels out, whatever it is.
That is to say: if we construe the grammar of the expression of sensation on the model of 'object and designation' the object drops out of consideration as irrelevant. (*PI* §293)

This argument (like many in Wittgenstein's writings) is an application of Occam's Razor. Positing a beetle, or some privately perceived inner object or process corresponding to 'C', serves no explanatory purpose. No doubt there are processes in the brain and the bum of the constipated person to which the unconstipated person is not privy, but brain or bum processes are not 'subjective' or 'private' – they may be observed or studied by any scientist inclined to do so. When people talk about private sensations, they mean such things as one person's pain that another cannot have, or my red sensation which is different from yours, a mental impression that is said to be had whenever a person looks at something red. It is the existence of *these* 'objects' that Wittgenstein is casting into doubt. The mind, as it is traditionally conceived, is some inner theatre populated by private inner objects and processes. This conception quickly loses its attraction if we cannot sustain our belief in such private entities. If they don't exist, they don't need any home.
We are able to learn constipation-speak because there are outward (public) criteria (*PI* §580) for feeling constipated. When, as young children, we cry out in pain, we are taught to use pain-talk as a substitute for crying out (*PI* §244). So, despite the fact that the utter-

107

ance 'I have a pain' seems, on the surface, to be a description of an (inner) object, it is really just a sophisticated groan. Wittgenstein does not deny the legitimacy of our ordinary sensation-talk. His quining of qualia[41] amounts only to denying that sensations are inner mental objects – taking a sensation for something other than what it is (*PI* §288). His target here is William James who talks of 'looking into our own minds and reporting what we there discover' (James, 1890, p. 185). James was not the first, and he certainly was not the last, to hold that, when talking of our mental lives, our sensations, emotions and other states of consciousness, we are reporting subjective inner states, so that the words we use in making such reports have a subjective or private meaning.

It is, perhaps, natural to suppose, because we can feel external objects, that when we feel a pain we are feeling an internal object. And one might further argue that a pain is subjective – it is yours or mine, his or hers – and that it is private in that it can belong to only one subject – I cannot have yours, you cannot have mine (Langsam, 1995). It is truly frustrating that I cannot free my beloved of her stomach pain by transferring it to myself. If I could do it, I would. But pains are not like that. There is no 'it' to transfer. I can feel my guide dog; the dog is *what* I feel. But to say 'I feel a sharp pain', is to say *how* I feel. The 'accusatives' of the verb 'to feel' are of different kinds: the dog, but not the pain, can exist without being felt. The dog is an object in its own right, but you cannot say the same of the pain on pain of infinite regress:

> 'To feel a table' describes one way a person may be aware of, or observe, an object. Now if a feeling, or more specifically a pain is itself an object, then to be aware of that feeling or pain, one needs to feel it, or sense it, or perceive it .... If one must sense or feel a pain, that feeling of the pain is in turn to be reified and becomes something that also needs to be sensed. One must now sense or feel the 'feeling' of pain and so on. (Douglas, *forthcoming*)

It may seem that, in denying inner states or objects, Wittgenstein is espousing behaviourism. His interlocutor questions him about this:

> But aren't you really only a behaviourist in disguise? For you say that nothing stands behind the avowal [äußerung, the verbal outpourings and other kinds of behaviour]. Aren't you at bottom really saying that everything except behaviour is a fiction? So do I therefore believe that we don't really feel pain, but rather only make faces?! But the fiction *is* the object behind the avowal. It is

a fiction that our words in order to be meaningful must refer to a something that I can exhibit to myself even if not to someone else. (Grammatical fiction.)

The statement 'Nothing stands behind behind the avowal' is a grammatical one – it doesn't therefore claim that we experience nothing ....

My critique consists in that I bring out that the whole (common, primitive) view of the function of words (in the language game // in the use of language //) is too narrow (MS 124, pp. 5-6, written in 1941. I have not recorded a couple of crossings out in the MS).

What Wittgenstein is denying is a world of inner objects (and of a mind in which to house them). This is not to deny our experiences, but just to deny a certain mistaken construal of our experiences. In the case of pain it is easy to see that an alternative construal is at least possible. For 'I have a pain in my stomach' conveys little more or less than 'My stomach hurts', yet the latter makes no mention of inner objects, and with no apparent loss – we can still ask where exactly it hurts (compare: where exactly is it raining?), how badly and so on, and we can ask why a punch on the nose hurts us but does not hurt a robot.[42]

Until the last quarter of the twentieth century, the 'object' conception of pain held sway in western medicine. The theory was that, above threshold levels of stimulation, pain receptors, situated mainly at the periphery of the body, delivered messages to a 'pain centre' in the brain, the resulting brain state somehow becoming the object of the subject's awareness and in turn giving rise to messages sent to the motor, the vocal and other systems so that remedial measures could be set in motion. It is now widely recognized that the picture is much more complicated. Whether, or to what extent, someone feels pain depends on such factors as emotional state and competing stimulations; pain may be felt at a location where there are no pain receptors. The neuroscientific enterprise of mapping the various brain subsystems and neural pathways implicated in the feeling of pain and other sensations is in its infancy, and the philosophical question of figuring out how it is *possible* for lumps of matter like us to feel, see and hear while other lumps of matter cannot (e.g., we hear; the tape recorder merely records) remains to be solved.

Seeing as, aspect-switching and experiencing meaning

In the writings on the philosophy of psychology done during his late, late period, and in his Cambridge lectures of that time, Wittgenstein

Clear and Queer Thinking

conducts an extensive investigation of seeing-as, a topic already adumbrated at *BB*, pp. 163-5 and developed in MSS 123 and 137 (1940-1, mainly 1948 respectively). Part II, sect. xi of the *Philosophical Investigations* is one of the most sustained discussions of a single topic within the whole book; 24 pages (pp. 193-216) exclusively on seeing-as. Yet, as Michel ter Hark (writing in 1990) notes, very few of the standard monographs on Wittgenstein devote a chapter to this topic. Some writers have incorporated Wittgenstein's views on seeing-as into a discussion of aesthetics; others into discussions within the philosophy of science on the theory-ladenness of observation,[43] and others into discussions of religious belief (Barrett, 1991, pp. 134-44). What has generally been missed is the link that Wittgenstein forges, in this section, between *seeing-as* and *meaning*.

Wittgenstein begins by noting two uses of the word 'see'. The first and more familiar sense occurs when I say that I saw some particular thing, such as a person or a drawing. In the second sense, the object of my seeing is a *likeness* or similarity – I might see a likeness between two drawings which another viewer fails to see. Wittgenstein writes: 'I contemplate a face, and then suddenly notice its likeness to another. I *see* that it has not changed; and yet I see it differently. I call this experience "noticing an aspect" ' (*PI*, p. 193). There are many examples of drawings which switch aspects as we look at them: the old lady in a shawl with a grossly ugly nose transforms into a beautiful young woman (the nose becomes a delicate chin); or the 'Necker Cube' where the near face suddenly switches to the rear. As Wittgenstein remarks, the *causes* of this aspect-noticing have been of interest to psychologists.[44] The example Wittgenstein works with is Jastrow's duck-rabbit, a drawing which one can see either as a serene duck or as a startled rabbit – the long bill switching to a pair of rabbit's ears. Most people switch back and forth between duck and rabbit. Someone who looks at the picture and just sees a rabbit will say 'It's a rabbit', and that is a report of a perception. But someone who sees the switch from a duck will say 'Now it's a rabbit', and that reports not a perception but what Wittgenstein calls 'the dawning of an aspect' (*PI*, pp. 195, 194). A person who is 'aspect-blind' never experiences such a switch.

Somewhat confusingly, a little later (p. 212), Wittgenstein says that we *perceive* the switch, but we can correct that slip by reading the verb as 'notice'. He writes: 'what I perceive in the dawning of an aspect is not a property of the object, but an internal relation between it and other objects.' This is rather gnomic. What is the 'it'; what are the 'other objects' ? Hark (1990, p. 182) usefully cites some MS protoversions. He argues that there could not be an *internal* relation between the geomet-

110

rical constellation (the drawing) and the duck or rabbit, because we can identify one without identifying the other. So what Wittgenstein seems to have intended is that the 'internal relationship' is between the change of aspect and whatever animal it is that is seen after the change. The drawing has, before my very eyes, turned, for example, from a duck-representation to a rabbit-representation, although, of course, nothing in the drawing has changed. This is a genuine visual experience; the task is to clarify in what sense it is (*PI*, p. 204); for example, to describe how it is different from seeing *simpliciter*.

In the end, Wittgenstein has little positive to offer on the proper way to describe aspect-switching. He writes:

> What is incomprehensible is that *nothing*, and yet *everything*, has changed, after all. That is the only way to put it .... But 'Nothing has changed' means: Although I have no right to change my report about what I saw, since I see the same things now as before – still, I am incomprehensibly compelled to report completely different things one after the other. (*RPP II* §474)

We flip-flop. Why? This seems to be a question for physiology. In aspect-switching, an object stays the same but our judgment of it changes – now it's a duck, now it's a rabbit – different people seeing the switch at different times, others (the aspect-blind), not seeing it at all. If we redrew a duck-rabbit, making it a bit more duck-like (say, by reducing the nick that represents the rabbit's mouth), then observers would not see the resulting figure as a rabbit. This is why dual-aspect drawings are not very common; it requires considerable skill to ensure that one's drawing falls within that narrow area of transition where it can be interpreted two ways.

Similarly, if we have a series of colour patches running from red to orange, with only an imperceptible difference between adjacent patches, there will be a small, indistinct, 'middle' range of patches in which observers are not consistent in their judgments about whether a patch is more red than orange.

Is there a 'perfect' duck-rabbit, a maximally ambiguous one such that each (non-aspect-blind) observer, gazing at the picture, switches between the two interpretations, seeing the rabbit aspect half the time and the duck aspect the other half? No – different observers react differently to the same picture just as they do to the Necker Cube. There is no uniformity of switching-behavior. And, perhaps for the same physiological reason as there is no 'perfect' duck rabbit, so there is no 'perfect' red-orange marking the exact boundary in the series of colour patches between those that are really, objectively red, and those that are really, objectively orange. Observers will switch differentially on different patches; there is no unique switching point, and there is typically no dramatic aspect-switch.[45]

One species of aspect-blindness is meaning-blindness. At *RPP I* §344, Wittgenstein writes: 'Anyone who cannot understand and learn to use the words "to *see* the sign as an arrow" – that's whom I call "meaning-blind". It will make no sense to tell him "You must try to *see* it as an arrow" and one won't be able to help him in *that* way.' Just as we become conscious of the duck-aspect when the change from rabbit-aspect occurs (see *LW I*, §169), so we become aware of a word's meaning when the meaning dawns. Wittgenstein makes this point at *PI*, p. 175 a little less clearly than at *RPP I* §175, from which I quote: 'If you say "As I heard this word, it meant ... for me" you refer *to a point of time* and *to an employment of the word* – the remarkable thing about it is of course the relation to the point of time. This relation would be lost on the "meaning-blind".'[46]

What is remarkable about a word's meaning something to me at a point in time? Well, just that the meaning of a word *in this sense of 'meaning'* is something occurrent, something that can be *experienced*. That is clearly not a sense covered by the 'meaning is use' formula, discussed in Chapter 2. To say that we can experience meaning seems – well – unWittgensteinian (at least, to those who do not know the corpus sufficiently). Yet it is a central tenet of his late, late philosophy.

At MS 180b, written in 1941, we find this remark: 'The meaning of a word, I said, is its use. But an important addition has to be made to this' (p. 7). Why the conception of meaning as use, as rôle in language-games is incomplete is, as Zemach points out, that 'it looks at a language-game as a whole, from the outside, not from the inside, not from the user's point of view, and therefore it cannot say how a user knows what term to use, what makes a use of a term correct or incorrect' (Zemach, 1995, pp. 480-1). For example, if I am familiar with the word 'bicycle', and have been around bicycles for a long time, but I now see one that I have never seen before, why will I call it a bicycle? The obvious answer is that I see it as a bicycle, that I see the word 'bicycle' as being suitable for that thing. It is this phenomenon of 'seeing-as' that needs to be explicated.

In *Philosophical Investigations* Part II, sect. ii, Wittgenstein raises this question: 'The words "the rose is red" are meaningless if the word "is" has the meaning "is identical with". – Does this mean: if you say this sentence and mean the "is" as the sign of identity, the sense disintegrates?' (*PI*, p. 175). The reader who has dutifully ploughed through the *Philosophical Investigations* up to this point naturally expects Wittgenstein's answer to this question to be 'No'. For to say that the sense disintegrates is tantamount to saying that its sense is sense-less, and Wittgenstein, at *PI* §500, expressly criticized that way of characterizing matters. Yet, after a paragraph of discussion, Wittgenstein, much to our surprise, says 'And yet there is something right about this "disintegration of sense" '. He elaborates: 'You get it in the following example: one might tell someone: if you want to pronounce the salutation "Hail!" expressively, you had better not think of hailstones as you say it' (p. 175). So what Wittgenstein is saying is that somehow the meaning of the salutation is destroyed if it has the wrong mental accompaniment. This position is utterly different from anything that he says in the first part of *Philosophical Investigations*. This is Wittgenstein the phenomenologist speaking.

Immediately after this, he talks about 'experiencing a meaning' – a phenomenon that he had discussed briefly in earlier writings (*PG* §3, p. 41; *PI* §§138-42). His initial attempt to characterize just what this is is inconclusive, but he seems to accept that, in normal circumstances where we say 'Hail', or use any sentence in the normal way without trying to do something peculiar at the same time, then we *do not* experience meaning; there is no 'parade of meanings before one's mind' (p. 176). In other words, experiencing a meaning, though unusual, is real. This point is made at *RPP I* §232: 'If I compare the coming of the *meaning* into one's mind to a dream, then our talk is ordinarily dreamless. The "meaning-blind" man would then be the one who would always talk dreamlessly.' By contrast, the rest of us experience meaning occasionally – such as when we succeed in finding the *mot juste* (see *LW I* §62).

It is clear that, at some stage, Wittgenstein himself had some doubts about this whole business of experiencing meaning (see *RPP I* §§184-

200); after all, it is a rather *nebulous* experience. But, in the end, he is in no doubt that this experience is not queerer than any other (*PI* Part II, sect. xi, p. 215), and gives several illustrations of when the experience occurs and how normal speakers differ from the 'meaning-blind'. For example, at *RPP I* §198, he says 'But it is true: with mental defectives we often feel as if they talked more automatically than we do, and if someone were what we called "meaning-blind", we should picture him as making a less lively impression than we do, behaving more like an automaton. (One also says: "God knows what goes on in his mind!",[47] and one thinks of something ill-defined, disorderly.' A little later (*RPP I* §202) he remarks that although it may seem that the meaning-blind person is not missing much, this is to overlook the fact that we sometimes say that some word in a communication meant one thing to us until we saw that it meant something else. The meaning-blind person would not be able to enjoy such revelations; nor to smell the definite slight aroma, the 'atmosphere' that surrounds words;[48] nor to hear the musical rhythm of a sentence (*PI* §527)[49] nor to feel as if the name 'Schubert' fitted Schubert's works and Schubert's face (*PI* Part II, sect. xi, p. 215) so that one can utter the name with reverence (*RPP I* §341).

Most people, I think, will be able to recall experiences of meaning from their own lives. Readers of the English satirical magazine *Private Eye* will be alert to the difference in 'feel' between the expression 'a sum of money adjacent to …' and 'a sum of money not unadjacent to …' when citing an outrageous but unconfirmed sum that a politician has acquired by dubious means. The words 'pull' and 'push' for me are easy to use; if forced to think about it, I should say that the first has a certain connotation of concavity, the second of convexity, whereas I have no such feel for the counterpart words in German, and so spend most of my time in Germany nursing broken wrists. The English word 'friable' (meaning 'crumbly') does not have the right sort of feel, so far as I am concerned. Wittgenstein is inclined to say that Wednesday is fat and Tuesday lean (*PI* Part II, sect. xi, p. 216); the German words ('Mittwoch' and 'Dienstag' respectively) have the same sort of 'feel' as their English counterparts. But the word 'unheimlich' seems to some to have a more sinister, threatening feel than 'uncanny' its usual translation (Clare, 1987).

Wittgenstein's diagnosis of the phenomenon of seeing-as, and his discussion of experiencing meaning, are sensitive and deep. And, when we review our own commerce with language, his reflections, or at least most of them, seems accurate and enlightening. Why does one associate the word 'cat' with cats? Because one sees the word *as* cat-involving. And, bearing in mind my story in Chapter 2 about the provenance of the word 'mama', it seems true that our early learning of language *is* a kind

114

of sensory experience. The rich associations of caring and cherishing with baby words for mother, explains why the following has an odd 'feel' to it: ' "Mumsey, tell me about weird love", begged Harry.' We can also now understand what makes swear words so difficult for the second-language learner – the learner has got to *feel* their appropriateness, to see one *as* fitting a certain situation, another as not. Grammar 'drills' do little to help a learner develop a feel for a new language; the learner needs to participate in, or at least to witness, language-games. And film subtitles are often unintentionally hilarious just because the translation hits the wrong register or tone. Wittgenstein, as Carnap reports (Schlipp, 1963, p. 26) had a deep loathing for Esperanto, because a language that has not developed naturally fails to have this aesthetic 'felt' dimension (*CV*, p. 52). On a standard theory of metaphor, one calls a cunning man a fox because foxes are supposed to be cunning. But that theory would not account for why we call a particular type of good-looking woman 'foxy'. This epithet *feels* right, no doubt, in part, because of the sound-association with 'sexy'.

Somatic proprioception

When playing a stroke in squash or tennis, I keep my eye on the approaching ball right until I strike it with my racket. But I do not keep my eye on the racket, nor on the hand that holds the racket. Yet I am aware of the position of hand and racket. I do not infer that my hand and arm are in a certain position, nor do I observe the position that they are in. Yet I know that they are in that position. More generally, I am aware of my posture and of the movement of my body. How – given that I do not infer or observe them? A natural answer, one popular in the writings of William James and other psychology texts of Wittgenstein's time (Candlish, 1996), a view which attracted Wittgenstein himself in his earlier late period (Hallett, 1977, pp. 640-9) and which is still very much alive today, is that there are 'kinaesthetic sensations' which inform me of the posture and movements of my body. The theory is that it is because of this feedback that I am able not only to know where my bodily parts are and how they are moving, but also to adjust my postures and movements in response to a changing situation, or to a request. Wittgenstein summarizes the theory in the following way: 'My kinaesthetic sensations advise me of the movement and position of my limbs' (*PI*, p. 185; *LW I* §386; *LW II*, p. 4). He discusses this view at length in the *Remarks on the Philosophy of Psychology*, but the discussion is inconclusive, even by his high standards. He seems tentatively to like the idea either that there are no such sensations or that, even if there are, we do not judge the position and movement of our limbs by the feelings that these movements give us (*RPP I* §§382-408, 698).

Extend your arm, pointing with the index finger. Now, with your eyes closed, quickly touch the tip of your nose with the tip of that finger. Unless there is something wrong with you, you will score a direct hit first time, or you won't be far off. Now, when you go through this exercise in proprioception, you do not *seem* to be aware of any sensations in your elbow by means of which you guide your fingertip to its destination. And in answer to the retort that there *must* be such a sensation, otherwise you would not be able to do it, Wittgenstein makes this telling comparison: 'I may be able to tell the direction from which a sound comes only because it affects one ear more strongly than the other, but I don't feel this in my ears; yet it has its effect: I *know* the direction from which the sound comes' (*PI*, p. 185). In each case, I obtain knowledge (of the position or movement of my body, of the direction from which the sound is coming, respectively) without any accompanying feeling or sensation. Another – of the many – considerations Wittgenstein advances against postulating kinaesthetic sensations is this: those sensations are supposed to be barely perceptible. Now, if you have a pain in the arm so severe that it drowns out all other sensations (including the alleged kinaesthetic ones) you still know the position and movement of your arm. So it cannot be the alleged kinaesthetic sensations that advise you on such matters (*RPP I* §386; *PI*, p. 186).

It is beginning to look as if the case against kinaesthetic sensations is overwhelmingly strong. Yet attention to certain other facts can start pumping our intuitions in the opposite direction. The twist on the handbrake or clutch lever of a motorbike, is set by swivelling the loosened clamp on the handlebar and tightening so that the lever is in a position where it can be grasped quickly and easily. When riding around, using these levers, you become very used to the lever positions. If, subsequently, a mechanic makes some clutch or brake adjustment, and resets the lever in a position which is twisted just a few degrees off its original setting, then, as soon as you ride the bike, you *feel* this difference; it feels strange. It does not seem far-fetched to say that this feeling 'advises' you that your hand is now in a different position for braking or declutching. Similarly, when teaching someone to row, you mention certain sensations that should occur at crucial points within each stroke. For example, only when you *feel* a strain at the back of the thighs do you break the legs and move forward on the slide. Thus, within the stroke pattern there are some clearly identifiable sensations It is not *too* outlandish to say that the beginner learns by becoming familiar with how the whole stroke feels – it is not a matter of jerking from one position of prominent sensation to another.

A response to this attempt to reinstate kinaesthetic sensations as respectable denizens of our mental world is to distinguish between sensations *associated* with movement and bodily posture from sensations *of* movement and bodily posture, the former being deemed real, the latter non-existent (Candlish, 1996). One can, for, example concede that singers have to learn the feeling *associated* with an open pharynx and similarly, it might be said, there are many sensations *associated* with biking and rowing, but that these are not sensations which *advise* the rider or oarsman in the required sense. This distinction is, it seems to me, hard to sustain. Kinaesthetic ability is very important for oarsmen, who practise and practise until each stroke is consistent and feels right all the way through. At any point t_i in the correct stroke pattern, my sensation S_i advises me about the position of my body in the sense that I am made aware that I am in the approved position P_i. If I'm in the wrong position, I sense it immediately, and sometimes acutely. This seems an acceptable construal of 'a sensation advises' – nobody would suppose that a sensation advises by sending a memo.

But what about the point that we usually know about our bodily postures and movements without feeling any particular sensations? It would not do to say that kinaesthetic sensations are unsensed – that would be a solecism. The idea of a subliminal sensing of what you don't sense appears to be so much mumbo-jumbo. The answer must be that we need to distinguish two senses of 'sense'. In the first, we sense something when our sensory receptors are stimulated and do their stuff – transmitting some signal to the interior. In the second, to sense is be sensorily *aware*. When I hear a sound over to my right, I am not (usually) aware of greater stimulation to the right ear than to the left, but I am aware of a sound off to my right. In the first sense of 'sense', it is my brain that gets the message; in the second sense, *I* do. A stimulation may have some effect on my brain and this in turn may effect some further change in brain state or in my behaviour without me being in the least aware that all this is going on. So – back to the rowing example – as an experienced oarsman, I become kinaesthetically aware in various (typically unpleasant) ways only when something goes wrong. Similarly, experienced typists and violinists are not normally aware of their hand positions – when they become aware of them, it's a sure sign that something is amiss.

Blindsight and bio-feedback, two well-accredited phenomena, also seem to depend on a kind of sensing which is not available to consciousness. Blindsight could be characterized thus: My senses advise me of

117

the visual presence of external objects, even though I am not conscious of being so advised.[50] The empirical evidence seems to show quite decisively that there are no phenomenal visual images in blindsight.[51] Bio-feedback patients learning to walk well make corrections in their posture and movement without being conscious of adjusting. It may be correct, in all such cases, to say that our sensory organs detect features of the external environment but that this detecting is not the same as sensing or having a sensation – recall Wittgenstein's example of detecting the direction of a sound. And, in fact, many modern textbooks and research papers on kinaesthesia refrain from mentioning sensations, and speak instead of 'information' that is passed to the brain. But the word 'information' suffers from the same sort of ambiguity as does 'sense'. If you inform *me* of something, then I am made aware of what you are telling me; but if I succeed in walking upright because of some 'messages' from my inner ear which 'inform' *my brain*, then I am completely unaware of (though thankful for) this flow of 'information'. By trading on this ambiguity, researchers in the field of Artificial Intelligence have managed to con governments out of millions of dollars in funding – for projects which promise artificial expertise, but deliver only high-speed data manipulation.

Colour

The experience of seeing colours can be wonderful, and what is intriguing is that, though science can tell us much about electromagnetic radiation, the interaction of light with surfaces and substances, and about the mechanism of vision, it apparently can tell us nothing about that experience. The point can be brought out by adapting a well known argument of Frank Jackson's. Mary, who has been monochromatic from birth – she only sees things in black and white – becomes a famous scientist, a specialist in, of all things, vision! She knows everything, yes *everything*, about visual perception. She knows about the differentiated sensitivities of retinal receptors, about colour opponent cells, about cortical area V_4; her knowledge of the amygdala and hypothalamus are a million miles ahead of what anyone knows today. She is familiar with all the theories there will ever be about depth perception, form vision, hallucinations, optical illusions ....[52] Mary works in a black and white room and, because a colour television would be wasted on her, she uses just a black and white set.

One day – a miracle – Mary, while working away, gets a shock when the laboratory cat jumps on her head, an event which suddenly restores her to full normal vision. She does not realise this until she leaves her room and beholds the wonderful world of colour. This first colour-visual experience of hers – let's call it WOW, COLOUR! – knocks her socks off. Now she knows what colours look like. *Before* WOW, COLOUR! – she understood why normal people could make visual discriminations that she couldn't, knew everything about what *gives rise to* colour vision and how it does so – but that did not in the least prepare her for WOW, COLOUR!. She didn't in the least know what WOW, COLOUR! would be like, even though she knew *everything* there is to know about vision, the complete science of visual perception. Therefore there is something which she now knows (what WOW, COLOUR! is like) that she did not know before. She thus now has a piece of knowledge *over and above all the relevant scientific knowledge*. Therefore the experience of seeing colours, knowing what colours look like, lies beyond the reach of scientific explanation.[53]

Look at a picture illuminated by white light. White light is incident on the picture, but what is reflected from it are rays of light of different frequencies and we see the picture as multicoloured. There seems to be the most intimate connection between the rays of reflected light and the colours seen. If the perceptual experiences of an observer could be explained wholly in terms of non-relational properties of the light and of objects (properties had by the light and the objects independent of her or of any observer), then Mary, pre-miracle, would know what the perceptual experiences of a normal observer are like. Newton advanced the view that 'colours in the object are nothing but a disposition to reflect this or that sort of rays more copiously than the rest' (Newton, 1952, p. 125). However, to say that colours are dispositions (John Locke and many subsequent philosophers have subscribed to this view), seems to overlook exactly what it is about colours that so stunned Mary when she emerged from her room – the way they look. Colours do not look like dispositions![54] She knew everything about dispositions to reflect this or that sort of rays but that left her, one might say, quite in the dark.

It was the thought that Newtonian science cannot explain colour, which inspired the poet Johann Wolfgang von Goethe to write a mammoth tome on the subject.[55] He remarked that 'the theory of colours, in strictness, may be investigated quite independently of optics' (Goethe, 1970, p. 725). Whether or not Goethe really grasped Newton's sophisticated theory is unclear.[56] Wittgenstein found Goethe's book 'partly boring and repelling, but in some ways also *very* instructive and philosophically interesting' (*LW-GW*, in *PO*, p. 475; *RoC* I.70), and was inspired to write on colour during the last year of his life.

Goethe pointed out that, in a picture showing a white piece of paper

119

under a clear blue sky, the sky is lighter than the paper yet, on the palette, white is the lightest colour; any shade of blue is darker than white (*RoC* I.2). This is an example of the sort of colour phenomenon that interested Wittgenstein, and he gives many further examples of his own devising, including (i) While it is an empirical matter whether one body is lighter than another, the proposition that a certain shade of colour is lighter than another is timeless; it states a logical or 'internal' relationship (*RoC* I.1). (ii) Blue obliterates yellow (*RoC* III.39). We have no idea what a bluish yellow would look like. But, in a way that's strange, because we can think of an *argument* for supposing that there must be a bluish yellow. After all, green is intermediate between yellow and blue, and we do not mind calling something a greenish yellow. Ergo ... (*RoC* III.40). Similarly, there is no reddish-green (*RoC* I.9-14, 21). (iii) There can be transparent green, but not transparent white (*RoC* I.17-20); no white sunglasses, no looking through a glass of milk. White does not 'lend itself' to transparency; green does. But can there be a green piece of paper which has *the same colour* as a piece of transparent green glass? (iv) Mental visual images are imperspicuous; they alter when inspected; you cannot 'zoom in' on a particular location and identify its colour. They are thus quite different from representations on a screen or on canvas (*RoC* III.257, 259). (So 'there is no need whatsoever to think of an image that appears before the inner eye' (*RoC* III.27), for having a mental image just is not like viewing a painting – there is no 'internal' screen or canvas, so we do not need an 'inner eye' to look at it.) (v) A 'blackish' colour, such as grey, does not shine (*RoC* I.55). 'Whatever *looks* luminous does not look grey. Everything grey *looks* as though it is being illuminated' (*RoC* I.36). (vi) The helmet in the Rembrandt picture looks gold, yet Rembrandt has used no gold paint on the canvas (*RoC* II.79). Another example in the same category was noted by the graphic artist M.C. Escher: a red surface, the same distance away as a blue one, looks closer.[57]

Quite clearly, Wittgenstein regards the investigation of such phenomena as lying outside the province of science. '[T]he fact that we cannot conceive of something "glowing grey" belongs neither to the physics nor to the psychology of colour' (*RoC* I.40; also III.234). We are dealing with phenomenological problems, but they are not to be solved by phenomenology, according to Wittgenstein, for (as he puzzlingly claims) there is no such thing (*RoC* I.53). What we need to establish is the *logic* of colour concepts; it is this that accomplishes what people unjustly expect a psychological or physiological theory to accomplish (*RoC* I.22).

People sometimes see beautiful coloured pictures when their eyes are closed and they are half asleep. Those pictures need not be complicated, and the half-sleeper may subsequently be able to give a rough description of them. But he cannot paint them, not through lack of skill but because of this weird difference in kind between 'inner' and 'outer' pictures. If I form a visual image and could paint it, then it should be possible for me to pick a spot on the painting, locate the corresponding point on my image, and say what colour that point has (*RoC* III.256-9). If you simply *assume* (without going through the phenomenological exercise) that a visual image is just like a painting on an internal screen, then you will not see any difficulty in painting it or matching the colours of points on the painting to points on the image. But forget about that preconception and *just try doing it*. You will not succeed. Why not? It is not clear how physics (or phenomenology) could set about answering this question.

Wittgenstein treats colour concepts as the concepts of sensations (*RoC* III.71, 72), and he is not arguing, in the style of McGinn (1993) that these problems about qualia are too difficult for science to solve but, in the style of Jackson (1986) that they are not scientific problems. It will be a matter for some future debate whether he is right about this. Even if he is not, the least that can be said is that *Remarks on Colour*, by drawing attention to a range of fascinating and puzzling colour phenomena, rewrites the agenda for all those working in the area of colour vision. Unfortunately, those working in that area do not generally seem to have realised this.

4

Mathematics

The background of Wittgenstein's interest in mathematics

Wittgenstein developed an amateur's fascination with mathematics in his late teenage years. There is no evidence of his having any aptitude for it in his early youth. His school record at the Realschule in Linz was fairly dismal, particularly in science subjects (Monk, 1990, p. 15). His early training at the Technische Hochschule in Berlin (1906-08) was in mechanical engineering, but what drove him in that direction was probably not any special interest in mathematics, but rather pressure from his father, a liking for machinery and a certain feel for materials – although he told Pinsent that he had 'neither taste nor talent' for engineering (von Wright, 1990, p. 6). As a ten-year-old child he had built, out of wood and wire, a working model of the house sewing machine,[1] as a student he designed and built kites and a propellor. During his unhappy sojourn as a schoolteacher in Trattenbach he performed a 'miracle cure' on a steam engine in the wool factory, by getting four workmen to tap the machine in rhythm – this was after the problem had defeated expert engineers who had been called in[2] – and he designed some of the fittings for the house he built for his sister Margarete ('Gretl') on the Kundmanngasse in Vienna. In his writings, Wittgenstein frequently makes a point by referring to some or other mechanical device.

Biographers are fond of recounting how Wittgenstein's engagement with mathematics as an engineer led him to an interest in the foundations of the subject and hence thence to Frege and Russell. This is a neat but unlikely tale. Wittgenstein's interest in the foundations of mathematics seems to have been independent of, and ultimately to have superseded, his engineering studies. At Manchester he started attending seminars and lectures on mathematics in 1908, and a friend introduced him to Russell's tremendous work *The Principles of Mathematics*, a philosophical discussion of fundamental mathematical and logical concepts. This is what got Wittgenstein hooked on foundational issues.[3]

Russell's *The Principles of Mathematics* stakes out the doctrine of *logicism*, the view that mathematics is derivable from logic. If it can be shown to be so, then we can rest secure in our mathematical knowledge, for we shall have generated mathematics out of self-evident logical axioms by the use of the most fundamental principles of reasoning (e.g., that from 'A' and 'If A then B' we can infer 'B') employing only a primitive notions, such as 'not', 'or', 'class' and 'identical'. The task of deriving arithmetic from logic was first attempted by Frege, and he failed in a most spectacular way, as was demonstrated in a letter that Russell wrote to him in 1902. Without going into the subtle technicalities of Frege's system (and even Russell got these slightly wrong) the basic problem can be set out as follows.[4] The bridge between arithmetic and logic occurs at the point where we express simple arithmetical statements about numbers as statements about classes or sets, employing purely logical notions. It seems as if nothing could be simpler than building this bridge, for consider the statement 'Dobbin is a horse'. The predicate in this statement is 'is a horse' – we are stating that the object, Dobbin, falls under the concept *being a horse* – and we can say, can we not, that anything is a horse if and only if it is a member of the class of horses. More generally, that x is a K if and only if x is a member of the class of Ks. So we can 'exchange' a concept-locution ('is a K') for a class-locution. The aim is to 'reduce' all the concepts of arithmetic to those of pure logic. In Frege's terminology, this bridge is 'the transition from a concept to its extension' and is codified in Basic Law V of his system.[5]

Yet, allow this apparently trivial truth, and everything goes downhill fast. For consider: Dobbin and other horses are flesh-and-blood creatures; a class is a mathematical entity which is certainly not made of flesh and blood. So no class is a horse; in particular, the class of horses is not a horse. Crossing the 'bridge', we can express that as: the class of horses is not a member of the class of horses. In short, the class of horses is not a member of itself. Now, is there a class which *is* a member of itself? Yes, lots. The class of things which are not horses, for example, is a member of itself – it is a member of the class of things which are not horses, i.e. (back across the 'bridge') it is not a horse. In short, there are some classes which *are not* members of themselves (call these the non-self-membered or NSM classes) and there are some classes which *are* members of themselves (the SM classes). Right, now let us form a class consisting of just the NSM classes, in other words, we are assembling a class – to be called the Russell Class R – which has classes as its members; specifically, all and only the NSM classes are members of the Russell Class. So, where y is a class, we can say that y is a member of R if and only if y is one of the NSM classes, which means, remember, that y is not a member of y. In symbols:

$$y \varepsilon R <-> \sim(y \varepsilon y)$$

To check whether some class – say the class of daydreams – is a member of R, just substitute 'the class of daydreams' for 'y' in the above formula. Since the only members of the class of daydreams are daydreams (no horses, classes etc.), we can say that the class of daydreams does not contain itself as a member, it is an NSM and therefore is a member of the Russell Class R whose members are just the NSM classes. But now ask whether the Russell Class R is itself a member of R. To find out, we have, in this case, to substitute 'R' for 'y' in the above formula. And the result?

$$R \varepsilon R <-> \sim(R \varepsilon R)$$

In other words, R is a member of R if and only if it isn't. Madness – just like my telling you 'I am a member of the Aristotelian Society if and only if I'm *not* a member of that Society'.

It really is quite amazing that an assumption as apparently innocuous as that captured in Frege's Basic Law V should lead so quickly to this absurdity. Frege consoled himself with the thought 'solatium miseris, socios habuisse malorum', that this problem was not peculiar to his system but besets everyone who is trying to lay logical foundations for arithmetic (Frege, 1964, p. 127). He tried to find a way around it but, in the end, it broke his heart. Russell made several attempts to escape the paradox – his struggle constitutes a very interesting chapter in the history of logic – and he ended up with a rather baroque theory, known as the Theory of Types, first sketched in an appendix to *The Principles of Mathematics*, set out in detail in Russell (1908), and incorporated in the mammoth *Principia Mathematica* (1910-13) he wrote with Alfred North Whitehead.

Logicism, though it has enjoyed something of a modern revival, is resisted by many philosophers of mathematics, including Wittgenstein, who takes the view that '[A] calculus cannot give us information about the foundations of mathematics ... work within the logical calculus can't bring to light essential truths *about* mathematics'.[6] He adds, parenthetically: 'Through Russell and Whitehead, especially Whitehead, there entered philosophy a false exactitude that is the worst enemy of real exactitude. At the bottom of this lies the erroneous opinion that a calculus could be the mathematical foundation of mathematics' (*PG*, p. 296).

We noted in Chapter 1 that a calculus is a scheme of rules or a mechanical device for manipulating signs. A logical calculus manipulates signs such as '→', '&', '~', 'p', 'x' in accordance with rules – called formation rules – which dictate which combinations of signs are to count as the 'well-formed formulae' (wffs), and typically there are further rules, called 'transformation rules' or 'rules of inference' showing how one wff may be inferred from another (e.g., 'A v B' from 'A') or from several (e.g., '~B' from 'A' and '~(A & B)'. '[A] calculus may be used to construct a tautology' (*WVC*, p. 106). This is all just a game with signs (*WVC*, p. 126), and it is *prima facie* difficult to see how such a game could be the foundation of mathematics, which has both content and application. Yet, even if one rejects the enterprise of reducing mathematics to a branch of logic, the Russell Paradox remains a thorn in one's side, for it is a really basic problem, independent of this system or that, or of any particular theory about the foundations of mathematics.

The Principles of Mathematics closes with the following remark about the paradox: 'What the complete solution of the difficulty may be, I have not succeeded in discovering; but as it affects the very foundations of reasoning, I earnestly commend the study of it to the attention of all students of logic' (Russell, 1903, p. 528). Ray Monk is surely correct in his speculation that this was the problem that grabbed Wittgenstein and sucked him into mathematical logic. As Monk says 'He had found a subject in which he could become as absorbed as his brother Hans had been in playing the piano, a subject in which he could hope to make not just a worthwhile contribution, but a *great* one' (Monk, 1990, pp. 30-2).

The reason for thinking that this was Wittgenstein's route into logic and the foundations of mathematics is that there is evidence that, when he was nineteen years old (or maybe even younger) he had worked out a solution to the paradox and sent it not to Frege or Russell – he may have been too shy, at that stage, to do that – but to the mathematician Philip Jourdain. In a notebook, recording a visit of Russell on 20 April 1909, Jourdain wrote:

Russell said that the views that I gave in reply to Wittgenstein (who had 'solved' Russell's contradiction) agree with his own. These views are: The difficulty seems to me to be as follows. In certain cases (e.g. Burali-Forti's case, Russell's 'class' $\hat{x}$ *(x~εx)*, Epimenides' remark) we get what seem to be meaningless *limiting cases* of statements which are not meaningless. Thus there may be

4. Mathematics

certain x's such that the statement (propositional function) of x, which is a (true or false) proposition for other x's, is meaningless: thus if $\phi x = {}'x$ is a liar', ϕx becomes meaningless if I put x = myself. Analogously, we see no contradiction in thinking of $\hat{x}$ $(x{\sim}\varepsilon x)$, where x is *restricted* to (say) finite integers; but when we drop this restriction the class w is such that $w\varepsilon x \leftrightarrow w{\sim}\varepsilon w$. Thus the first problem is to find a principle to exclude those and only those limiting cases.[7]

The passage is very interesting as indicating a possible source of Wittgenstein's early idea (discussed in Chapter 1) that tautologies and contradictions are meaningless (sinnlos) *limiting cases* of statements (T 5.143) but it tells us virtually nothing about his teenage solution to the paradox. He gives a quick and rather dismissive solution of Russell's Paradox in the *Tractatus* (3.331-3),[8] but the problem continued to plague him. Russell's paradox plays a central rôle in the course of Wittgenstein's thinking about mathematics and he returned to the topics of paradox and contradiction throughout his philosophical career.

What can philosophy do for mathematics?

Most of the time, Wittgenstein is wise enough to take a 'hands off' approach to the practice of mathematics. It is surely not for philosophers to tell mathematicians how to do their work. '[Philosophy] leaves mathematics as it is, and no mathematical discovery can advance it' (*PI* §124). At the beginning of the first of his Cambridge lectures of 1939 on the foundations of mathematics, Wittgenstein asks 'How can I – or anyone who is not a mathematician – talk about this? What right has a philosopher to talk about mathematics?' (*LFM*, p. 13), and he answers that his intention is 'not to interfere with the mathematicians', not to dispute their results, but only to 'deal with puzzles which arise from the words of our ordinary everyday language, such as "proof", "number", "series", "order", etc.' (p. 14).

Yet Wittgenstein seems to have had a visceral dislike for certain branches of mathematics, and, on occasion, he seems willing to interfere with mathematical practice, or, at least to cast aspersions or take cheap shots. Earlier in the decade, when, lionized by the Vienna Circle and revered at Cambridge, he seems to have been at his most arrogant, he wrote such things as: 'A philosopher feels changes in the style of a derivation which a contemporary mathematician passes over calmly with a blank face. What will distinguish the mathematicians of the future from those of today will really be a greater sensitivity, and *that*

127

will – as it were – prune mathematics; since people will then be more intent on absolute clarity than on the discovery of new games' (*PG*, p. 381). He thinks, then, that philosophy will have the salutary effect of curbing the excesses of mathematicians: 'Philosophical clarity will have the same effect on the growth of mathematics as sunlight has on the growth of potato shoots. (In a dark cellar they grow yards long.)' (*PG*, p. 381). More abuse and gratuitous insult: 'The stupid pursuit of elegance is a principal cause of the mathematicians' failure to understand their own operations; or perhaps the lack of understanding and the pursuit of elegance have a common origin' (*PG*, p. 462); 'Mathematicians nowadays make so much fuss about proof of the consistency of axioms. I have the feeling that if there were a contradiction in the axioms of a system it wouldn't be such a great misfortune. Nothing easier than to remove it' (*PG*, p. 303). This, of course, is ridiculous posturing. Proving consistency is not an obsession, but an important area of mathematics in which interesting techniques have been developed. And as for there being 'nothing easier' than removing inconsistency, it proved to be the devil's own job to remove the inconsistency from Frege's *Grundgesetze* theory, as Wittgenstein was perfectly well aware. Yet Carnap tells us that '[Wittgenstein's] influence on some students in Vienna was so strong that they abandoned the study of mathematics' (Schilpp, 1963, p. 28).

At *PG*, p. 295, Wittgenstein says 'Time and time again I would like to say: "What I check is the *account books* of mathematicians".' He specifically denies that he is concerned with 'their mental processes, joys, depressions and instincts as they go about their business'. So what does he mean? It would seem that what he wants to do is to check the accounts that mathematicians give of what they are doing; he thinks, for example, that set-theoreticians are prone to perpetrating 'the crudest imaginable misinterpretation' of set theory (*PG*, p. 469). Cantor's Proof (that the natural numbers cannot be put into 1-1 correspondence with the reals) is not invalid; it's just that the usual ways of reading the result (e.g. that some infinities are bigger than others, that the reals outstrip the natural numbers) give it a certain specious 'charm', a misleading conception of number – for example, a mistaken idea about the similarity between the finite cardinals and transfinite numbers (*LC*, p. 28). He thinks that we get confused about notions such as the actual infinite and the continuum 'because language leads us into applying ... a picture that doesn't fit' (*PG*, p. 471).[9] More strongly: 'There is no religious denomination in which the misuse of metaphysical expressions has been responsible for so much sin as it has in mathematics' (*CV*, p. 1). He also has criticisms of mathematicians' views about the nature of mathematics.

The philosophical interest of mathematics

What is the philosophical interest in mathematics; what are the sorts of problems which incite philosophical enquiry? There are many, but a broad, embracing one is 'What is the nature of mathematical knowledge?', and that can be subdivided into questions about the objects of mathematical knowledge, how we acquire such knowledge, and whether what is thus known is contingent or necessary, synthetic or analytic. It was Kant who, by sharpening the issue of how, though not obtained through experience or experiment, mathematical knowledge can be substantial (more than just a matter of definitions), wrote the agenda for subsequent philosophy of mathematics.[10] First, there is a very basic question about numbers. For all of us, the entry point into mathematics is arithmetic.[11] We learn to count at an early age: by reciting a series of sounds we can determine the number of objects placed before us. Very soon, we learn to add numbers together, then to subtract one number from another. This is of great practical value. The numbers are something different from the objects counted and added; different too from the sounds made in counting them. It is commonly said that sounds or marks *represent* numbers so, for example, '3', 'III', 'drei', 'sam' all are used, in various contexts, to stand for the same number. If we accept this way of seeing things, then the the question we are asking is an ontological one: exactly what are numbers?

How do we acquire mathematical knowledge? Again, there is a dominant conception – the mathematician David McCarty calls it 'the locked room' – which makes our access to mathematical knowledge seem a mysterious phenomenon. If we are inclined to assimilate mathematical beliefs to geographical beliefs, then it can seem as if there is a real difficulty in explaining how we can acquire mathematical knowledge. Someone studying geography acquires beliefs about (say) the black hills of Dakota; the hills are quite separate from the beliefs about them. If mathematical belief is like that then, on the one hand, we shall have mathematical beliefs, and, on the other and quite separate from those beliefs, a body of nonconceptual mathematical fact. In the traditional (Platonistic) conception, this land of mathematical truth is not situated anywhere near the black hills of Dakota; it is not situated anywhere in space and time.[12] So how can we establish contact with this non-physical mathematical realm; how can we so much as glimpse it? On the 'geographical' conception, as McCarty says, in order for our beliefs to record the goings-on in a place, there must be some means of physical access to that place. We must somehow be able to peek in, or, if not a real peek, there must at least be some physical avenue into the place where the facts are kept. [Thus] the realm of mathematics takes on the aspect of a locked room: we are cut off from its inside and we cannot get in. And, yet, we seem to know something of the inside; we certainly know some mathematics. Hence, we cannot really be locked out. (McCarty, 1993)

It is noteworthy that, even by the time of his transitional period, Wittgenstein had managed to free himself from this vision of mathematics as a remote territory. In *PR* §109, he says (a trifle enigmatically) 'Arithmetic doesn't talk about numbers, it works with numbers'. In *PG* p. 365, he explains the difference between a mathematical expedition and a geographical expedition:

How strange it would be if a geographical expedition were uncertain whether it had a goal, and so whether it had any route whatsoever. We can't imagine such a thing, it's nonsense. But this is precisely what it is like in a mathematical expedition. And so perhaps it is a good idea to drop the comparison altogether.

We might set out on a 'mathematical expedition' to find out whether (for example) there are four consecutive 7s in the decimal expansion of π, but, so Wittgenstein wants to say, we don't even know the meaning of that question (we don't know the 'goal') until we have a proof of the answer, and there is no telling now whether such a proof will be forthcoming (*PG* pp. 475-7, *RFM* V-9, *PI* §516). This seems like an extremely strange view, and we shall have to see, later, if it makes any sense.

At this stage in his career, Wittgenstein had come back into philosophy under the influence of a lecture by the intuitionist L.E.J. Brouwer, and arguably it is intuitionism (taking its lead from Kant) which breaks most cleanly with the 'geographical' conception of mathematics.[13] In Brouwer's view, expressing it as crudely as possible, we are blessed with a 'primordial intuition of time' – a sense of the present as *one* moment which is at the junction of *two* phases – the going (receding into the past) and the becoming (as the future unfolds); hence our most fundamental number concepts are acquired once we can recognize change. We construct the mathematical world out of our concepts; it's not a matter of struggling to bring our conceptual resources to bear on

4. Mathematics

a mind-independent mathematical realm. In his later writings, Wittgenstein repeatedly insists that the mathematician is not someone *discovering* previously uncharted territory, but is rather a creative individual *inventing* new terrain (*RFM* Appendix II-2, p. 111) – as in land reclamation of the waterfront, where the coastal contour is for us to shape. This idea goes beyond Kant and Brouwer, for whereas they confronted the problem of how we acquire mathematical knowledge, of how we apprehend mathematical truths, Wittgenstein regards mathematics as not, generally speaking, a species of knowledge – there can be no knowledge of mathematical truths when mathematics deals not in truths of the kind that we come to know, but in *rules*, which we lay down.[14] The distinction is a subtle one. We regard 'The bishop moves only along diagonals of its own colour' as a *rule*, whereas 'The Bishop of York breeds goldfish' is not a rule but a proposition or statement. Now, is Wittgenstein right to categorize mathematical results as rules? This, again, is a problem to which we shall return.

Number

The question one feels most immediately impelled to ask about numbers is 'What are they?' If they are not concrete things – and they do not seem to have concrete properties like weight, shape and colour – then perhaps they are abstract entities. Prominent among the many who have subscribed to this latter view are Plato and Frege.[15] A modern exponent of the view is, oddly enough, W.V. Quine, lover of desert landscapes, whose conception of what there is is: only as much as we absolutely cannot do without (Quine, 1953). Quine thinks that by refusing to posit abstract mathematical objects, we deprive ourselves of the ability to furnish scientific explanations: 'The numbers and functions contribute just as genuinely to physical theory as do hypothetical particles' (Quine, 1981, p. 150). He says that words like 'five' and 'twelve' 'name two intangible objects, numbers, which are *sizes of* sets of apples and the like' (op. cit., p. 149).

Russell's view – which was inspired by Peano – appears to be superior to all those mentioned so far. Suppose we have several different sets each containing n objects (so each member of one of the sets corresponds 1-1 with a member of any other of the sets). Then we can say that what all these sets have in common is only their n-ness. On this Russellian view, numbers are not themselves either physical or abstract objects; they are *abstracted* objects – we abstract (or isolate) what is common to all sets containing the same number of members. A number is, on Russell's account, a class; for example, the number 2 is the class which contains classes as its members; specifically, it contains as its members all those classes which contain just 2 members. If this is supposed to be a definition of the number 2, then, to avoid circularity, we had better say what it is to contain 2 members without using the number 2. And Russell shows how to do this: A class contains just 2 members if it contains x as a member and y as a member, and, if z is a member, then z is identical with either x or y.

In his early period, Wittgenstein took the view that 'number is *the* fundamental idea of calculus and must be introduced as such'.[16] In the *Tractatus*, he argues that the word 'number' signifies a *formal* concept (4.1272). A concept is formal if it is unthinkable that the objects that fall under it should fail to do so;[17] (for example, it is unthinkable that 8 should fail to be a number). Wittgenstein's account of numbers starts with two definitions:

$$x = \Omega^{0\prime}x \quad \text{Def.}$$
$$\Omega\Omega^{v\prime}x = \Omega^{v+1\prime}x \quad \text{Def.}$$

(*Tractatus* 6.02). These can be stated non-technically as follows:

Do nothing (0 things) to an x and it remains the same.
Do something to an x to which you've already done the same thing n times, and you've now done it n + 1 times.

The key notion in these definitions is that of doing something (performing an operation) repeatedly (n times). For example, complex propositions can be generated from elementary ones by successive applications of an operation N (*T* 6-6.002).[18] Wittgenstein says that 'a number is the exponent of an operation' (*T* 6.021); the exponent indicates how many times the operation is performed. He says that these definitions are rules which deal with signs, and his idea seems to be that if there are a certain number of operator signs 'Ω' in front of 'x' (where 'Ω' is an operation variable, for which one can substitute the designation of any operation) this *shows* that x is operated on that number of times. Armed with these definitions of '0' and '+ 1', it is now trivial to define each of the natural numbers, viz.

$$0 + 1 = 1 \quad \text{Def.}$$
$$0 + 1 + 1 = 2 \quad \text{Def.}$$

and so on.

In his transitional phase, 1929-33, Wittgenstein abandons as 'nebulous' (*PR* §109) the *Tractatus* introduction of the concept of number by means of the general form of operation. He is right to do so. The idea that the number 0 can somehow be explained or defined in terms of *doing nothing* is a bit optimistic. *Indolence*, perhaps, could be so defined. And to define '+ 1' in terms of the repetition of an operation is not exactly helpful, since to repeat an operation is to do it *one more time*, so the definition is circular. Wittgenstein came to see that there is a much more concrete way of getting to grips with numbers, and this is via the numerals that represent them. For (and, in some ways, this is a *Tractatus*-like idea) there is a way of perspicuously picturing the numbers such that the essential characteristics of the pictured are captured in the picture. This perspicuous notation involves not arbitrary marks, such as 'one', '2', 'trois', but brushstrokes (or strokes of a pen etc.) – one stroke to represent the number 1, two strokes for the number 2 etc. (In Chinese, the first three numerals look like that.) The internal, or essential, properties of numbers are made manifest in this perspicuous stroke notation – four strokes are *visibly* one more than three. This is a kind of geometricization of arithmetic in which the nature of numbers is made transparent.[19]

The following slightly less babyish example came upon me, for no apparent reason, while I was reading *RFM*. (It was new to me, though I am sure it is not new.) Consider a square grid of dots, with (n + 1) dots on each side:

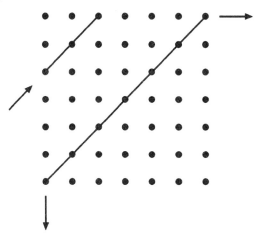

There are (n + 1) rows, each containing (n + 1) dots, so the number of dots in the grid is $(n + 1)^2$. But there is another way of counting. First count the dots on the main diagonal: n+1. Symmetrical about this diagonal are two sets of dots, which can be counted by starting at the corner dot and adding each subdiagonal, giving a total of $2\Sigma n$. So, the total number of dots on the grid is $(n+1) + 2\Sigma n$, and this equals $(n + 1)^2$, obtained by counting the 'normal' way. So here we have a 'geometrical' proof that $\Sigma n = n(n + 1)/\,2$, a result standardly proved by mathematical induction – a method which is both boring and requires that the formula be known in advance. Wittgenstein writes: 'You could say arithmetic is a kind of geometry; i.e., what in geometry are constructions on paper, in arithmetic are calculations (on paper). – You could say it is a more general kind of geometry' (*PR* §109).

Wittgenstein inherited from Russell, and from nineteenth-century authors such as Frege and Dedekind, the problem of defining 'number'. All of those authors took numbers to be objects (although they differ vastly over what kinds of objects they are), as did Wittgenstein in the *Tractatus*. Since numbers are not physical things, one may seem to be driven to the Platonistic view that they are abstract objects. One difficulty with this Platonistic conception is that abstract entities are causally inert – they can't impinge on our senses even to the extent of provoking us into recognizing them and giving them names. Hilary Putnam (following Jody Azzouni) provides a telling criticism of Quine's defence of the view that positing such abstract entities is necessary for understanding the application of mathematics to scientific theorizing:

> Wouldn't mathematics have worked exactly as well even if the 'intangible objects' didn't exist? For, since the supposed mathematical objects are causally inert, the ordinary empirical objects would have behaved just as they do, and our applied mathematics would have succeeded and failed just when it does succeed and fail. But doesn't this already show that postulating immaterial objects to account for the success of mathematics is a useless shuffle?[20]

In his early transitional period, Wittgenstein appears to be getting uncomfortable with the idea that numbers are objects. At *PR* §107, he says that numbers are 'structures' and thinks it best not to try to say directly what numbers are, but to say that they are what numerals represent: 'That is to say, I take (so to speak) the number schemata of the language as what I know, and say numbers are what these represent.' In other words, numbers are the *je ne sais quois* for which numerals stand. This seems rather evasive – we are left wondering how numbers differ from the sorts of thing for which words other than numerals stand. It is interesting that Wittgenstein himself got worried by this difficulty, for, sometime later, at this very point in the text, he wrote a note in the margin: 'Instead of a question of the definition of number, it's only a question of the grammar of numerals.'[21] This is highly significant and very close to a Formalist position.[22] It is like a move away from agnosticism to atheism – from saying that you do not know what numbers are (except that they are what numerals stand for) to saying that numerals do not stand for anything, that there are no objects or 'structures' for which they stand.

The claim that numbers are not objects was defended by Paul Benacerraf in a well-known paper (Benacerraf, 1965). He points out that some mathematicians have identified the numbers 1, 2, 3, ... with the sets [Ø], [[Ø]], [[[Ø]]] ... while other mathematicians have identified these numbers with the sets [Ø], [Ø,[Ø]], [Ø, [Ø], [Ø,[Ø]]] ... (where Ø is the empty set). Other admissible identifications are possible and, importantly, working with any of them you get identical results in number theory. So, if you can equally well identify the number series with many different progressions of sets, it would be arbitrary and incorrect to identify the number series with *any* such progression. A similar kind of 'indifference' argument for the indeterminacy of translation is propounded by Quine (1960, ch. 2). Both arguments have the form 'If X can equally well be identified with Y_1, Y_2, Y_3 ..., where the Y_i are non-identical, then X should not be identified with *any* of the Y_i'. In Quine's case, X = the meaning of 'gavagai', a word in the language of a certain tribe; the Y_i are various translations, all compatible with all behavioural evidence, documented in mutually incompatible translation manuals. In Benacerraf's case X = the integers; the Y_i are various set-theoretic progressions. Quine's conclusion is that there is no such thing as the meaning of an expression, Benacerraf's that there are no such things as numbers (though he adds, gnomically, 'which is not to say that there are not at least two prime numbers between 15 and 20' (Benacerraf, 1965, p. 294).

Benacerraf's argument, even if correct, does not entitle him to the strong conclusion he draws. He succeeds in showing that numbers are not to be identified with sets. But sets are only one kind of object; Benacerraf has not shown that there are no objects of any kind to which numbers could properly be identified. That stronger conclusion is, I contend, established shortly and sweetly in Wittgenstein's later writings. He argues that we can attain a perfectly clear understanding of the rôle of numerals and other number words without supposing that these words stand for any kind of thing.

Wittgenstein undercuts the discussion of the nature of number by casting doubt on the assumption that numbers *have* a nature. If we look at the history of number, we shall see that what counts as a number is not fixed over time. For the ancient Greeks, numbers were just the integers and ratios between integers (Heath, 1949, 209-11). The negatives were not generally accepted as numbers – on the contrary, they were, well into the nineteenth century, condemned as 'absurdities' by distinguished authors including William R. Hamilton.[23] Whether to call such exotica as irrationals and imaginaries, when they appeared on the mathematical scene, *numbers*, was determined not by measuring them against fixed conditions for numberhood, but by seeing whether they bore sufficient 'family resemblance' to what was already being counted as numbers. This is not fixed other than by human decision-making, and is just as much a matter for dispute as (say) whether feminism sufficiently resembles racism for it to be classified as pernicious discrimination, or whether abortion sufficiently resembles a premeditated fatal knifing for it to be classified as murder. The doctrine of family resemblance (or family likeness (*BB*, p. 17), which has subsequently been used to attack essentialism and realist theories of universals, is set out in *Philosophical Investigations* at §67:

I can think of no better expression to characterize these similarities than 'family resemblances'; for the various resemblances between members of a family: build, features, colour of eyes, gait, temperament, etc. etc. overlap and criss-cross in the same way. – And I shall say: 'games' form a family.

And for instance the kinds of number form a family in the same way. Why do we call something a 'number'? Well, perhaps because it has a – direct – relationship with several things that have hitherto been called number; and this can be said to give it an indirect relationship to other things we call the same name. And we extend our concept of number as in spinning a thread we twist fibre on fibre. And the strength of the thread does not reside in the fact that some one fibre runs through its whole length, but in the overlapping of many fibres.

But if someone wished to say: 'There is something common to all these constructions – namely the disjunction of all their common properties' – I should reply: 'Now you are only playing with words. One might as well say: Something runs through the whole thread – namely the continuous overlapping of those fibres.'

The *Philosophical Investigations* discussion of family resemblance (*PI* §§65-78) is exceptionally clear and fine. The import is that we can converse perfectly intelligibly about numbers (or games etc.) even though numbers (or games etc.) do not have a nature specifiable by means of necessary and sufficient conditions. As the marginal note at

4. Mathematics

PR §107 indicates, there is no definition of 'number' and no need for one. 'But', someone might object, 'although we may not know in advance of decisions that we make what is going to count as a number, surely *three* is a paradigm case of a number; the word "three" stands for something different from what the word "four" stands for, and both words must have meaning, for they are used in meaningful sentences.' The reply is that we have this unfortunate tendency to think that a substantive must correspond to a thing (*BB*, p. 5). A word like 'three' can be used grammatically as a noun, but that means that it can be the grammatical subject or object of a verb; there is no requirement that it stand for some object. Let us imagine ourselves at that point in history when it is being debated whether to count i (the square root of −1) as a number. It is true that here one is making a comparison between i and uncontroversial examples of numbers, such as 3. But making such a comparison seems in no way like comparing two *objects* of any sort. Rather, we are looking at questions such as whether i can be comfortably embraced within standard mathematical procedures like adding and subtracting, whether working with i as a number produces results unacceptably disruptive of existing number theory etc. What is evident, when we look into the matter, is that what is crucial, in deciding whether to incorporate i within the number system, is to investigate what we do with i, how we use it.

It is not in virtue of standing for an object that a number word has meaning. The word 'three' does indeed have a meaning (it is not a meaningless mark), and if we wish to determine the meaning that word has, then, true to *PI* §43, we should observe how it is *used*. The integers, for example, are frequently used for *counting*, for numbering off objects. Likewise the gradations on a ruler are used for measuring length. In Benacerraf's words: 'Questions of the identification of the referents of number words should be dismissed as misguided in just the same way that a question about the referents of the parts of a ruler would be seen as misguided' (Benacerraf, 1965, p. 292). The shopkeeper at *PI* §1 gets the correct number of apples by uttering different sounds for each of the apples he takes from the drawer. The numerals he enunciates stand neither for the apples nor for any abstract objects. At least, we have no reason so far to suppose that they do, and a very good reason (Occam's Razor) to suppose that they do not. That the numerals have such standard and practical uses as in counting and sharing things out is quite sufficient to guarantee that they have a meaning, and we discern what meaning they have by observing their rôle in such ordinary activities.

It could be argued that certain nouns, such as 'gold' and 'tiger' stand

137

for *natural kinds* whose nature, or characteristic structure – chemical or biological – it is for experts to discover. Such discoveries would then be instrumental in enabling us to furnish accurate definitions of those nouns. For example, one might define 'gold' as 'element with atomic weight 79', 'tiger' as – well, nobody has yet come up with a satisfactory definition. Now, even if one accepted this view,[24] there is good reason, given the history of the series of decisions about what to include under the term 'number', to deny that number has any hidden structure which it is up to experts to reveal. For sure, it has no chemical or biological structure, and it is mere prejudice to assume that, by analogy with natural kinds, number must have *some* kind of essence, that anything we properly call a number must possess this essence. Why accept such an analogy? The alternative, once one gets used to it, is attractive (though possibly disheartening to lexicographers of a certain ilk): one finds out more about numbers by doing more and more advanced arithmetic, not by conducting a metaphysical investigation into the hidden nature of number; there are no properties common to all numbers, and hence no definition of 'number' in terms of characteristic or essential properties.

Wittgenstein is not offering a theory of number, but is discouraging theorizing about the nature of number. Yet such 'quietism', if reasonable, has significant consequences. Numbers begin to lose their Pythagorean mystique. And we shall not be able to continue to regard arithmetical equations (and inequalities (*PR* §201, p. 249) as asserting relationships between timeless entities. But then we should want to ask what kind of a beast an equation is; more generally, what job do the propositions of mathematics do?

Mathematical 'propositions'

A true mathematical proposition is surely not one that corresponds to empirical reality, for mathematics is independent of empirical contingencies. So (it seems natural to say) true mathematical propositions express necessary relationships among objects in a non-empirical realm. For the Platonist, a true mathematical proposition corresponds to some aspect of a non-physical, mind-independent reality.

Does Wittgenstein have a plausible alternative to the standard Platonistic account of mathematical propositions? In the *Tractatus*, he had maintained that mathematics does not *describe* (any kind of) reality, but makes manifest certain essential features of reality: 'The logic of the world, which is shown in tautologies by the propositions of logic, is shown in equations by mathematics' (*T* 6.22).[25] The late Wittgensteinian view can best be explained by starting from a very simple example. Suppose that I lay one stick on the ground, then add another. Then I count the resulting collection, using a series of sounds of which, in this instance, I need only the first two members: 'one' and 'two'. That the result of thus adding 1 and 1 is a collection the counting of which requires not less than and not more than the first two sounds in the series is a truth which has the same status as (say) the truth that nothing can be red and green all over or that one thing cannot be simultaneously in two places. So, if we agree to use the words 'One plus one equals two' to state this truth, we are in effect saying that it is constitutive of the meaning of 'one', 'two' 'plus' and 'equals' that we rate it ungrammatical, nonsensical, to deny that one plus one equals two. The proposition cannot be overturned in the light of any empirical observation. The proposition 'one plus one equals two', then, has the status of a rule of grammar; such propositions, as Wittgenstein neatly puts it, are 'dependent on experience but made independent of it' (*LFM*, p. 55).

Of course, if we think that what is characteristic of propositions is that they are true or false, then we may be reluctant to call rules of grammar 'propositions' and will seek to contrast mathematical 'propositions' with genuine propositions (*PR* §122, p. 143, *LFM*, p. 111). Wittgenstein asks: 'Might we not do arithmetic without having the idea of uttering arithmetical *propositions*, and without ever having been struck by the similarity between a multiplication and a proposition?' We do shake our heads when we are shown a multiplication done wrong, just as we might shake our heads when somebody tells us something we know to be false – but we also shake our heads when someone behaves stupidly. The head-shaking is no indication that, in all three cases, we are denying the truth of a *proposition*. Wittgenstein continues: 'We are used to saying "2 times 2 is four", and the verb "is" makes this into a proposition, and apparently establishes a close kinship with everything that we call a "proposition." Whereas it is a matter only of a very superficial relationship' (*RFM* Appendix III-4, p. 117).

It would be unlike Wittgenstein to maintain, for very long, a general theory to the effect that everything that looks like a proposition in mathematics is really a rule of grammar. And indeed, by a little later in *RFM*, he has overcome his 'craving for generality'. At *RFM* VII-6, he says 'There is no doubt at all that *in certain language-games* mathematical propositions play the part of rules of description, as opposed to descriptive propositions. But that is not to say that this contrast does not shade off in all directions. And *that* in turn is not to say that the contrast is not of the greatest importance.' If we already know what

139

words like 'square', 'hypotenuse', 'right angle', 'triangle' and 'sum' mean, then the proposition 'The square on the hypotenuse of a right-angled triangle is equal to the sum of the squares on the other two sides' is a *description* of a property of a right-angled triangle. By contrast, if someone says to you 'This trio is larger in number than that quartet', we should conclude that his mistake was one concerning the meaning of words: if you don't know that three is less than four, you don't yet know what 'three' and 'four' mean. In this case, '3 < 4' is plausibly regarded as a rule for the use of those words; it is thus that 'mathematics is normative' (*RFM* VII-61). Here 'the mathematical proposition is to shew us what it makes SENSE to say' (*RFM* III-28). One could say that, despite having an empirical provenance, some propositions of arithmetic have a non-empirical, non-descriptive *status*, that of rules for the use of signs. This seems to me a by no means crazy option.

Mathematical proof

If you want crazy (or apparently crazy), turn to Wittgenstein's discussion of mathematical proof. The question is: how should one regard a proof in mathematics? There is a common – perhaps even commonsense – belief that a valid mathematical proof establishes a truth, a true mathematical proposition about relationships between non-empirical objects (such as numbers). Since these objects are atemporal, any relationship which holds between them must exist independently of the proof that it does so hold, hence the proof, when it is first performed, is a discovery of the relationship. This is the Platonistic conception of mathematical proof which, though it may rarely be articulated by working mathematicians, is the one most would endorse if pressed. Of course, some mathematicians have endorsed that conception quite explicitly. For example, G.H. Hardy, a Cambridge contemporary of Wittgenstein, writes: 'I believe that mathematical reality lies outside us, that our function is to discover or observe it, and that the theorems which we prove, and which we describe grandiloquently as our "creations" are simply our notes of our observations' (Hardy, 1967, pp. 123-4).

The Platonistic account weaves together a view of the nature of mathematical objects, a geographical conception of our relation to mathematical reality, a conception of the truth of mathematical propositions and an account of the function of mathematical proof. Pick at one thread, and the fabric is likely to fall apart. We have already seen that a Platonistic conception of numbers is not compulsory, and that Wittgenstein is able to provide an alternative by replacing the question of what number words stand for by the question of what they are used to do. We have also seen that he rejects the standard conception of a mathematical proposition. It should come as no surprise, then, that his views on mathematical proof are somewhat deviant.

Wittgenstein says that proving mathematically is a matter of creating new concepts – 'the proof puts a new paradigm among the paradigms of language' (*RFM* III-31, p. 166; I-165-7, pp. 98-9) – or modifying old ones; that the proof determines the sense of a question or a conjecture, changes the meaning of what is proved; the sense of the result is read off from the proof (*RFM* III-25, p. 162; III-29, p. 164; cf. VII-10, p. 367). All this seems manifestly false. Some time ago, I made the following conjecture: if one produces alternate sides of any hexagon inscribed in a conic section and joins the opposite pairs of the six points where those lines cross, then the resulting three lines meet at a point.

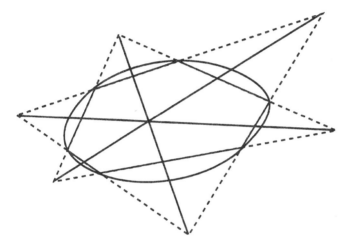

Because the conjecture made entirely good sense, a mathematician friend, many years later, understood it, and he proved it to be true. The proof did not create any new concepts, and both of us immediately and rightly accepted it as valid, without needing a community of mathematicians to confer necessity on it by their endorsement of a new way of talking. Anyone who defends Wittgenstein's late conception of mathematics should at least show how to shoot down this sort of rather obvious objection.

An objection along similar lines is raised by Wittgenstein himself. Consider Fermat's Last Theorem: that there are no integral values of x, y, z such that for any integer n greater than 2, $x^n + y^n = z^n$.[26] The concepts of *integer*, *power* etc. are entirely familiar. Surely the sense of the theorem is perfectly plain and we understand the problem before us if we are asked to prove the theorem. Wittgenstein says: 'Suppose prizes are offered for the solution – say – of Fermat's problem. Someone might object to me: How can you say that this problem doesn't exist? If prizes are offered for the solution, then surely the problem must exist' (*PG*, p. 362). In other words, surely the meaning of the problem is clear when it is stated, and is not resolved only after a solution is found. To this Wittgenstein responds:

> I would have to say: Certainly, but the people who talk about it don't understand the grammar of the expression 'mathematical problem' or of the word 'solution'. The prize is really offered for the solution of a scientific problem; for the *exterior* of the solution (hence also for instance we talk about a Riemannian *hypothesis*). The conditions of the problem are external conditions; and when the problem is solved, what happens corresponds to the setting of the problem in the way in which solutions correspond to problems in physics.
>
> If we set as a problem to find a construction for a regular pentagon, the way the construction is specified in the setting of the problem is by the physical attribute that it is to yield a pentagon that is *shown by measurement* to be regular. For we don't get the concept of *constructive division into five* (or of a *constructive pentagon*) until we get it from the construction.
>
> Similarly in Fermat's theorem we have an empirical structure that we interpret as a *hypothesis*, and not – of course – as the product of a construction. So in a certain sense what the problem asks for is not what the solution gives.

This response is, I think, entirely unsatisfactory. It amounts to no more than the observation that, in setting the problem, we do not supply the solution. That in solving a problem we learn something new, even that we learn something necessarily true, does not show that we didn't know what we were talking about before the proof, or that we must have been talking about something different.

Wittgenstein next tries a different tack:

> Imagine someone set himself the following problem. He is to discover a game played on a chessboard, in which each player is to have 8 pieces; the two white ones which are in the outermost files at the beginning of the game (the 'consuls') are to be given some special status by the rules so that they have a greater freedom of movement than the other pieces; one of the black pieces (the

142

'general') is to have a special status; a white piece takes a black one by being put in its place (and vice versa); the whole game is to have a certain analogy with the Punic wars. Those are the conditions that the game is to satisfy. – There is no doubt that is a problem, a problem not at all like the problem of finding out how under certain conditions white can win in chess. – But now imagine the problem: 'How can white win in 20 moves in the war-game whose rules we don't yet know precisely?' – That problem would be quite analogous to the problems of mathematics (other than problems of calculation). (*PG*, p. 363)

The idea here is that, in order to solve the war-game problem, we have to *make up* some rules; without such rules, we cannot play the game; these new rules, together with those that are already given are *constitutive* of the new game. Now, is this 'quite analogous', as Wittgenstein claims, to solving mathematical problems by furnishing a proof? There is a competing, but in Wittgenstein's view, misleading analogy the lure of which we need to resist:

We must first ask ourselves: is the mathematical proposition proved? If so, how? For the proof is part of the grammar of the proposition! – The fact that this is so often not understood arises from our thinking once again along the lines of a misleading analogy. As usual in these cases, it is an analogy from our thinking in natural sciences. We say, for example, 'this man died two hours ago' and if someone asks us 'how can you tell that?' we can give a series of indications (symptoms). But we also leave open the possibility that medicine may discover hitherto unknown methods of ascertaining the time of death. That means that we can already describe such possible methods; it isn't their description that is discovered. What is ascertained experimentally is whether the description corresponds to the facts. For example, I may say: one method consists in discovering the quantity of haemoglobin in the blood, because this diminishes according to such and such a law in proportion to the time after death. Of course that isn't correct, but if it were correct, nothing in my imaginary description would change. If you call the medical discovery 'the discovery of a proof that the man died two hours ago' you must go on to say that this discovery does not change anything in the grammar of the proposition 'the man died two hours ago'. The discovery is the discovery that a particular hypothesis is true (or: agrees with the facts). We are so accustomed to these ways of thinking, that we take the discovery of a proof in mathematics, sight unseen, as being the same or similar. We are wrong to do so because, to put it concisely, the mathematical proof couldn't be described before it is discovered.

The 'medical proof' didn't incorporate the hypothesis it proved into any new calculus, so it didn't give it any new sense; a mathematical proof incorporates the mathematical proposition into a new calculus, and alters its position in mathematics. The proposition with its proof doesn't belong to the same category as the proposition without the proof. (*PG*, pp. 370-1)

This example of Wittgenstein's is not a particularly good one since, as we are nowadays aware, there are competing criteria for death. He writes as if there is no disputing whether someone is dead, and hence that there is a clear, unambiguous sense of the proposition that a man died two hours ago. But the sense of that proposition is not independent of the means we use to establish its truth, such as checking the pulse or scanning for signs of brain activity just as, as he wants to say, the sense of a mathematical theorem is dependent on *its* method of proof. Setting this quibble aside, what does seem true is that while, in the medical case, we can make conjectures about methods that might be used for establishing the truth of the proposition (and, with luck, at least one of these conjectures will be correct), in the mathematical case, we cannot. Yet Wittgenstein could not (or, at least, should not) be arguing that this difference is explained by the fact that the medical proposition is a fixed target, while the mathematical one is moving until fixed by the proof. For this 'explanans' is itself what needs to be explained.

The illustrations that Wittgenstein gives in support of his thesis that the sense of a mathematical conclusion gets altered after, and as a consequence of its being proved, are not particularly compelling. Perhaps the following more homely example may be of some help. In squash, as in many games, there are rallies which end when one player hits an illegal shot; this means that his opponent wins the rally and earns the right to serve. There are two systems of scoring in squash. In the 'English' system the first player to reach 9 points wins a game, whereas in the 'American' system, 15 points are needed. Another difference between the English and American scoring systems is that the latter awards one point for winning a rally irrespective of who serves, whereas the former allows only the server to gain a point. In both systems, the player winning the match is the first to win three games. It might be thought that a game score of 9:3 (English) is equivalent to 15:5 (American), i.e. that any player who typically scores a certain fraction of the number of points of his opponent in the English system will typically score that same fraction of the number of points of his opponent when they are using the American scoring system. However, that turns out, empirically, not to be the case, and this raises the theoretical problem of finding, for each English score, its American equivalent. In other words, we need to find a function f(x) and a proof that an English score of 9:x is equivalent to an American score of 15:f(x). What emerges, however, when one attempts the proof, is that *there is no such function*, although we can prove that *for any particular pair of players*, there is a key for translating their English scores into American (Goldstein, 1992b). *Before* the proof, we were looking for a mapping between two sets of scores, each score in one set being matched with its equivalent in the other; *after* the proof, we continue to use the phrase 'equivalent score' but mean it in a different way. Wittgenstein's term of art 'grammar' is apposite for describing the situation. The proof teaches us something about the grammar of the phrase 'equivalent score': to say that an English score and an American score are equivalent is as ungrammatical as a transitive verb used without an object; we have to say 'the equivalent of English score 9:n *for players A and B* is 15:f$_{AB}$(n) American'.

According to Wittgenstein, that's how it is with mathematics: the effect of a proof is to modify the concepts with which we are operating and hence to alter the sense (the grammar) of the conclusion at which we are driving. Or better, since we alter the senses of those conclusions in the very process of driving towards them, it seems reasonable to say that we are inventing new destinations.[27] This is a theme to which Wittgenstein repeatedly returns. Someone who thinks that there could be a round square has not acquired the concept of *square*. Similarly, someone who talks of 'the trisection of an angle by means of straight edge and compass' does not have a proper grasp of the relevant concepts (*RFM* IV-30, p. 239). After grasping the proof of the impossibility of such a construction, a person will recognize as nonsense the phrase 'the trisection of an angle by means of straight edge and compass' just as surely as he so recognizes the phrase 'round square'. That person has achieved conceptual enlightenment.

Perhaps what Wittgenstein had in mind can be illuminated by a comparison with what Thomas Kuhn has termed 'revolutionary' science, a conceptual revolution in which an old paradigm is abandoned and a new set of conceptual tools and research methods adopted (Kuhn, 1970). In relativity physics, we have conceptions of *mass* and *length* that are quite different from their classical counterparts. For example, we now take length not to be an absolute measure but to depend on the relative velocity of the object being measured and the measuring device. So Newton wouldn't be able to *understand* a conjecture in relativity theory *before* he understood the concepts, and he'd acquire that understanding by learning the theory. Similarly, when doing a new proof in mathematics, we create new concepts, and the proposition proved cannot be understood independently of an understanding of those concepts and that proof. The comparison with Kuhn should not be pushed too far. Kuhn thinks that 'conceptual revolutions' are rare, and that, most of the time, we are doing 'normal science'. For Wittgenstein, the normal state for mathematics is revolutionary.

David McCarty draws attention to the great variety of diverse kinds of mathematical proof, thereby giving the lie to the belief (which philosophers of mathematics tend to take for granted) that proof consists in the derivation of theorems from axioms. He claims that proofs in mathematics of the strictly axiom-and-rule-bound kind 'are, within the great mass of proofs, relatively few in number and lacking in significance' (McCarty, 1993, p. 286). I'm not sure that I would call Euclid's *Elements* lacking in significance, but it is probably true that the *Elements* are so famous that people who know very little about actual mathematical practice assume that Euclid's proofs are the exemplar – that they set the standard for what is to count as respectable proof in mathematics. Yet if one observes, for example, Euler's solution to the 'Seven Bridges' problem or Cantor's diagonal method for showing that the reals are non-denumerable, or Paul Cohen's forcing technique for proving the independence of the continuum hypothesis, or the heavily computer-assisted demonstration that plane or sphere maps of whatever complexity need only up to four colours to guarantee visible boundaries between distinct adjacent areas, one soon becomes aware that mathematical proofs are not, in general, axiomatic.[28] McCarty says 'When I finally "get" a truly deep proof, I have learned a manner of proceeding, a manner from which I can create an array of answers to an indefinite variety of *other* mathematical questions' (McCarty, 1993, p. 287).

This is a mathematician speaking in a distinctly Wittgensteinian tone, although for McCarty it is only the 'truly deep' proofs that furnish us with new conceptual resources. Wittgenstein sometimes talks as if each new proof in mathematics redraws the conceptual boundaries, sets up new rules, lays down new paradigms. But, as we saw in the previous section, in the later sections of *Remarks on the Foundations of Mathematics*, dating from around 1941, he acknowledges that some mathematical propositions are descriptions – I offered, without his endorsement, the example of Pythagoras' Theorem, most proofs of

146

which do not, presumably, involve any concept-stretching. It is not, anyway, as if there is a sharp distinction to be made between proofs which alter a concept and those from which we learn about connections between unaltered concepts. For the concept of 'concept' is itself vague – 'too vague by far' (*RFM* VII-45, p. 412).

Wittgenstein describes mathematics as a 'motley' of techniques of proof – 'upon this is based its manifold applicability and its importance' (*RFM* III-46, p. 176); 'a family of activities with a family of purposes' (*RFM* V-15, p. 273; also VII-33, p. 399). He wants to give an account of this motley (*RFM* III-50, p. 182). Forming concepts may be characteristic of certain areas of mathematics, but it is not essential to all; 'it plays no part in other regions. This insight by itself will of course have some influence on people once they learn to see mathematics in this way' (*RFM* VII-33, p. 399). Here, yet again, we find Wittgenstein showing us *differences*, encouraging us to resist seeking a unified account, to resist seeking the *essential* thing about mathematics (including resisting the essentialist claim that Wittgenstein himself was inclined to make, about mathematics consisting in the forming of concepts (ibid.) This is a hard lesson to learn, for we seem to have a gnawing suspicion that mathematical proof *must* have an essential nature, and that one theory will lay this bare. Yet the 'essentialist' viewpoint is at odds with what we know, empirically, about the differences in content and methodologies between different regions of mathematics such as (say) number theory, topology, statistics and algebra. It is quite usual for a mathematician to be great in some areas of the subject but hopeless in others, just as a philosopher might be great at (say) applied ethics, but useless at philosophical logic or theory of mind. Had Wittgenstein claimed that philosophy is a motley, nobody would have batted an eyelid.

Contradiction

In the preceding sections, we have considered some Wittgensteinian theses in ascending order of apparent craziness, and have concluded, in each case, that, after considerable transitional waywardness, Wittgenstein's mature position is (at least) worthy of serious consideration and (at best) puts mathematics and mathematical practice in an interesting new light. We shall now ascend further and, by the end of this section, arrive at a similar verdict about his views on contradiction, views which, in the words of Crispin Wright (1980, p. 295) give a first impression 'not so much that of ordinary attitudes or assumptions questioned, as of good sense outraged'. The outrageous position, stated most starkly, is that contradictions are not false.

As we noted, at the beginning of the chapter, Russell's Paradox was Wittgenstein's point of entry into mathematical logic. This paradox, and various others, continued to plague him throughout his career. For example, we find him, in a 1946 manuscript MS 130 (p. 32), trying to contrive a new paradox in the region of both Russell's and Grelling's.[29] (After going through a few steps in the deduction, he gives up and – rather violently – crosses out the last line of the derivation.) The Liar paradox, arising out of the sentence 'This statement is false', exercised him sporadically, as did the associated incompleteness theorem of Gödel's, to the effect that arithmetic (if it is consistent) contains truths which are unprovable. And, as we saw in the previous chapter, extensive reflection on Moore's paradox occupied him during the late, late, period.

Wittgenstein's contribution to the struggle to solve these 'insolubilia' deserves a monograph of its own,[30] but our concern here is with a thesis of his which, if correct, would lead to a very general re-evaluation of our attitude towards paradoxes. Typically, in a paradox, we are led from apparently true premises, by simple and straightforward steps of reasoning, to a contradiction. The natural reaction is to regard this as a disaster, and to scrutinize the reasoning to see what has gone wrong. If something has gone wrong, this would show that there is a fundamental flaw in how we reason – fundamental since, as we said, the reasoning steps are utterly simple, almost unquestionable. Suppose, however, that we could persuade ourselves to react less unfavourably towards contradictions, to positively embrace them – as some religions advocate – to accept that they are true (even if false too) as 'dialetheists' urge we should.[31] Then maybe we would no longer regard paradoxes as so vexing and threatening, but just as interesting examples of *valid* reasoning. The main reason why we do not like our reasoning to lead us from premises that seem to be true to contradictory conclusions is that we think that contradictions are plain false.[32] So if Wittgenstein can disabuse us of that 'superstitious dread and veneration' in face of contradiction (*RFM* III-17; *A*, p. 71), he will have performed a service.

In each period of his work, Wittgenstein makes the claim that contradictions are not false and, except for the last six years of his life when he defended it in a different way, defends it by maintaining that *contradictions are not statements*. He held that contradictions (and tautologies) are logically quite separate from ordinary statements – they form a 'logical island'. Peter Geach (from whom I have borrowed that phrase) thinks that this insulation doctrine is incorrect and, moreover, that the attribution of it to Wittgenstein is incorrect too. Geach locates, as the likely source of the alleged misattribution 'a misreading of the doctrine of truth-functions, particularly as presented in Wittgenstein's *Tractatus*'. He writes, '... I must say that the grounds for ascribing the insulation doctrine to Wittgenstein seem exceedingly shaky', and adds: 'In any event, only by confusion could anybody suppose that the doctrine of truth-functional compounds requires such insulation: it requires the very opposite, and therefore could not also require the insulation doctrine unless it were internally inconsistent, which nobody is going to show' (Geach, 1979, p. 233).

There is, as I shall show, an overwhelming volume of evidence against Geach, and the importance of examining this evidence is (at least) fourfold:

(1) Most commentators agree with Geach that, in the *Tractatus*, Wittgenstein is presenting what has now become the classical truth-tabular semantics for the propositional calculus, thereby effecting what Russell, in his introduction to the book (*T*, p. xvi), calls an 'amazing simplification' of the classical theory of inference. Most commentators do not even bother to debate the matter; Robert Fogelin, who does, ends up, like Geach, rejecting the insulation view (Fogelin, 1987, pp. 45-7). Now, undoubtedly, the semantical theory of truth-functions does play a crucial role in the *Tractatus*. And it is quite clearly maintained in that work, that contradictions, like tautologies, are truth-functions of elementary propositions. But whether this theory buttresses the classical theory of inference is open to serious doubt when it is remembered that its author, while still in his post-Tractarian flush, espoused such non-classical principles as 'p & contradiction = p' (*DL*, p. 56). (Classically, the conjunction of any proposition with a contradiction is a contradiction.) Whether the *Tractatus* Wittgenstein would have accepted the non-classical principle as part of logical proof (as opposed to proof in logic – for this distinction, see below) or whether he would have simply banned tautologies and contradictions from this kind of proof is not clear. Either route is non-classical. Far from supporting the classical theory, Wittgenstein, in the *Tractatus*, repeatedly *attacks* its key tenets. He maintains that 'laws of inference' which are supposed to justify inferences have no sense and would be superfluous (*T* 5.132); that the procedure for introducing 'primitive statements' is illicit (*T* 5.452) – there is not a privileged set of logical statements that are essentially underived – for all the statements of logic are of equal status (*T* 5.43, 6.127, 6.1271); that *self-evidence*, to which Frege and Russell appealed, is a sham (*T* 5.4731, 6.1271). This rejection of logical classicism is one of the reasons why the *Tractatus* theory is relevant to the construction of those modern

formal logics designed to displace the classical system. What is needed is a correct interpretation of the theory of truth-functions which accommodates the insulation view and illuminates Wittgenstein's criticisms of central doctrines of Frege and Russell. Only then can one appreciate the connection of this theory with Wittgenstein's theory of the nature of a Satz, a theory the construction of which he once regarded as his 'whole task' (N, p. 39).

(2) It was not until many years after its publication that Wittgenstein's famous doctrine of what can be *shown* but not *said* got to be properly understood, and the credit belongs to Geach for first properly explaining the doctrine and drawing attention to its indispensability for Wittgenstein (Geach, 1976; also Dummett, 1981). Since tautologies and contradictions do not *say* anything (T 4.461, 5.142, 5.43, 6.11, 6.121) but something is *shown* by them (T 4.461, 6.12-1202), further light on the unsayability thesis is likely to be thrown by a clear understanding of the 'unique status' (T 6.112) which Wittgenstein accords them.

(3) As I have already suggested, Wittgenstein, in his later writings on mathematics, has some *prima facie* strange things to say about contradictions; for example, that they are 'harmless' (WVC, pp. 139, 194-201; LFM, pp. 184, 231; RFM App. III-11, 12), that a contradiction is 'no worse than a tautology' (WVC, p. 131; also LFM, p. 187; Z §689) and that some day 'people will pride themselves on having emancipated themselves from consistency too' (WVC, p. 139). These claims are not idling animadversions that someone seeking an understanding of the Wittgensteinian *corpus* can afford to neglect, but are essential parts of the jigsaw. We need to find out what problems Wittgenstein was grappling with and how these led him to solutions requiring the abandonment of the common sense view that contradictions are false propositions.

(4) Last, but not least, the thesis that contradictions are not false may actually be *correct*!

Since distinguished commentators such as Geach and Fogelin have got it wrong, it will be worth spending some time setting the record straight on this important topic. There are several related ways in which, in his early writings, Wittgenstein separates tautologies and contradictions from mainland Sätze.

• A Satz *says* that things stand in a certain way, it describes a state of affairs (T 4.022, 4.023, 4.5). Tautologies and contradictions say nothing – they do not represent reality (T 4.462, 4.463). Whereas the totality of true Sätze is the whole of natural science, when the logical

Satz acquires the characteristics of a Satz of natural science, this is a sure sign that it has been construed wrongly (*T* 4.11, 6.111). One learns nothing of any meteorological substance from being told 'Either it is raining or it is not'; one learns less than nothing from being told 'It is raining and it isn't'.

• Ramsey, writing about the *Tractatus* position, correctly remarks that, for Wittgenstein, a tautology is not a significant sentence (Ramsey, 1978, p. 53). Every significant Satz has sense (*T* 3.1431, 3.3, 3.34, 4.031, 4.064 etc.); metaphorically, 'Names are like points, Sätze like arrows – they have sense' (*T* 3.144).[33] To have a sense *is* to present a possible situation (*T* 4.031), so a statement *says* something in that it presents such a situation. The German word 'Sinn' is ambiguous between 'sense', 'significance' and 'direction'. Wittgenstein's point is that a fully-fledged sense-ful ('sinnvoll') statement is intentional; it is directed towards a possible situation (*T* 4.027, 4.03). By contrast, tautologies and contradictions lack sense, 'like a point from which two arrows go out in opposite directions to one another' (*T* 4.461). The conjunction of A and ~A 'says nothing in the proper sense of the word. For in advance there is no possibility left that it can correctly present' (*N*, p. 59).[34] In a contradiction, the mind would be both directed towards and away from the same situation – an impossibility. (There is a discussion of this conception of a contradiction as 'jamming' the mind in *LFM*, pp. 178-9.) Perhaps a dislike of syllogistic, or of Camestres in particular, blinded Geach to the conclusions of the following arguments:

(a) Every Satz has sense (*T* 4.064)
Tautologies and contradictions lack sense (*T* 4.461)
Therefore ...
(b) A Satz is a picture of reality (*T* 4.01)
Tautologies and contradictions are not pictures of reality (*T* 4.462)
Therefore ...

Others who have a problem with Camestres might prefer the following more direct indication of the conclusion: 'I actually think that the fear of contradictions is connected with taking a contradiction to be a Satz' (*WVC*, p. 131).
• A statement determines a unique place in logical space (*T* 3.4-3.42). By contrast: 'A tautology leaves open to reality the whole – the infinite whole – of logical space: a contradiction fills the whole of logical space leaving no point of it for reality. Thus neither of them can determine reality in any way' (*T* 4.463). Without even being able to understand

what 'determines a unique place in logical space' means, we can see that these remarks of Wittgenstein's entail 'Contradictions (and tautologies) are not statements'.

- Tautologies and contradictions are neither true nor false, at least not in the sense that contingent statements are. This claim is first developed in the *Notebooks 1914-16*, where Wittgenstein points out that to have sense *means* to be true or false (*N*, p. 112), hence tautologies and contradictions, which lack sense, cannot have either truth-value (*N*, p. 108).[35] This explains why, at *T* 6.125, Wittgenstein uses scare quotes to talk of the 'truth' of logical Sätze. The thesis is repeated at *A*, pp. 139-40: 'Because we see the similarity of ~*(p & ~p)* and *p v ~p* to true propositions, we make the mistake of saying that they are true.' And at *LFM*, p. 222 there is the complementary claim that 'the contradiction itself need not be called false at all'. In a letter to Wittgenstein, dated 13 August 1919, Russell writes: 'I am convinced you are right in your main contention, that logical prop[osition]s are tautologies, which are not true in the sense that substantial prop[osition]s are true' (McGuinness and von Wright, 1990).

- There are no inferences from tautologies and contradictions to contingent Sätze and vice versa.[36] This is a claim that Wittgenstein defends in the six propositions that form the 6.126s of the *Tractatus*. After first introducing the truth-tables and the notions of *truth-possibilities* and *truth-conditions* at *T* 4.3, 4.45, Wittgenstein devotes a large section (*T* 4.46-4.4661) to considering the 'extreme cases' (*T* 4.46) of tautology and contradiction. Here we are told that the truth-conditions of a Satz determine the range that it leaves open to the facts (*T* 4.463) but that a tautology has no truth-conditions (*T* 4.461) and cannot even be considered a combination ('Verbindung') of signs (*T* 4.466). Sätze just are such combinations of signs (*T* 4.031, 4.0311), so they are different in kind from tautologies and contradictions, and we should not be surprised to discover that, in Wittgenstein's view, logical relations fail to obtain between the two different *genera*. At *T* 5.101, Wittgenstein gives the name 'truth-grounds' of a Satz to those truth possibilities of its truth-arguments (which are elementary Sätze – see *T* 5.01) that make it true. Immediately afterwards, he states the conditions for valid inference: 'The truth of a Satz "p" follows from the truth of another Satz "q" if all the truth-grounds of the latter are truth-grounds of the former' (*T* 5.12). Now, one can reason that since, by *T* 5.101, a contradiction has *no* truth-grounds, nothing follows from it. So the classical 'spread' principle *ex falso quodlibet* 'A & ~A ⊢ B' would not, for Wittgenstein, be an allowable inference. It might be objected that, since a contradiction has no truth-grounds, it is (vacuously) *true* that all its truth-grounds are included in the truth-grounds of any Satz and hence that all Sätze *do* follow from a contradiction. But not only does Wittgenstein never assert this conclusion, he flatly *denies* it, both early (*N*, p. 59) and late (*LFM*, pp. 209, 243). This, of course, represents a major departure from classical logic.

There is, so far as I can see, just one short section in the *Tractatus* that appears to support Geach's no-island view. Having given a precise account of the notion of *following from* at *T* 5.12, Wittgenstein, for no apparent reason, gives an additional loose, metaphorical account: 'If one Satz follows from another, the latter says more than the former, and the former less than the latter' (*T* 5.14). It is from this that he concludes, at *T* 5.142, that a tautology follows from all Sätze on the grounds that it says nothing. This is clearly the wrong conclusion to draw, for similar reasoning would force Wittgenstein into accepting the unacceptable principle that a contradiction follows from all Sätze since it too says nothing (*T* 4.461). This mistake is easily avoided by noting that, since *T* 5.14 deals with Sätze, and tautologies and contradictions are not Sätze, one is committed to *neither* principle. The deduction of 'p v ~p' from 'p' by means of the Law of Addition (A ⊢ A v B) is blocked by rejecting an unrestricted rule of substitution, since the substitution p/A, p/B would yield a non-Satz and hence remove us from the domain of the deducibility relation. The 'Lewis Proof' of *ex falso quodlibet* would be blocked, in Wittgenstein's scheme, at the very first step, for we should disallow A & ~A ⊢ A (i.e., that a contradiction entails a constituent conjunct) for the very same reason.[37]

What gives succour to Geach is no more than an aberration, for at all other times, Wittgenstein is absolutely insistent on demarcating inferences involving tautologies (or those involving contradictions – see *T* 6.1202) from inferences involving contingent, i.e. *sinnvolle* (sense-ful) Sätze. He calls the former kind 'proof in logic' (*T* 6.1262, 6.1263) and contrasts this with the *logical proof* of a sense-ful Satz, where what is stated in the Satz is shown by its proof to be so (*T* 6.1264). *Proof in logic* is characterised as merely a mechanical expendient to facilitate the recognition of tautologies in complicated cases (*T* 6.1262) – we produce logical Sätze out of other logical Sätze by successively applying certain operations that always generate further tautologies out of the initial ones (*T* 6.126). Thus (*T* 6.1263):

Indeed, it would be altogether too remarkable if a Satz that had sense could be proved *logically* from others, and *so too* could a logical Satz. It is clear from the start that a logical proof of a Satz that has sense and a proof *in* logic must be two entirely different things.

The emphases are Wittgenstein's. There could hardly be a more explicit commitment to the doctrine of logical islands.

From the textual evidence marshalled above, and more that is available (Goldstein, 1986), we can safely attribute to Wittgenstein the claim that logical Sätze are not Sätze.[38] This claim, this insulation doctrine, is of central importance to him, as is evident from the frequency with which it recurs in his logical writings. As to the particular version of the doctrine that is set out in the *Tractatus*, what we want, but are not given, is a system of logical proof. What would be its formation rules and its rules of inference? In the case of the former, there would, I have suggested, be non-standard prohibitive rules ruling out tautologies and contradictions as well-formed formulae; in the case of the latter, there really are not enough hints to allow us to reconstruct what system (if any) Wittgenstein may have had in mind. It might seem that fidelity to his theory would require him to deprive himself of the proof procedure 'Constructive Dilemma' which involves taking a tautology of the form 'p or not-p', deriving a conclusion C from 'p' and then, independently, from not-p. But perhaps this rule can be stated in such a way as to make no mention of a tautology: If C can be derived on assumption p, and also derived independently on assumption not-p, then C may be inferred just from any additional assumptions made in those two derivations.

In his 'transitional' period, Wittgenstein toys with the rather boring idea that there are two senses of the word 'contradiction'; the first referring to a configuration of signs occurring in a 'calculus'; the second to some kind of conflict occurring in 'the true/false game'. Since, as we saw earlier, a calculus is only a game with signs, there is nothing to get excited about if a sign such as '0 ≠ 0' should crop up (*WVC*, p. 119). If we do not want such a sign to occur in a particular calculus, then we can stipulate various permissions and prohibitions to ensure that it doesn't (*WVC*, p. 175); equally, we might be happy to play a game in which this configuration occurs regularly. 'But', says Wittgenstein, 'the game is a game, and I cannot understand in any way why people want to attach so great a significance to the occurrence of this configuration; they behave as if just this configuration was "tabu" ' (*WVC*, p. 119).[39] It is not signs that, properly speaking, get into conflict. So a contradiction in a calculus is only a 'contradiction', and Wittgenstein suggests that we call it a 'Z' (*WVC*, p. 176) to distinguish it from a contradiction proper. It is *people* who contradict each other when they make statements, and this is contradiction in the primary sense, contradiction arising in 'the true/false game'.

When, in the transitional period, Wittgenstein says that he is 'prepared to predict that there will be mathematical investigations of calculi containing contradictions, and people will pride themselves on having emancipated themselves from consistency too' (*WVC*, p. 139), he is talking only about Zs; and his prediction has turned out to be accurate: the study of formal systems of paraconsistent logic, which began with Jaśkowski in 1948, has flourished (Priest, Routley and Norman, 1989) and continues to be a very active field of research. His attitude to contradictions which show up in the true/false game – in the *application* of a calculus – appears to be different. The rules of a game are, he says 'in a certain sense – statements' and two rules can contradict one another. He gives as an example a game similar to chess but containing both the rule that, under certain conditions, the knight may be taken, but also the rule that the knight may *never* be taken. 'What do we do in such a case? Very simple – we introduce a new rule and the conflict is resolved' (*WVC*, pp. 119-20). In a slightly later work, he again takes the line that a contradiction can occur in the 'higgledy-piggledy' zone of the rules, and there it can easily be removed, but offers the stronger view that a contradiction is inadmissible: 'Why may not the rules contradict one another? Because otherwise they wouldn't be rules' (*PG*, p. 305).[40]

In Wittgenstein's later writings, there is a much more radical, dialetheist, strain. That is to say, he comes to *accept*, and accept as *true*, some contradictions in the true/false game. This is not as astonishing a view as may appear at first sight. It stems from two sources; first, his anti-essentialism, second his methodological conviction that philosophy's real task is simply that of *describing* language games, leaving everything as it is (*PI* §§124, 654, 655). If we can resist our 'craving for generality' (*BB*, p. 17), we will recognize that there is no essence of negation, that the symbol 'not' is not always used in one way (*RFM*, pp. 102-10, *A*, pp. 115-16, *LFM*, pp. 80-2, *PI* §§547-557). He insists

> There is *one* mistake to avoid: one thinks that a contradiction *must* be senseless: that is to say, if e.g. we use the signs 'p', '~', '&' *consistently*, then 'p & ~p' cannot say anything. – But think: what does it mean to continue such and such a use consistently. ('A consistent continuation of this bit of curve.') (*RFM* VII-15)

This reference to the fact that a finite bit of curve can be extended in any number of different ways as illustrating that the future use of a word is not determined by past usage, is the Kripkensteinian analogy discussed in Chapter 2. Now, if we are merely describing language use, we can hardly deny that propositions such as 'I like it and don't like it' and 'Well, it is fine and it is not fine' are sometimes used (*A*, p. 71; *LFM*, p. 176); we can't say that such propositions are forbidden by the rule for the correct use of 'not'; that consistency with how we use the word 'not' in other contexts dictates that we can't use it thus in these. We might, deny, though, that these are examples of genuine *contradictions*. Yet Wittgenstein wants to insist that, for certain purposes, we *can* accept contradictions. When his interlocutor expostulates 'But you can't allow a contradiction to stand', Wittgenstein replies

> Why not? We do sometimes use this form in our talk, of course not often – but one could imagine a technique of language in which it was a regular instrument.
>   It might for example be said of an object in motion that it existed and did not exist in this place; change might be expressed by means of a contradiction. (*RFM* VII-11)

I take it that here he is alluding to Zeno's Paradox of the Arrow (the arrow is flying *between* the time when it was shot and when it strikes its mark, but *at* any (and at every) moment inbetween it does not move … yet all the time it is in continuous motion) and is offering the Hegelian suggestion that at any given point on its path, the arrow is both moving and not moving. Wittgenstein does not seem to be suggesting that this is a *solution* to the paradox, but merely to be recommending a way of using a contradiction to make a true statement about motion or change. Yet, so far as I can see, this is a recommendation that has little to recommend it.

As we saw, when discussing Moore's paradox in the previous chapter, there are certain special circumstances under which an assertion of the form 'p is not the case, yet I believe p' makes entirely good sense. Likewise, as Wittgenstein says (*RFM* VII-11, quoted above), we sometimes use contradictions – but 'of course, not often'. Why 'of course'? Well, if someone utters a contradiction and is *not* trying to show his indecision, or to opt for a middle way, or to be funny, or one of the several other things one can do with a contradiction, then one just doesn't know how to take his words, and, if he is being serious, you have to seriously doubt whether he understands what he's saying. He says 'I'll go with you to the movie tonight, and I won't go with you to the movie tonight' – but that doesn't make sense: you certainly can't make your evening arrangements on the basis of what he said.

4. Mathematics

It might be objected here that all of the speaker's words are quite standard and have definite meanings, so that what he says when he assembles these words in his utterance is, however infelicitous, still meaningful and *false*. Now, behind this objection lies a certain *compositional* view of meaning: the meaning of 'and' is such that the result of joining two sentences by this connective is a sentence that is false unless both the original sentences are true; negating a sentence results in a sentence with truth-value opposite to that of the original unnegated sentence. Therefore the result of conjoining a sentence with its own negation is a sentence that must be false. This compositional account, then, purports to offer an *explanation* of why a contradiction is false. But is it true, as the compositional account supposes, that expressions have fixed, context-independent meanings? Wittgenstein may have believed so in the *Tractatus*,[41] but, as we have seen (Chapter 2), in later writings he expressly repudiated such a view. If there is no preservation of the 'literal meanings' of expressions in, for example, metaphor, euphemism and hyperbole, how likely is it that these alleged meanings are preserved in such nonstandard utterances as candid assertions of contradictions?

Mastery of language involves the grasping of rules (permissions and prohibitions). 'Following according to the rule is FUNDAMENTAL to our language-game' (*RFM* VI-29). Our grasp of the rules for 'and' and 'not' is manifested *inter alia* by our excluding contradictory assertions, except where these words are used in nonstandard senses, or where we can supply 'completing surroundings' for what would otherwise be a defective performance. Hence to candidly affirm 'p and not p' is to use words *incorrectly* and this is quite different from using them correctly to make a necessarily false assertion. Should somebody sincerely utter a straight contradiction, it would be wrong to say that his assertion is true or false. Since the utterer does not possess a command of the language, we cannot ascribe sense to what he says, his utterance is not available for truth-evaluation. Similarly, if we have attempted to teach someone the word 'pain' (by pricking him with a pin etc.) and he now says 'Oh, I know what "pain" means: what I don't know is whether *this*, that I have now, is pain' then, as Wittgenstein puts it, 'we should merely shake our heads and be forced to regard his words as a queer reaction which we have no idea what to do with.'[42] Someone who asserts a contradiction, or who denies, for example, that he has a body, is not regarded as making a mistake, for 'in order to make a mistake a man must already judge in conformity with mankind' (*OC* §156; also *OC* §§128-9 and *PI* §§241-2). The person who does not conform in this way fails to satisfy the prerequisites for making a judgement, and 'we should

157

regard him as demented' (*OC* §155, see *RPP I* §957, *Z* §371), as a 'half-wit' (*OC* §257; also *OC* §§350, 467), or, as Aristotle would have it, 'a vegetable' (*Metaphysics*, 1006a16, 1008b11).

In his late, late period, Wittgenstein thinks that we can give no *explanation* of the unacceptability of contradictions. It is obviously no explanation to say that we exclude mutually contradictory conclusions *because* they are contradictory (*RPP I* §1132). And there would be an obvious circularity in a *reductio ad absurdum* proof of the unacceptability of contradiction because that proof-procedure, as its name suggests, *presupposes* that a contradiction (to which we 'reduce' an assumption) is absurd. So it may seem that Wittgenstein is right in holding that the justification for excluding contradictions cannot go beyond saying that we just have no use for them (*RPP I* §§44, 1132; *RPP II* §290), for '[a] contradiction prevents me from getting to act in the language-game' (*Z* §685). But I want to argue that, while it is perfectly true that justification must come to an end somewhere, it does not come to an end where Wittgenstein says it does. We can, I think, say something more to explain why contradictions are unacceptable, and the explanation consists in saying what *purpose* the word 'not' serves. (The meaning of the word 'and' should also feature in the explanation, but I am going to concentrate on 'not'.)

Wittgenstein does not like the idea of any such explanation because he thinks it invokes a mysterious entity – the sense or the meaning of a word, 'an atmosphere accompanying the word, which is carried with it into every kind of application' (*PI* §117). True, we are inventive in our uses of words. But the very fact that we can recognize cases where a word is being used abnormally (as Wittgenstein acknowledges we can – see *PI* §§141, 142) indicates that there is a *normal* use for that word. If we can say what the normal use for 'not' is, then we shall be able to see why, unless special conditions prevail, we cannot assert a contradiction. This normal use need not be any entity, not any 'atmosphere' nor any set of rules in the mind of a normal speaker. A fruitful way of establishing the normal use of 'not' is to ask why we have that word in ordinary language – what is the word *for*, what is its function? When the word is serving that function, then it is being used normally.

Aristotle, in a parenthetical remark at *Categories* 12b5-12b15, argues that there are oppositions in nature that precede, in the order of being, our statements which reflect them:

Nor is what underlies an affirmation or negation itself an affirmation or negation. For an affirmation is an affirmative statement and a negation a negative statement, whereas none of the things underlying an affirmation or negation is a statement. These are, however, said to be opposed to one another as affirmation and negation are, for in these cases too, the manner of opposition is the same. For in the way an affirmation is opposed to a negation, for example 'he is sitting' – 'he is not sitting', so are opposed the actual things underlying each, his sitting – his not sitting.

(There is further elaboration in the *Metaphysics* (1004a31-b10, 1018a20-38, 1051a5-13, 1061a7-14)). Aristotle is here contrasting the world of things (*ta onta*) with the world of words (*ta legomena*). But there is a level intermediate between these two. The *recognition* of an opposition in nature is pre-linguistic. Camouflage is important in nature just because predators can recognise the boundary between different colour patches. To recognise such a boundary, say between brown and red, is to notice (without necessarily being able to say) that brown is *not* red. Accepting one of two options perceived to be opposed involves recognizing that the other must be rejected. Accepting and rejecting are also ontologically more fundamental than statement-making. Statements are used as a means of expressing, indicating or conveying our acceptances or rejections. As Huw Price explains, there is a primitive awareness of incompatibility; it is this that gives us the occasion for rejection and hence, with the development of language, for the use of the word 'not'. He writes:

To signal significantly, one needs to be capable of discrimination. One needs to signal in some circumstances and to remain silent in others. One needs a sense that these are mutually exclusive possibilities ... [A]t ... times nature offers us an opportunity, and our choice is simply to accept or to decline. To have a sense that there is a decision to be made in such a case seems already to have a sense of the incompatibility of the options. Once language comes to be associated with the activity of agents, there is thus a need for negation in formulating, offering and expressing choices. (Price, 1990, pp. 227, 226)

As Price shows, agents need to make choices, often choices between mutually excluding options. We recognize the incompatibility between such options, and use the word 'not' as a linguistic marker of this recognition. Wittgenstein himself remarks 'Negation ... is a gesture of exclusion, of rejection' and he points out that 'such a gesture is used in a great variety of cases' (*PI* §550).

My acceptance that Socrates is sitting excludes my rejection of the

159

same proposition, so I cannot assert both that he is sitting and that he isn't. We cannot assert a contradiction because acceptance excludes declension. If someone asks me whether it is raining, and I reply 'It is and it isn't', then my hearer would be an idiot if she failed to grasp, for example, that I was trying to convey that we were not in the middle of a prolonged downpour. But, of course, my assertion on this occasion is not properly described as a case of simultaneously making a claim and withdrawing it. On the other hand, what would we say of a person who says 'Yes' to our question 'Is your name Zeno?' while vigorously shaking his head? That he is communicating something true, or that he is communicating something false? Our answer can only be that he is giving incompatible indications, so we cannot make any truth-evaluation of his performance. This is by no means the same as claiming that what he is communicating is untrue (any more than failing to make a telephone connection is the same as getting the wrong number).

On the question of paradoxes (from where this discussion of contradiction started) Wittgenstein vacillates. There is a particularly interesting section of MS 124 (1944) in which (on March 7 or 8), he says that paradoxical utterances (such as 'heterological is heterological') are not significant statements (*RFM* VII-28), yet, just four or five days later, he says that they are proper statements, and notes the difference between this and his *Tractatus* view (*RFM* VII-36). We can certainly use Wittgenstein's views on contradiction as a starting point for a solution to the paradoxes. Consider the Liar. Although we can *utter the words* 'S is not true', we cannot use those words self-referentially to assert S. 'S' cannot be the name of the statement 'S is not true', for otherwise, in asserting S, we should, at the same time be rejecting it (in saying that it is not true). So, one might argue, in the Liar paradox, one does not *derive* a contradiction; contradiction is present right from the start. A contradiction fails to be a true statement, so Wittgenstein urges, so the solution to the Liar is that the original utterance has no truth-value. Of course, much more needs to be said in elaboration of this solution (Gaifman, 1992, Goldstein, 1992c, Simmons, 1993) and the discussion has progressed way beyond the point at which Wittgenstein left it.

5

Wittgenstein the Man

Mandy Rice-Davies on interpretation

There are many excellent biographies of Wittgenstein, long and short.[1]
This chapter, while not itself a biography, is an attempt to (begin to)
answer the question of the extent to which knowledge of certain facts
about Wittgenstein's life and persona can aid in an interpretation of his
writings. That may seem to be a curious, even misguided enterprise.
Read an article in (say) a journal of physics and one's understanding of
it is quite independent of any knowledge one may have of its author.
The authors of most academic articles are known only by name to most
readers, yet the reader's understanding of the text is not impaired by
ignorance of the author's personality. Indeed, it would be ludicrous to
suggest that, in general, in order to gain a proper appreciation of the
content of an academic text, one needs to delve into the life of the person
who wrote it. In Wittgenstein's case, however, things are different, or so
I shall argue. In a way difficult to characterize, Wittgenstein's writings
are informed by his personality, and without an understanding of him,
it is impossible to gain a proper grasp of them. This makes interpretation difficult. The ideal solution would be to become so thoroughly
attuned to his personality that, when confronted with any of his remarks, one can readily see why, in the words of Mandy Rice-Davies (or
near enough), 'Being him, he would say that, wouldn't he?'[2] So our
problem becomes one of achieving a clear sense of what being Wittgenstein was like. Not the easiest of tasks. Momentous events occurring
during Wittgenstein's formative years had a profound influence on the
development of his character, and I shall concentrate on that period.
Wittgenstein was, I think it's fair to say, a late developer (some have
said, less charitably, that he 'never grew up'), and we shall need to
accompany him right up to the 1930s.

Anyone reasonably well versed in the secondary literature on
Wittgenstein is acutely aware that interpretations of his views are
extremely various and divergent. His writing is hermetic, sometimes
apparently wilfully so. One of Wittgenstein's most ardent admirers,

161

Georg Henrik von Wright, who succeeded Wittgenstein to the Chair of Philosophy at Cambridge, has a positive evaluation of this: 'I have sometimes thought that what makes a man's work classic is often just this multiplicity [of possible interpretations], which invites and at the same time resists our craving for a clear understanding' (Malcolm, 1958, p. 22). With great respect to von Wright, this is nonsense. Wittgenstein himself vilifies unclarity, perhaps most famously in the Preface to the *Tractatus*: 'what can be said at all can be said clearly, and what we cannot talk about we must pass over in silence' (*T*, p. 3; also in the book's finale, Proposition 7). In *CV*, p. 76, an entry written at the other end of his working life (in 1948), he writes: 'Are you a bad philosopher then, if what you write is hard to understand? If you were better you would make what is difficult easy to understand – But who says that's possible?! [Tolstoy].' A little later he said to Maurice Drury: 'Every sentence in the *Tractatus* should be seen as the heading of a chapter, needing further exposition. My present style is quite different; I am trying to avoid that error' (Rhees, 1984, p. 159). Ramsey said that some of the propositions of the *Tractatus* are 'intentionally ambiguous' but in the sense of 'having an ordinary and a more difficult meaning which he also believes' (Letter, dated 20.9.1923, in *LO*, p. 78). Speaking about Wittgenstein's later method, Drury says that there is 'nothing obscurantist, woolly or mystical' about it (Fann, 1978, p. 70). Kripke is right to point out that 'purely stylistic and literary considerations meant a great deal to Wittgenstein. His own stylistic preference obviously contributes to the difficulty of his work as well as to its beauty' (Kripke, 1982, p. 5). But to sometimes sacrifice perspicuity for beauty hardly amounts to obfuscation.

It seems not to have been Wittgenstein's intention, then, either to lay himself open to variant interpretations or to deliberately invite misunderstanding. He was trying, so far as the intrinsic difficulty of the thoughts allowed, to say what he had to say clearly. That disputes still rage about the reading of his writings is at least partly attributable to the fact that readers don't know who he was, and what he was trying to do. I can report that my own understanding of Wittgenstein's work has improved immeasurably as a result of developing an empathy for the man (insofar as this is possible for someone who, unlike Wittgenstein, is not homosexual, misogynistic, truculent or morbidly depressed), and I wish to encourage those who would consult the primary sources to try likewise to get under his skin. By so doing, one also discovers, as Monk puts it, 'what his work has to do with *him* – what the connections are between the spiritual and ethical preoccupations that dominate his life, and the seemingly remote philosophical questions that dominate his work'.[3]

5. Wittgenstein the Man

Working on oneself

In 1931, Wittgenstein wrote:

> Work on philosophy is – as work in architecture frequently is – actually more of a //a kind of// work on oneself. On one's own conception. On the way one sees things. (And what one demands of them.) (*TS* 213 §86 and *CV*, p. 16)

He is not, of course, making the general point that doing any kind of intellectual work is good for the soul. There is, he is saying, something specific about doing architecture and philosophy that fosters self-improvement. In architecture this is simply a matter of improving one's aesthetic judgment, one's 'feel' for the construction of three-dimensional spaces, awareness of the importance of detail and a sense of the difference between what doesn't quite satisfy and what is just perfect.[4] In philosophy, it is a matter of learning to live better, more decently, of recognizing and fulfilling one's duties to oneself and to others. That such was Wittgenstein's view is illustrated by the angry retort, quoted below, that he made to Norman Malcolm:

> What is the use of studying philosophy if all that it does for you is enable you to talk with some plausibility about some abstruse questions of logic etc., and if it does not improve your thinking about the important questions of everyday life, if it does not make you more conscientious than any ... journalist in the use of the dangerous phrases such people use for their own ends. (Malcolm, 1958, p. 39)

The offending phrase that Malcolm had used was 'the British national character'.

It hardly needs emphasizing how dangerous can be the bandying about of cheap labels and slogans, yet Wittgenstein himself, earlier in life, had been guilty on just this count. Under the influence of Otto Weininger's mad book *Sex and Character*, he was quite prepared to talk of 'the Jewish character', describing this as unpoetic, valuing the power of money and inclined towards secretiveness. And he says, with touching modesty: 'Even the greatest of Jewish thinkers is no more than talented. (Myself for instance.)' (*CV*, pp. 6, 21, 22, 18). His criticism of Malcolm applies in spades to his own former arrogant, racist self, as he is well aware. 'You see', he adds to Malcolm, 'I know that it's difficult to think well about "certainty", "perception", etc. But it is still more difficult to think or try to think, really honestly about your life and other people's lives. And thinking about these things is not thrilling, but often downright nasty. And when it's nasty then it's most important.' By doing philosophy, 'working on himself', Wittgenstein sought to exorcize his demons. There were, as we shall see, demons a-plenty.

Wittgenstein and Hitler

A domineering father, a mother who took no interest in her children,[5] seven older brothers and sisters all more talented than he, ignorant of his Jewish ancestry and baptized a Catholic – Wittgenstein was off to a bad start in life. Three of his brothers committed suicide, and he himself soon acquired suicidal tendencies.[6] As a young child, he seems to have had a reasonably cheerful disposition. His father, Karl, was one of the wealthiest industrialists in Austria, and Wittgenstein was raised in the lap of luxury, in a household which was one of the great centres of Viennese cultural life. Until the age of fourteen he was educated at home, but, not having achieved much, was sent away in 1903 to a Realschule in Linz, a school for dayboys. He lodged at the house of one of the teachers at the local Gymnasium, Dr. Strigl, and seems to have developed a sexual attraction towards Pepi, the son of the family. At Linz, things started to go sour.

For one thing, at the K.u.k. Realschule in Linz, Wittgenstein met Adolf Hitler and may have inspired in him a hatred of Jews which led, ultimately, to the Holocaust. This, naturally enough, weighed heavily on Wittgenstein's conscience in later years. While it is well known that Hitler and Wittgenstein were similar in age, Hitler being the older by just six days, and that they overlapped for one year at the Realschule (though Hitler was in the 3rd class, Wittgenstein in the 5th), biographers have said almost nothing about their influence on each other. Monk flatly states: 'There is no evidence that they had anything to do with one another' (Monk, 1990, p. 15), a view shared by Hans Sluga (Sluga and Stern, 1996, p. 4). Even if this were true, it is a well known fallacy (*argumentum ad ignorantiam*) to infer from there being no evidence that p to the conclusion that p is not the case. In the absence of direct evidence, a reputable historian needs to try to establish, by whatever indirect means are available, whether some historical claim or its opposite is more likely to be true. It is overwhelmingly probable that Hitler and Wittgenstein did meet, and with dire consequences for the history of the world. The evidence (admittedly circumstantial) for believing so has been assembled by Kimberley Cornish, a journalist trained in philosophy, in an important recent book called *The Jew of Linz* (Cornish, 1997). The following account follows Cornish closely and adds a bit more evidence. If the story is correct, then much of Wittgenstein's very strange subsequent behaviour becomes intelligible.

In *Mein Kampf*, Hitler recounts that his home background was not antisemitic:

> Today it is difficult, if not impossible, for me to say when the word 'Jew' first gave me ground for special thoughts. At home I do not remember having heard the word during my father's lifetime. I believe that the old gentleman would have regarded any special emphasis on this term as cultural backwardness. In the course of his life he had arrived at more or less cosmopolitan views which, despite his pronounced national sentiments, not only remained intact, but also affected me to some extent. (Hitler, 1969, p. 47)

Yet we learn from a school colleague of Hitler's, Herr Keplinger, that, at school

> Adolf shouted at another boy, 'Du Saujud!' ('You filthy Jew!') The boy concerned was staggered; he knew nothing of his Jewish ancestry at the time and only discovered it years later ... (Jetzinger, 1956, p. 71)

There is, in the whole of *Mein Kampf*, just one reference to an individual Jew whom Hitler knew:

> At the Realschule, to be sure, I did meet one Jewish boy who was treated by all of us with caution, but only because various experiences had led us to doubt his discretion, and we did not particularly trust him .... (Hitler, 1969, p. 48)

There were only a few, perhaps fifteen, Jewish boys at the Realschule in Linz at that time, but only one who, so far as we are able to tell, was persecuted. If there is one type of person hated by schoolboys, it is the 'snitch', someone who can't keep a secret, someone who tells. Now, we know that in the 1930s, Wittgenstein went around making formal, soul-baring 'confessions' to people who were variously embarrassed or irritated to hear them,[7] but it seems that he was already doing this sort of thing as a 15-year-old! From his own notes:

Realschule class first impression. 'Muck.' Relation to the Jews. Relation to Pepi. Love and pride. Knocking hat off. Break with P.

Suffering in class.

Halfway reconciliation and further break with P. Seeming inno-
cence I learn the facts of life. Religiosity, G's influence on me, talk
about confession with my colleagues. Reconciliation with P. and
tenderness.

Inventions

Halfway confessions to Mining but ones in which I manage to
appear to be an excellent human being.[8]

Such confessions would have seemed to be in flagrant disregard of the
schoolboys' 'code of honour', and to say that his colleagues would have
'doubted the discretion' of someone who went in for this sort of disclo-
sure, that they 'did not particularly trust' him, would be to put it mildly.

But, apart from this, there were so many other ways in which
Wittgenstein was markedly different from regular boys at the school
that, things being as they were (and are), it is no wonder at all that he
should have been the prime target for their abuse and execration. For
a start, they were mostly local lads, working-class boys from a small
town, whereas he was patently upper crust, from one of the most
prominent and highly cultured families in the capital, a huge, unbridge-
able social distance away from them. Private tuition at home, instead
of a normal public education, had reduced his opportunities for the
development of interpersonal skills. Further, he joined the school not at
the usual age of entry, but as a late outsider, after others had already
had four years to forge friendships.

... he did not find it easy to find friends among his predominantly
working-class fellow pupils. On first setting eyes on them he was
shocked by their uncouth behavior. 'Mist!' ('Muck!') was his initial
impression. To them he seemed (as one of them later told his sister
Hermine) like a being from another world. He insisted on using
the polite form 'Sie' to address them, which served only to alienate
him further. They ridiculed him by chanting an alliterative jingle
that made play of his unhappiness and of the distance between
him and the rest of the school: 'Wittgenstein wandlelt wehmutig
widriger Winde wegen Wienwarts' ('Wittgenstein wends his woeful

166

windy way Viennawards'). In his efforts to make friends, he felt, he later said, 'betrayed and sold' by his schoolmates. (Monk, 1990, pp. 15-16)

Now, Hitler also considered himself a cut above the rest. He too refrained from using the familiar 'du' form of address to his school colleagues (except, it seems, when he was calling them filthy Jews!), and remained 'stiff, aloof, a stranger' (Fest, 1982, p. 19). His family were reasonably well off, and he liked to be seen at the opera in Linz, dressed immaculately and obviously expensively. How his nose would have been put out of joint by the arrival at school of a boy who not only attended the Vienna opera, but who had Brahms and other great musicians as frequent visitors to his family home (Hayek, 1953, p. 2), a boy whose immense wealth would have made Hitler seem, in comparison, a pauper.

In *Mein Kampf*, Hitler accuses Jews of trying to pass themselves off as 'Germanic', when, in reality, they possess 'nothing but the art of stammering its language' (Hitler, 1969, p. 283). Wittgenstein thought of himself as thoroughly German – he once wrote 'I am German through and through' (MS 101, entry for 21.10.1914; Monk, p. 114). Also, he stammered, at least until early adulthood, when the stammer had been replaced 'with the clear high voice not uncommon among those who have overcome an impediment' (McGuinness, 1988, p. 52). He

... was delicate and sensitive in temperament, and almost certainly in health also. By the age of 14 it is known that he had to be excused gymnastics at school and his history even before the hardships of the First World War is one of minor operations and surgical appliances (he had apparently a double rupture). At this time of his life he both needed and invited affection. (McGuinness, 1988, p. 32)

As research has now shown, the English schoolboy rhyme was correct (at least, as it applied to Hitler); Hitler was monorchid,[9] and was intermittently impotent. He was vicious and aggressive; his basic sex drive was sado-masochistic; he got his kicks with Geli Raubal, the only woman he ever loved, by having her urinate on his face (Hayman, 1997). We are not here looking at a person who would have reacted with sympathy to Wittgenstein's multiple afflictions and would generously have offered the kind of affection that this small, unathletic boy so craved. Rather, Hitler would have viewed with envy, hatred and mistrust that stammering, precious, precocious, aristocratic upstart who suddenly appeared in the school disdainfully flaunting his wealth and superiority. That filthy Jew.

The disgust that others felt for him was matched by the disgust he occasionally felt for himself. A bitter passage in the *Remarks on Frazer's 'Golden Bough'* gives eloquent expression to this self-disgust:

> I could imagine that I had had the choice of picking a creature of the earth as the dwelling place for my soul, and that my spirit had chosen this unattractive creature as its residence and vantage point. Perhaps because the anomaly of a beautiful residence would be repugnant to it. One's spirit would certainly have to be very sure of itself to do this. (*PO*, p. 135)

Wittgenstein, as we have already seen, was a Jew-hater. Eddy Zemach (personal correspondence) has the following hypothesis about the genesis of his antisemitism: Even as a child, Wittgenstein was tormented by a sense of intellectual inadequacy, filthy sinful desires, freakish body, etc. There was something warped, something rotten, something stinking at the core of his being. What? What? Then a dark secret was revealed: he was not what he seemed to be; his blood was poisoned – a disguised Jew in nobleman's clothes, a Meyer posing as a Wittgenstein, a viper. That explains it all! That is why he is so different! He'll renounce the Judas in him and try for salvation, but that, he knew, was impossible: he is doomed.[10]

Theodore Redpath reports that

> when talking with Wittgenstein [in 1938 about the imminent war] I said I thought the problem was hard for Britain in view of her military weakness, and that she might have to temporize in order to gain time to re-arm. On the other hand it was a terrible thing to sacrifice the Czechs and their fortress, and it is hard to estimate the rights and wrongs of Munich, about which Wittgenstein himself told me later that the issue was a 'personal one'. (Redpath, 1990, p. 72)

One of the things that Wittgenstein 'confessed' to in the 1930s was his Jewishness – or, at least, of being more Jewish than he thought he had led people to believe (Rhees, 1984, pp. 35-6). If he was, indeed, the Jewish boy referred to in *Mein Kampf*, and believed himself to be the individual who first stirred antisemitic sentiments in Hitler, would it have been rational for him to take personal responsibility for the dislocation and destruction of European Jewry which began some twenty years after the Linz episode? Cornish suggests, with some plausibility, that at certain points in *Mein Kampf* where Hitler seems to be raging against Jews in general, it is the individual young Ludwig Wittgenstein whom he has in mind.[11] Nevertheless – so it might be said – Wittgenstein could hardly blame himself for being the catalyst of Hitler's subsequent poisonous reaction against the Jewish race.

Such a response might trip lightly off the tongue of someone who is not himself a member of a racial minority, but, for those who know of visceral racism through being victims of it, that Wittgenstein might have felt a deep guilt would make perfect sense. For one is aware, as a member of a racial minority, that one's behaviour is under particular scrutiny. Aspects of one's character perceived as repellent, are likely to be attributed by unthinking people to one's whole minority group, making that whole group the object of a festering resentment or hatred. So, for the sake of other members of that minority, it is wise to take precautions, to watch how one acts, even to over-compensate. A black man walking on a pavement at night who sees signs of fear in a woman walking towards him, may cross the street simply to help destroy the image of black men as dangerous; a Jew may spend over-generously in an effort to dent the stereotype of Jews as mean. Such action may be supererogatory, but it is surely better to act in a way that will tend to allay, rather than to create or reinforce, a prejudice. After Hitler had embarked on his programme of persecution, one can easily imagine Wittgenstein being haunted by the thought of what a difference it might have made had he taken the trouble to behave less obtrusively and obnoxiously as a schoolboy in Linz. To have done so would have required a degree of self-awareness (including the awareness of his Jewishness) and the ability to see oneself through the eyes of another, that Wittgenstein, at that time, did not possess. Pride, arrogance, petulance and vanity (some of his early vices) thrive on one's being unable to see the reflection of oneself in others' perceptions. It takes effort to see yourself as others see you, and Wittgenstein spent a lot of the rest of his life trying to make that effort. By 1908 he had come to recognize and dislike certain aspects of his character, without yet being able to correct them (McGuinness, 1988, p. 71).

Love and despair

For the six years after leaving school, when he studied mechanical engineering at the *Technische Hochschule* at Charlottenburg, Berlin, and subsequently worked on aeronautical engineering at Manchester, Wittgenstein was constantly unhappy, or so he told von Wright

(McGuinness, 1988, p. 54). This is, of course, an exaggeration, as well as being gratuitously insulting to the several good people whose company he enjoyed during that period. Prominent among these was William Eccles, an engineer, an honest, straightforward man who remained a lifelong friend. If Wittgenstein was unhappy for much of the time, this was no doubt connected with his not having found for himself a vocation, some career in which he could excel. He was nervous, restless, over-reactive and prone to self-indulgent temper tantrums:

> He seemed an odd fish ... Bamber and Mason, then of the Engineering Department, both describe him as charming but as of nervous or excitable temperament. This indeed was his oddity to an English eye – the extreme formality and charming manners in everyday matters coupled with an intensity, a concentration, and an extreme dislike of being interrupted or thwarted in things that mattered to him. 'He was doing work' (Bamber says) 'on the combustion of gases and his nervous temperament made him the last person to tackle such research, for when things went wrong, which often occurred, he would throw his arms about, stamp around and swear volubly in German'. (McGuinness, 1988, p. 70)

As we saw in Chapter 1, it was mathematical logic that gave Wittgenstein the new intellectual direction he needed, a pursuit in which he could gain satisfaction, find salvation from loneliness and thoughts of suicide (von Wright, 1990, p. 6) and achieve greatness. And it was love that temporarily tempered his temper. At Cambridge in 1912, at one of Russell's 'squashes' (these were weekly evening social gatherings) he met David Pinsent and, within a month, had invited him on holiday in Iceland.[12] They travelled in great style (money was no object for Wittgenstein) and this was followed by their expedition to Øystese in Norway.

Pinsent had been awarded a scholarship in mathematics, went up to Trinity College, Cambridge in 1910 and gained a first class degree. Sir George Thomson, who became Master of Corpus Christi College, wrote that: 'David was the most brilliant man of my year, among the most brilliant I have ever met .... He was by way of being a pure mathematician with a leaning to philosophy.... He opened my eyes to some of the possibilities of philosophy, on which till then I had held the naivest ideas.' Pinsent, in turn, had an extremely high opinion of Wittgenstein's intellect. 'He is really remarkably clever', wrote Pinsent, 'I have never yet been able to find the smallest fault in his reasoning: and yet he has

5. Wittgenstein the Man

made me reconstruct entirely my ideas on several subjects' (von Wright, 1990, p. 11; diary entry for 18.9.12).[13]

While Pinsent liked and admired Wittgenstein, he was not sexually attracted to him; there is no reason at all to suppose that Pinsent was homosexual. Monk is surely correct in saying that 'it is doubtful whether Pinsent ever realized how much Wittgenstein was in love with him, and almost certain that he did not return that love' (Monk, 1990, p. 361). Pinsent, contemplating the pleasures of the proposed visit to Iceland, regarded it as the height of delight that 'all inland travelling has to be done on horseback, which would be supreme fun!' (von Wright, 1990, p. 5). The word 'fun' frequently occurs in the diary record of his times together with Wittgenstein – Pinsent enjoying his swimming, hiking, photography and music-making, the jolly boyish fun of a well-bred Englishman – blithely oblivious to the possibility that the dark moods of sulkiness and depression that he often observed in his travelling companion were the symptoms of a brooding yearning for physical contact with his slim, fragile body, and of the corrosive agonies of unrequited lust. That would never have crossed David Pinsent's mind. Homosexuality was taboo; among those whose 'perverted disposition' drove them to shame and suicide were Wittgenstein's own brother Rudolf, and the great English mathematician Alan Turing who attended some of Wittgenstein's lectures on the foundations of mathematics in 1939. His eroticism was a subject about which Wittgenstein would have been unable to speak with Pinsent.[14]

Ten days after arriving back from their Norwegian adventure, Wittgenstein returned to Norway, this time for a lengthy stay and without Pinsent. It was in Norway more than anywhere that Wittgenstein had the peace to work on improving himself. He described Skjolden as 'the only place I know where I can have real quiet' (Malcolm, 1958, p. 129). Many of the self-reflective remarks now assembled in *CV* were written during his stay there in 1936-37. Marguerite de Chambrier (formerly Respinger), a Swiss woman whom Wittgenstein met at Cambridge and once planned to marry,[15] said that he had great respect for Skjolden's simple way of life: 'He admired the Norwegians' simple human decency .... He demanded simplicity of everybody' (Johannessen et al., 1994, pp. 12-13). Wittgenstein found that in Cambridge there were too many distractions and interruptions. Pinsent records that Wittgenstein wanted to live alone in Norway, first because he thought that he could work better there, but secondly because he did not consider himself fit to live in a society:

... he feels that he has no right to live in an antipathetic world (and of course to him very few people are sympathetic) a world where he constantly finds himself feeling contempt for others, and irritating others by his nervous temperament – without some justification for that contempt etc., such as being a really great man and having done really great work. (von Wright, 1990, p. 80)

Another reason, based on Weiningerian principles, is suggested by Monk. According to Weininger, a person who fails to achieve greatness has achieved nothing; love is conducive to greatness, sexual desire inimical to it and 'sexual desire increases with physical proximity; love is strongest in the absence of the loved one; it needs a separation, a certain distance to preserve it' (Weininger, 1906, p. 239). The possibility of greatness, therefore, demands a separation from the loved one (Monk, 1990, p. 90).

Some of these principles are false and there is no telling whether Wittgenstein really was influenced by them.[16] His moral behaviour was not determined by principles. As Russell says, 'he would not practise any cold-blooded immorality. His outlook is very free; principles and such things seem to him nonsense, because his impulses are strong and never shameful'. Wittgenstein, he said, 'abominates ethics and morals generally'.[17] So it may not be sensible for us to foist upon Wittgenstein a train of reasoning resting on general moral principles. What does seem certain is that, encouraged both by what he had so far achieved and by Russell's adulation,[18] he felt that he was within grasping distance of producing a great work in logic. For the sake of his sanity, he needed to calm his desire for Pinsent. And he needed to pay serious attention to his moral development, particularly to the way in which he treated others. In a letter to Russell which seems to have been written at Christmas 1913, Wittgenstein says

> ... deep inside me there's a perpetual seething, like the bottom of a geyser, and I keep on hoping that things will come to an eruption once and for all, so that I can turn into a different person. I can't write you anything about logic today. Perhaps you regard this thinking about myself as a waste of time – but how can I be a logician before I'm a human being? *Far* the most important is to set myself straight. (*LRKM*, pp. 57-8. The letter was previously, and probably incorrectly, assigned the date June/July 1914)

The ambition to do good logical work in Norway was fulfilled. At Skjolden, Wittgenstein lodged with the family of the local postmaster, Hans Klingenberg, and was left to think, undistracted. The logical core of the *Tractatus* was in place by the time that G.E. Moore visited in March/April 1914. But what about his moral development?

After April, Wittgenstein, mentally exhausted, suspended his thinking on logic and began the construction of a wooden hut for himself on a mountain slope reached by rowing across Lake Eidsvandet which is situated about one mile above Sognefjorden.[19] Much of his subsequent time in Norway was spent living and working in this hut. Ivar Oxaal passes a harsh judgment on Wittgenstein for his building of the hut:

> ... if anything its situation and the immense difficulties which must have attended its construction ... might be interpreted as signs of the tendency towards exhibitionism with which he periodically heedlessly castigated himself, and as an architectural folly which only a heedlessly wealthy young man, as he then was, could possibly have entertained. (Johannessen et al., 1994, pp. 72-3)

Oxaal is referring not only to the difficulty of the site, but also to the fact that Wittgenstein insisted on the labourers using, for the initial rock-blasting, not the relatively safe dynamite (which would have put money into the pocket of its inventor Alfred Nobel against whom Wittgenstein had a gripe), but gunpowder.[20]

It is indeed very tempting, at times, to interpret much of Wittgenstein's behaviour as simply childish exhibitionism. But by living in seclusion in his hut, whom would he be trying to impress? Himself? The handful of people in the Skjolden settlement? That really would be going to extraordinary lengths. No, to work in that hut, especially through a Norwegian winter, as he did on a later visit, required fantastic dedication and mental toughness, and, as McGuinness notes, 'some courage too – Wittgenstein was of a nervous enough disposition to spit into the lake for luck when he took his little boat across on a stormy day' (McGuinness, 1988, p. 202). Wittgenstein did impress the people in Skjolden, but not as being a wealthy playboy, a mad eccentric or a show-off. What they really thought of him is conveyed in a wonderful letter, written in an archaic dialect, that the Klingenberg family sent to him after the First World War. The outbreak of war had prevented him returning to Skjolden, as planned, at the end of the summer of 1914. Even those who speak not a word of Norwegian cannot fail to be moved by the simple, exquisitely tender tone of this letter. It is reproduced here on pp. 174 and 175 with the original Norwegian on the left-hand page and the English translation on the right (Letter from Skjolden, dated Christmas 1919; Johannessen et al., 1994, pp. 120-2).

173

Hr. Witgenstein

Ja De kan tro vi har ventet at høre fraa Dem, for De skrev altid det før, at saasnart krigen var slutt vilde De komme hertil igjen. Det var derfor med sorg vi hørte av Halvard at De aldrig vilde komme her mer. Jeg har altid sagt og trot at De kom saa snart alt kom i god orden igjen og jeg vil endnu tro det, naar det en dag ved Guds hjelp oprinder rolige velsignede tider for deres Fædreland, da vil de tage dere en tur hertil aa hilse paa kjendte og *Venner.* Vi har talt saa ofte om Dere ja Det har ikke gaat en dag uten vi har husket Dem De som var saa ædel og god at De vilde ikke have fiskeret i EidsVandet for De vilde ikke dræbe noget levende undtagen Mygg. De som var saa Ædel: Deres karakter De har nu maatet se paa saa meget uendeligt meget ondt, aa - hvor vi har husket Dem og vi har ønsket havde De bare været her i denne lange tunge tid. men Ingen kunde tænke eller ane noget sligt. Men bare De for være frisk og De ikke har faaet noget varigt skade, saa vil nok alt blive godt igjen med tiden. Aa matte Gud faa Velsigne Dem og Deres fædreland og os alle, for det er hans vilje, at gjore oss lykkelige i tiden og salige i Evigheten.

Vi er alle som sedvanlig friske Vesle *Sverre Hess* er vor største glæde, han er saa morasom og kvikk han synger mange julesalmer alene, han var 2 aar 17de november, han var med og gik rundt juletræ og sang, saa han er som ein solstraale i vort hjem. Kari var 12 aar den 4 oktober og hun er nu høyere av vekst end jeg er men gran som et lys. Jeg sender et kort av Kari og Sverre der er Sverre 11 maneder og Kari er 11 år. Aa hvor gildt og hygeligt det havde været om vi havde havt et fotografi av Dere, det havde været den kjæreste erindring Vi kunde tænke os Da havde vi altid havt Dem levende for os vaer dag, vi har nok dere i levende erindring endnu allikevell; men da havde det aldrig blegnet.

Arne Bolstad er hjemme nu men har vaeret på Gartner Skole og i sommer var han på Østlandet saa han er nu en stor, stram, kjek ungdom. Vi har sendt deres bøker og alt deres tøy skal blive sendt. Eller skal vi vente svar fra Dem først? saa snart vi for utførselstilladelse. Her er igjen 16 par brkte strømper 3 par underklæder 3 badetørkla 3 handtørkla 3 par støvler 1 par *store* støvler 2 par gamle Putteser 1 badekåbe 1 uljefrakke 1 vinjakke med hetta 1 stav 2 gamle utapaabukser 1 trøye graa, 1 slirekniv 2 slips og en bordlampe mer tror jeg ikke det er. Men vi havde altid haabet at De havde komet igjen og hentet Deres tøy selv; men vi vil haabe at De engang nar alt er komet i orden efter denne ruinerende krig at de da vil finde veien hid til Norge. Velkomen skal De være. Hjertelig hilsen fraa Sofia, Hans, Kari og Sverre

Klingenberg

Mr. Wittgenstein,

You can be sure that we've been longing to hear from you. Earlier you always wrote that as soon as the war was over, you would come back here again. It was, therefore, with regret that we learned from Halvard that you will never come back anymore. I have always said and believed that you would come as soon as everything was all right. And I still want to believe that one day, with the help of God, when quieter and more prosperous times return to your native country, then you will make a journey up here to meet acquaintances and *friends*. We have spoken about you so often. Indeed, not a day has gone without us thinking of you. You, who were so noble and considerate that you didn't want your fishing rights in Lake Eidsvandet, because you didn't want to kill any living thing except mosquitos. You, who were so noble: Your character. And now you've had to experience so much evil. Oh, how we've remembered you and wished that you were here during this long and difficult time. No one could think or foresee anything like this. But as long as you are healthy and haven't been permanently wounded, everything will be well again in the course of time. Oh, may God bless you and your country and all of us, because it is His will to make us happy in time and blissful in eternity.

We are all well as usual. Little *Sverre Hess* is our greatest joy, he is so amusing and bright and can sing several Christmas carols all by himself. He was 2 years old on November 17th, and walked around the Christmas tree singing songs with us. So he is like a sunbeam in our home. Kari was 12 on October 4th, and she is now taller than me, but as slender and fair as an angel. I am sending you a photograph of Kari and Sverre in which Sverre is 11 months old and Kari 11 years old. Oh, how nice it would be if we had a photograph of you; that would be the dearest memory we could imagine. Then you would be present to us every day. As it is, we still have you vividly in our minds, but then our memory would never fade.

Arne Bolstad is at home now, but has attended a gardening school, and this summer he went to Eastern Norway. He is now a fully grown, handsome youth. We have forwarded your books and all your clothes are to be sent. As soon as we get the exportation permit. Or should we wait for your reply first? 16 pairs of used socks, 3 sets of underwear, 3 bath towels, 3 hand towels, 3 pairs of boots, 1 pair of *heavy* boots, 2 pairs of old puttees, 1 bath robe, 1 mackintosh, 1 windproof jacket with a hood, 1 stick, 2 old pull-on trousers, 1 grey vest, 1 sheath knife, 2 ties and a table lamp are left. I don't think there's anything else. But we had always hoped that you would return to fetch your clothes yourself. We hope that when everything has settled after this ruinous war, you will find your way back to Norway. You shall be very welcome. Cordial greetings from Sofia, Hans, Kari and Sverre

Klingenberg

It is difficult to read this letter without being moved to tears. Even though, with the people at Skjolden, Wittgenstein managed generally to enjoy open, warm friendship, the seething within him had not quieted and, in his dealings with others, he was still a time bomb waiting to explode. After receiving from Moore news that the 'Logik' he had written needed to clear some regulations before it could be counted as a dissertation towards a Cambridge B.A. degree, Wittgenstein sent the following charming note in reply:

> Your letter annoyed me. When I wrote Logik I didn't consult the Regulations, and therefore I think it would only be fair if you gave me my degree without consulting them so much either! As to a Preface and Notes: I think my examiners will easily see how much I have cribbed from Bosanquet – If I'm not worth your making an exception for me *even in some* STUPID *details* then I may as well go to Hell directly; and if I *am* worth it and you don't do it then – by God – you might go there. (*LRKM*, p. 150, letter of 7.5.14)

The gentle, genial Moore had not written the regulations governing the award of Cambridge degrees, nor was it within his power to waive them. Wittgenstein's letter made him sick to his stomach and he resolved not to reply and to avoid contact in the future. It was only a chance meeting on a train in 1929 that brought the two of them together again.

There was, then, much further self-examination left for Wittgenstein to do when he went off to the war, plenty of scope for self-improvement. Danger and the nearness of death would provide him with 'the chance to be a decent [anständig, upright] human being', so he thought (Diary entry, discussed in Rhees, 1984, p. 192). He served first on a ship called the *Goplana* on the Vistula river, and was loathed by the crew. Then, at his own (repeated) request, he was sent to the battlefront, where, attached to the Austrian Eleventh Army, he (both geographically and spiritually) found himself in the middle of colossal carnage in the fight against the Russians. By the beginning of 1918 he was, on his own reckoning, *'slightly* more decent' but only in a metadecent kind of way: 'I only mean that I am slightly clearer in my own mind about my lack of decency' (Engelmann, 1967, p. 11; letter dated 16.1.18). In the intervening years, and under the profound influence of Tolstoy's *Gospel in Brief*, he had undergone a religious conversion, something not uncommon among people suffering extremes of adversity.[21] The soldiers called him 'the one with the Bible' (Leitner, 1973, p. 19).

Since 'the heart of a true believer understands everything' he even

5. Wittgenstein the Man

made the effort to understand rather than to hate the 'malicious and heartless' men in his unit, who hated him. But he came to recognize that that faith had been a sham. In the letter to Engelmann just cited, he says: 'If you tell me now I have no faith, you are *perfectly right*, only I did not have it before either. It is plain, isn't it, that when a man wants, as it were, to invent a machine for becoming decent, such a man has no faith'. As Wittgenstein may have learned from Nietzsche, the eighth volume of whose *Collected Works* he had purchased in Kraków at the beginning of the war, the mark of a certain character lies not in the profession of a set of beliefs, but in living a certain way.[22]

Just before the war, Wittgenstein made a charitable donation of 100,000 crowns, distributed, with the help of Ludwig von Ficker, editor of the avant-garde literary journal *Der Brenner* (*The Burner*), among various Austrian artists including Georg Trakl, R.M. Rilke and Carl Dallago.[23] After the war, he realised that spiritual self-purification required not magnanimous benefaction, but living simply, as he had as a soldier, not cossetted by the soft trappings of luxury. Embracing a life of hardship and deprivation entailed getting rid of all his wealth, and this he proceeded to do, sharing the huge fortune he had inherited from his father amongst his sisters Hermine and Helene and brother Paul. From this point on, he lived frugally, eating sparely and staying in humble lodgings, earning a little money from various kinds of work, including gardening and making wooden crates. Even when he was elected to the Chair of Philosophy at the University of Cambridge (11.2.39), he declined the rather sumptuous accommodation to which this post entitled him, and continued to live in his small rooms at Trinity.

Hermine, writing about how his relatives (and the notary) did not understand why Wittgenstein was so anxious to ensure that no part of the fortune should belong to him in any form, explains the situation thus:

However, they also could not know that to this mentality of Ludwig's belonged a completely free and relaxed possibility of permitting his brothers and sisters to help him in any situation. Anyone who knows *The Brothers Karamazov* by Dostoevsky will remember the place where it is said that .... Alyusha, who knows nothing about money and has none, would not starve because everyone would gladly share with him and he would accept from them without hesitation. I, who knew all this for a fact, did

177

Clear and Queer Thinking

everything to fulfil Ludwig's wishes down to the smallest detail. (Leitner, 1973, p. 19)

This diagnosis, it seems to me, does Wittgenstein an injustice. Hermine is, in effect, saying that Wittgenstein could play at being poor, knowing full well that his relatives would always be there to bale him out if the going ever got rough. But Wittgenstein never fell back on his relatives, nor would he have dreamt of doing so. When, ten years later, the authorities at Trinity, aware of his family wealth, were reluctant to give him a research grant, Wittgenstein insisted (in capital letters) that although his relatives would gladly give him money 'I will not ask them for a penny' (*LRKM*, p. 154, letter to Moore dated 18.6.29). Even when sick, he returned invalid food parcels sent by his relatives.

Frank Ramsey, the young Cambridge mathematician and first translator of the *Tractatus*, was staggered to discover, after first visiting the family home in March 1924, the astonishing opulence of the Wittgensteins' style of life. Ludwig was not on bad terms with them, Ramsey noted, but refused, on principle, to accept their money (Letter from Ramsey to Keynes, dated 24.3.24; see Nedo and Ranchetti, 1983, p. 191). That attitude is easy to understand. To have accepted money from his relatives (especially from those among whom he had distributed his fortune) would have been as crass as asking for the return of a gift, and would have rendered his rejection of comfort and privilege an empty gesture. He was happy, however, to accept financial assistance from *friends* for specific purposes; not for luxuries (*LRKM*, pp. 128-9, letter to Keynes dated May 1929). When able to do so, he gave freely to others, and was digusted when others did not show similar generosity.[24]

As with goods and money, so with ideas. These too are to be shared. Hence it really was a matter of indifference to Wittgenstein, as he indicates in the Prefaces to both the *Tractatus* and the *Philosophical Investigations*, that he was not the 'owner' or originator of some of the thoughts he published; so he didn't trouble to mention the names of the authors who were. In the world of ideas, he seems to hold, one should be able to take without even having to ask, and to acknowledge would be the height of bad taste.[25] Curiously, though, he was sometimes embittered when he felt that his own ideas had been purloined (Rudolf Carnap and Gilbert Ryle are two he accuses). Perhaps he thought that an acknowledgment of refusal to acknowledge was acknowledgment enough; anything less, not. He also complained that his results, as circulated by others, were 'variously misunderstood, more or less mangled or watered down' (Preface to *PI*).

There is another reason why the names of other authors rarely appear in the works that Wittgenstein prepared for publication. This can be traced to a revealing argument he believed to be 'unanswerable' which he put to Russell in 1920, at the time when there was difficulty in finding a publisher for the *Tractatus*:

> Either my piece is a work of the highest rank, or it is not a work of the highest rank. In the latter (and more probable) case I myself am in favour of it not being printed. And in the former case it's a matter of indifference whether it's printed twenty or a hundred years sooner or later. After all, who asks whether [Kant's] Critique of Pure Reason, for example, was written in 17x or y.[26]

Wittgenstein was obsessed with the difference between those composers, writers, philosophers who are geniuses, and those who are merely talented (*CV, passim*). Kant's *Critique* or Beethoven's late quartets are everlasting – they won't go out of fashion or be forgotten. Clearly, if your ambition is to publish a work of the highest rank, which is timeless, you do not put in names of transient figures that will mean nothing to readers in a hundred years' time. Passages from Wittgenstein's published writings are frequently misinterpreted (and misinterpreted wildly) simply because commentators are unaware that Wittgenstein is not contriving a new doctrine, but is confronting the views of a particular (non-stellar) author. The true import of such passages can often be discerned by going back to the original MS sources, where the author is identified.[27]

The immediate post-war period was (again) a desperately unhappy time for Wittgenstein. David Pinsent, who, in a letter home, had bemoaned the fact that his war work, investigating the causes of aeroplane accidents, was insufficiently dangerous, was killed in the process of such an investigation on 8 May 1918. Mrs. Pinsent wrote a very moving letter to Wittgenstein, informing him of the tragedy. In his reply, Wittgenstein says that David had been his first and only friend, that the hours spent with David had been the best in his life, and that to David he owed 'far the most part of the happy moods that made it possible for me to work' (Monk, 1990, pp. 154-5). Two years later, he was still thinking of Pinsent every day. 'He took half my life away with him', he told Russell, 'The devil will take the other half' (*LRKM*, p. 91, letter to Russell dated 6.8.20). It was twelve years before Wittgenstein fell in love again. But although the physical attraction was, this time, mutual, the relationship with Francis Skinner was, in many ways, less healthy, for Skinner became merely a willing slave to Wittgenstein's whims, and Wittgenstein, by his own admission, behaved badly towards him.[28]

Soon after replying to the letter from Ellen Pinsent, Wittgenstein was discovered at a railway station, apparently ready to set off for a destination appropriate for suicide. He was talked out of that by his uncle Paul, who took him to Hallein, where he finished writing the *Tractatus*. But the text was not understood by those whom Wittgenstein hoped would understand it. After returning to the Italian front, where he had first been posted to a mountain artillery regiment in early 1918, Wittgenstein was taken prisoner, and ended up in a prisoner-of-war camp in Cassino in January 1919.

The village schoolmaster

By the time of his release, on 21 August 1919, Wittgenstein had decided, after considering becoming a priest, to train as a schoolteacher. After a year's training, he received his teaching certificate, spent the summer of 1920 working as a gardener at the Klosterneuberg Monastery on the outskirts of Vienna, and then headed for Lower Austria, to teach at rural village schools. The School Reform Movement had, at that time, captured the imagination of many Austrian intellectuals, but Wittgenstein did not share its ideals. He had, in Monk's words, 'a rather Tolstoyan conception of what it would be like to live and work among the rural poor .... The ideal that emerges from his teaching, whether in the Austrian countryside or at Cambridge University, is a Ruskinian one of honest toil combined with a refined intelligence, a deep cultural appreciation and a devout seriousness; a meagre income, but a rich inner life' (Monk, 1990, p. 192). He gets a very favourable 'school report' from sister Hermine:

> In many respects, Ludwig is a born teacher. He is interested in all things himself and he knows how to sum up the most important aspects of everything and make them clear. Several times I myself had the chance to watch Ludwig teaching, since he devoted a few afternoons to the boys' occupational school. It was a rare delight for all of us: he not only lectured, but tried to steer the boys toward the right solution by means of questions. Once he let them invent a steam engine, then draw a sketch construction of a tower on the blackboard, or another time depict moving human figures. The interest which he aroused

was tremendous. Even the untalented and usually inattentive boys gave surprisingly good answers, and they literally crawled over each other in their desire to be chosen for answers or demonstrations. (Leitner, 1973, pp. 19-20)

Hermine seems to have been lucky in catching Wittgenstein on his good days, when he was giving 'model' lessons. She must have missed the bad days when he was tearing the hair of out of children (both boys and girls) who were rather slow on the uptake, or bashing them hard on the ears. Hermine says that it was a lack of patience with lazy students and with unsympathetic parents, that brought an end to Wittgenstein's teaching career. But really, it was his violent temper. He moved from his first school in Trattenbach to a secondary school in Hassbach, where he lasted one month, then to a primary school in Puchberg and finally, in September 1924, to a village school in Otterthal, incurring the wrath of parents, and of many of his fellow teachers, wherever he went. It was an incident at Otterthal, where a weak, sickly child called Josef Haidbauer collapsed after Wittgenstein had struck him with two or three blows to the head, that caused the 'born teacher' to resign from schoolteaching. Although, at the trial, he was cleared of misconduct, his behaviour as a teacher was something about which Wittgenstein felt a deep sense of shame and guilt; this was another of those subjects included in the confessions he made in the 1930s.

Yet Hermine is evidently right that, in several ways, Wittgenstein was a good and conscientious teacher. He gave extra tuition, outside school hours, for some of the gifted or diligent students and apparently became something of a father figure to them. He went to considerable trouble to broaden students' career aspirations, encouraging the more able to look beyond the local farm or factory to which they seemed destined. But arrangements that he tried to make for children to enjoy further, subsidised education were typically rejected by parents. He expended a lot of effort in trying to ensure that students had a wealth of practical, hands-on experience inside and outside the classroom. He had them constructing animal skeletons, identifying botanical species on walks through the countryside, and he took them on trips to Vienna, to look at the architecture. This was learning through observation and experiment. Throughout his life, he had more confidence in scientific experimentation than in theory. He was, for example, enthusiastic about experimentation in psychology but became very critical when psychologists took off into theoretical or metaphysical flights of fancy.

181

Wittgenstein broke away from the rote learning method then prevalent in rural schools, preferring that children learn by working out their own solutions to problems. Much later in life, referring to those studying his philosophy, he writes: 'Anything your reader can do for himself leave to him' (*CV*, p. 77) This injunction can strike a reader as extremely conceited and patronizing. Or it can be read as a self-addressed reminder of the pedagogical ideals that had informed his schoolteaching and of the successful coaching of his 'lover', young Mr Kirk.

It was during this period of teaching in Lower Austria that Wittgenstein compiled the *Wörterbuch für Schüler*. The content of this dictionary was determined, as he notes in the preface, by the needs of the kind of student he was teaching. Thus certain German words not common in Austria are omitted, while a number of words in the Austrian dialect are included. Also included were explanations of elementary distinctions (e.g. between 'das' and 'dass') that children often got wrong. These are explanations of *meaning*. But what is the meaning of 'dass'? One can easily imagine, and perhaps it's true, that Wittgenstein was suddenly struck by the thought that, while the difference between 'ant' and 'spider' can be explained to a child by taking it on a walk through the woods and showing it samples, most words are not like that. This may have sown some seeds of doubt about his simplistic *Tractatus* theory. That there is a great multiplicity of kinds of words, learned in different kinds of ways is, of course, one of the themes of Wittgenstein's later philosophy.

Entirely absent from his early writings, but prominent in the later, are considerations concerning learning. In lectures given while he was making the transition to his mature philosophy, he uses the example of *teaching a child language* to illustrate that the semantic tools of the *Tractatus* (the notions of *proposition*, *language*, *logic* etc.) were unnaturally rigid (*A*, pp. 11-12). The *Philosophical Investigations*, as we saw in Chapter 2, begins with a discussion of what Wittgenstein takes to be an unrealistic account of how children learn their first language, and the later writings contain many more references to language development. One cannot tell the extent to which Wittgenstein's involvement, as a schoolteacher, with applied linguistics (language teaching, the compiling of a dictionary) helped determine the 'pragmatic' turn of his later philosophy, with its emphasis on actual language *in use* (language-games). My sense, like that of William Bartley III (1973), is: a great deal.

During his last summer vacation as a schoolteacher, Wittgenstein, encouraged by a letter from Eccles, visited England and renewed his acquaintances in Cambridge and Manchester. After the Otterthal deba-

5. Wittgenstein the Man

cle and a few more months working as a gardener in Hütteldorf (where he lived in the toolshed), he enjoyed two years of therapeutic architecture in Vienna, building a house for sister Gretl. His attention to minute detail combined with a rejection of anything ornate both in this project and in earlier work on furniture design that he had done with Eccles is echoed in the attention to details of linguistic usage in his late philosophy, and in his austere, economical style of writing. The house is an aesthetic experience to be reverently savoured, certainly not the sort of place in which to put one's feet up after a hard day's work.

Towards the end of this Vienna period, Wittgenstein got enticed by Moritz Schlick into attending meetings with a group of intellectuals who formed the core of what was to become known as the 'Vienna Circle'. Emerging from the obscurity of life as a village schoolmaster to find himself fêted by the greatest minds in Vienna who regarded the *Tractatus* as a masterwork did absolutely nothing for Wittgenstein's humility. Finding himself in the position of hero worshipped, he played it to the hilt. He agreed to meet with only an inner circle of the Circle, comprising Schlick, Friedrich Waismann, Herbert Feigl and Rudolph Carnap, and insisted that he be allowed free rein in the choice of topics to be discussed. Carnap gives us this portrait of a prima donna:

> Before the first meeting Schlick admonished us urgently not to start a discussion of the kind to which we were accustomed in the Circle, because Wittgenstein did not want such a thing under any circumstances. We should even be cautious in asking questions, because Wittgenstein was very sensitive and easily disturbed by a direct question. The best approach, Schlick said, would be to let Wittgenstein talk and then ask only very cautiously for the necessary elucidations. (Schilpp, 1963, p. 25)

Carnap ventures the opinion that Wittgenstein's behaviour was not caused by any arrogance. But Monk (1990, p. 243) tells us that sometimes Wittgenstein would turn his back on the audience and read them poetry out loud, in particular the 'mystical' poems of Rabindranath Tagore. When he deigned to face them and talk philosophy, it was a performance. Carnap says that the audience often felt the internal struggle and witnessed 'an intense and painful strain which was even visible on his most expressive face. When finally, sometimes after a prolonged arduous effort, his answer came forth, his statement stood before us like a newly created piece of art or a divine revelation' (Schilpp, 1963, p. 26).

With Wittgenstein, the philosopher-scientists of the Vienna Circle

183

hadn't quite got what they bargained for. They, as a group, were committed to the ideal of an exact philosophy which aspired to generate precise results by employment of the techniques of mathematics and logic – an enterprise continuous with science, and which is supposed to expose as nonsensical all discourse in metaphysics, ethics and religion. They regarded the *Tractatus* as the flagship text. However, when they met its author, they found him to be antipathetic towards science and sympathetic to the very kinds of discourse they condemned. Yet Carnap found his remarks 'always illuminating and stimulating', and he reports that Schlick in particular was strongly influenced by Wittgenstein, both philosophically and personally (Schilpp, 1963, p. 27).

In a 1930 notebook, Wittgenstein writes: 'Man has to waken to wonder – and so perhaps do peoples. Science is a way of sending him to sleep again' (*CV*, p. 5). He later says: 'I may find scientific questions interesting, but they never really grip me. Only *conceptual* and *aesthetic* questions do that. At bottom I am indifferent to the solution of scientific problems; but not the other sort' (*CV*, p. 80). But sometimes he expresses his distaste more strongly – he calls 'our disgusting soapy water science' an 'evil', and talks of the 'infinite misery' caused by science and industry (*CV*, pp. 49, 56, 63). The late Wilfrid Sellars once said (to Julian Young): 'Fundamentally, Wittgenstein objected to scientists telling us how to live.' He was antagonistic towards the '*wissenschaftliche Weltauffassung*' (scientific world view) which he linked with the decline of western civilization and which permeated philosophy of the 1930s.[29] This is not to say that there is anything wrong with the methods of science; it is just that it is dangerous, in Wittgenstein's view, to make a fetish of scientific progress, and dangerous to convey to schoolchildren the idea that scientific learning is the only kind of learning of any value. As we saw in Chapter 1, in his later writings, Wittgenstein wanted philosophy 'to get something done, to get something settled' (Rhees, 1984, p. 110). He wanted to achieve conceptual clarity, but by a technique quite different from the methods used in science, methods which he regarded as *inappropriate* for philosophy (*BB*, p. 18). Picking at the knots in a ball of wool (which is one of the similes Wittgenstein used for explaining his *modus operandi*) can have a beneficial effect (if you want the wool untangled) but the activity calls for no conjectures or hypotheses, nor does it result in the formulation of any laws. Hence Wittgenstein's constant insistence, in the late works, that he is not offering *theories*.

Members of the Vienna Circle would have found Wittgenstein's views on science and scientists quite alien to their own outlook. And their crude way with ethics would have left no space for the subtle position that Wittgenstein wanted to occupy. For although Wittgenstein agreed with them that *talk* of ethics is nonsense, *doing* it, and doing it well, is all-important; improving one's moral being is an inside job. As for religion, the Vienna Circle dismissed it as waffle, whereas Wittgenstein confessed: 'I am not a religious man but I cannot help seeing every problem from a religious point of view.'[30]

By 1929, Wittgenstein had completed a major, innovatory architectural project in the heart of Vienna. He had composed an instant philosophical classic. Great thinkers (the chosen ones) gathered to gaze in awe at his back as he read whatever poetry struck his fancy and waited with bated breath for words of philosophical wisdom to fall from his lips. He was a legend in his own lifetime (or perhaps just a legend in his own mind). Working in monastery gardens and in poor village schools obviously had not done the trick; he was still, to use one of his own favourite words, intolerable. Yet, with the rise of Nazism in Europe, his outlook began to change. No ugly antisemitic remarks, of the sort with which his early notebooks are peppered, appear after 1931. To what extent this change was brought about by a perception of his own contribution to Hitler's malignant programme, one can only speculate. It is interesting to note, however, that his rejection of racial generalization coincided with his abandonment of grand, general, philosophical theory.

Discussion with the Vienna Circle, with old Cambridge friends, and the inspiration of a lecture given by the Dutch mathematician L.E.J. Brouwer, propelled Wittgenstein back to philosophy and back to Cambridge in 1929. He there worked his way out of his old views and out of the style of thinking that had produced them. In the Foreword to his transitional work, *Philosophical Remarks*, he writes:

> This book is written for such men as are in sympathy with its spirit. This spirit is different from the one which informs the vast stream of European and American civilization in which all of us stand. *That* spirit expresses itself in an onward movement, in building ever larger and more complicated structures; the other in striving after clarity and perspicuity in no matter what structure.

Peter Hacker, borrowing from Isaiah Berlin, borrowing from the Greek poet Archilochus, characterises this spiritual development as the transformation from hedgehog to fox (Hacker, 1996a, p. 98). The fox knows many things, but the hedgehog knows one big thing. Wittgenstein was temperamentally, a hedgehog. The *Tractatus*, like Plato's theory of Forms, presents a magnificent unifying vision, a single key to unlock

185

the mysteries of the mind, value and the fundamental structure of the world. In his later philosophy, Wittgenstein actively resists generalisation and theory construction. He values the minutiae, investigates the details. This is the way of the fox. It is a more humble approach, the work of a more humble man. He considered taking as a motto these lines from Longfellow:

> In the elder days of art,
> Builders wrought with greatest care
> Each minute and unseen part,
> For the gods are everywhere. (*CV*, p. 34)

Wittgenstein's ethics

A somewhat confused picture seems to have emerged concerning Wittgenstein's views on ethics. On the one hand, we have it, on Russell's authority, that Wittgenstein abominated ethics and thought it all nonsense; he also told Moritz Schlick 'I think it definitely important to put an end to all the claptrap about ethics' (*WVC*, p. 69). On the other hand, we find Wittgenstein insisting on the importance of ethics, and going so far as to say that the point of the *Tractatus* is ethical. And saying the same thing, on another occasion, to Schlick![31] Traditionally, ethics is thought of as a subject to be pursued by rational argumentation, with the end of achieving a defensible account of what is good, and of what, as good people, we ought to do. One way (the best way, I think) of resolving the apparently conflicting views about ethics that Wittgenstein expresses, is to see him as seeking to undermine this tradition.

In the *Tractatus*, Wittgenstein says that ethics cannot be put into words; that there are no ethical propositions (*T* 6.421, 6.42). Descriptions of matters of fact are the only genuine propositions recognized by the *Tractatus*. Ethical propositions are not reducible to these, for we can have a complete physical description of an action but that won't tell us whether that action has value, whether it is worthwhile. 'The world is independent of my will' (*T* 6.373); we cannot make anything happen just by willing it to do so, even with the best will in the world (see *T* 6.374, 6.43). 'Ethics is transcendental' (*T* 6.421). 'There are, indeed, things that cannot be put into words. They *make themselves manifest*. They are what is mystical' (*T* 6.522). That's just about the whole *Tractatus* account of ethics – a mere handful of propositions. Yet Wittgenstein, in a letter to von Ficker, characterizes the work thus:

The book's point is an ethical one. I once meant to include in the preface a sentence which is not in fact there now but which I will write out for you here, because it will perhaps be a key to the work for you. What I meant to write, then, was this: My work consists of two parts: the one presented here plus all that I have *not* written. And it is precisely this second part that is the important one. My book draws limits to the sphere of the ethical from the inside as it were, and I am convinced that this is the ONLY *rigorous* way of drawing those limits. In short, I believe that where *many* others today are just *gassing*, I have managed in my book to put everything firmly into place by being silent about it. (Engelmann, 1967, p. 143)

The idea seems to be that ethics is ineffable, so we should maintain a pregnant silence on the subject. This passage has been cited on many occasions, but nobody has remarked just how silly it is: Wittgenstein is saying that the important part of his book is the part that cannot be written – the silence is supposed to ring out loud; the nothingness is supposed to have a being, indeed, to be the whole point of the work. Questions of ethics, religion and the meaning of life became important to Wittgenstein after March 1916, and he may have much *wanted* the *Tractatus* to be seen as an ethical work. But the fact is that it isn't one, and should not be so seen.

Logical Positivists wedded to the Verification Principle – that an apparently empirical proposition is meaningful only if it is in principle verifiable or refutable – would conclude that, on *Tractatus* principles, ethics is meaningless. For if, as Wittgenstein claims, one can't *say* anything about ethics, then, *a fortiori*, one can neither verify nor refute an ethical 'proposition'. In the 'transitional' phase of his philosophical development, Wittgenstein himself endorsed the Verification Principle. He said, for example, that ethical judgments 'are not propositions because they cannot be verified' (*DL*, p. 66). But, whereas for the positivists the term 'meaningless' is pejorative (roughly equivalent to 'junk'), Wittgenstein maintains the seemingly unstable view that what is meaningless may be important. He defends this view, at substantial length, in the only popular lecture he ever gave, a lecture on ethics (*LE*) to the Heretics Club at Cambridge in November 1930.

In this lecture, Wittgenstein uses the term 'ethics' broadly enough to include aesthetics, and offers what he calls 'a number of more or less synonymous expressions' to get his audience to appreciate 'the characteristic features of ethics': He writes:

... instead of saying 'ethics is the enquiry into what is good' I could have said ethics is the enquiry into what is valuable, or, into what is really important, or I could have said ethics is the enquiry into the meaning of life, or into what makes life worth living, or into the right way of living. I believe if you look at all these phrases you will get a rough idea as to what it is that ethics is concerned with. (*LE*, p. 5)

One might say, anachronistically, that Wittgenstein is here depicting 'ethics' as a family resemblance term. Ethics deals with absolute judgments of value – categorical imperatives – and Wittgenstein explains what these are:

Supposing that I could play tennis and one of you saw me playing and said 'Well, you play pretty badly' and suppose I answered 'I know, I'm playing badly but I don't want to play any better,' all the other man could say would be 'Ah then that's all right.' But suppose I had told one of you a preposterous lie and he came up to me and said 'You're behaving like a beast' and then I were to say 'I know I behave badly, but then I don't want to behave any better,' could he then say 'Ah then that's all right'? Certainly not; he would say 'Well, you *ought* to want to behave better.' Here you have an absolute judgment of value. (*LE*, p. 5)

So a *relative* (or hypothetical) judgment has the form 'If you want so and so, then you ought to do such and such'. The 'ought' here is not really a moral 'ought', for the hypothetical can be reformulated as 'Doing such and such will help you achieve goal so and so', and no moral terms feature in this reformulation. No mention is made here of whether so and so is a *worthy* goal. But ethics is concerned precisely with identifying what goals are worthy; with specifying how we ought to conduct our lives. Thus, it is *absolute* judgments that are the stuff of ethics. Now, Wittgenstein argues, a science of ethics is impossible:

What Hamlet says ['Nothing is either good or bad, but thinking makes it so'] seems to imply that good and bad, though not qualities of the world outside us, are attributes of our states of mind. But what I mean is that a state of mind, so far as we mean by that a fact which we can describe, is in no ethical sense good or bad. If for instance in our world-book we read the description of a murder with all its details physical and psychological, the mere description of these facts will contain nothing which we could call an *ethical* proposition. The murder will be on exactly the same level as any other event, for instance the falling of a stone. Certainly the reading of this description might cause us pain or rage or any other emotion, or we might read about the pain or rage caused by this murder in other people when they heard of it, but there will simply be facts, facts, and facts but no ethics. And now I must say that if I contemplate what ethics really would have to be if there were such a science, this result seems to me quite obvious. It seems to me obvious that nothing we could ever think or say should be *the* thing. That we cannot write a scientific book, the subject matter of which could be intrinsically sublime and above all other subject matters. (*LE*, pp. 6-7)

This is fairly clearly a misinterpretation of Hamlet's words, but let that pass. To put murders and falling stones on a moral par may seem disconcerting, even wicked. It is fairly easy to see what Wittgenstein has in mind. We can give a 'cold' description of a chain of events: 'He had come home drunk for the last three weeks and smashed everything in sight – she waited until he had fallen asleep – she got a sharp knife from the kitchen – she *intended* to cut off his penis – she did cut off his penis – ....' This description includes statements about states of mind, but no *ethical* statement has entered the picture. Yet we strongly feel that this particular chain of events does give rise to moral considerations in a way that some other chains don't. Science deals exclusively with *natural* phenomena. Moral statements – absolute judgments – are not about natural phenomena but are about what we *ought* to do, about 'the right way of living'. To suppose that what we ought to do is reducible to, or is determined by natural phenomena is to commit a 'naturalistic fallacy'. As Wittgenstein puts it, 'no statement of fact can ever be, or imply, a judgment of absolute value' (*LE*, p. 6) Therefore although there certainly is a non-natural, 'sublime', realm of ethics – we find ourselves in moral binds almost every day – these problems are not for any science, physical or psychological, to resolve.

We are tempted, says Wittgenstein, to use such expressions as 'absolute good' and 'absolute value' because we have a strong sense that there are certain experiences which defy naturalistic explanation: experiences such as *wonderment at the existence of the world*, or *feeling guilty* or *feeling absolutely safe*. But, in each case, when we come to examine how we describe these experiences, we discover that we are talking nonsense. In the case of *feeling absolutely safe*, for example, Wittgenstein says 'To be safe essentially means that it is physically impossible that certain things should happen to me, and therefore it's nonsense to say that I am safe *whatever* happens' (*LE*, p. 9). And he says to his audience: 'I want to impress on you that a certain characteristic misuse of our language runs through *all* ethical and religious expressions.' So Wittgenstein's diagnosis is that ethics is nonsense and the cure, presumably, is that we should hold our tongues whenever we have the inclination to wax ethical.

It has to be said that Wittgenstein's argument in this 'Lecture on Ethics' is far from satisfying. At the time of writing the lecture, his view on ethics was highly idiosyncratic: 'What is good is also divine. Queer as it sounds, that sums up my ethics. Only something supernatural can express the Supernatural' (*CV*, p. 3, comment written in 1929). In the lecture, he gives a few examples of descriptions of 'supernatural', quasi-religious experiences and suggests that these descriptions turn out, on inspection, to be nonsensical. But those experiences are hardly *typical* of the moral troubles we get ourselves into, and Wittgenstein has given us no justification for thinking that *all* moral problems lie outside the realm of sensible discussion.

After 1932, when he was leaving his 'transitional' and entering the 'late' phase of his work, Wittgenstein wrote nothing in the philosophy of morality, apart from one parenthetical remark at *PI* §77. Do his late writings offer a more principled account of the need to be silent on ethics? Colin Radford levels a most serious charge against Wittgenstein; he in effect accuses him of intellectual dishonesty. Radford suggests that what accounts for Wittgenstein's silence on ethics is that he had something to hide. In Radford's view, the existence of moral discourse – and nobody can deny that people do talk about moral issues – undermined Wittgenstein's later philosophy; that Wittgenstein realised this, but, instead of coming clean, he fraudulently kept quiet. So much for Wittgenstein's much vaunted integrity and his unwavering pursuit of truth!

In a nutshell, Radford's argument is this: Wittgenstein held that the 'therapy' he offered in his late writings applied to philosophers' misuses of language; he thought that ordinary, uncorrupted discourse is perfectly in order and stands in no need of treatment. Now, moral discussion – trying to figure out how we should or should not behave – is an ordinary part of our everyday lives, a form of life, as Radford puts it, 'into which we are inducted from earliest infancy, and as we grow we may see it as impinging on almost everything we are and do' (Radford, 1989, p. 102). Therefore Wittgenstein has no business condemning ethics as nonsense. Suppose it is objected here that, although moral discourse is commonplace, it is philosophical (in the bad way that Wittgenstein condemns) because moral claims are typically made with indicative sentences, and this *misleads* us into thinking that they are used to make statements which are objectively true or false. If it is a mistake so to construe moral sentences (and Wittgenstein was by no means the only person to think that) then perhaps it is right, after all, to stamp ethics 'unsayable'. But Radford claims that, *even if we grant this*, there are still devastating consequences for Wittgenstein's late philosophy. For consider (Radford's example) a girl who accidentally gets pregnant and sees that having a baby will impair her education and her career prospects. After a long, serious conversation with her sister, she decides that she must not terminate the pregnancy: 'I cannot have an abortion, I cannot kill this two month foetus. It would be wrong.' Her sister passionately disagrees, insisting that an abortion would not be wrong. Suppose, now, that the sisters acquaint themselves with Wittgenstein's late writings. They learn, and accept, that it is a mistake to think that moral claims are right or wrong. So the pregnant girl now sees that she was mistaken in thinking that having the abortion is wrong, and this makes it much easier for her to do what her sister advises and go ahead with the termination. Radford concludes that 'philosophy *will* or *should* interfere with how people think, say, and with what they do'. Thus Wittgenstein's non-interventionist claims about philosophy, a direct consequence of the methodology of his mature work, are refuted.

This notion of Radford's, that embracing a Wittgensteinian conception of morality ought to spare us agonizing over moral problems, is kind of laughable, given that Wittgenstein spent half his own waking hours agonizing over just such problems. Radford seems to think that Wittgenstein wants to *write off* ethics as all nonsense, but Wittgenstein's point is only that moral *theory*, traditionally conceived as the determination of general principles of right behaviour, is of no help in our practical moral affairs. This raises two interpretative questions. First, what, in Wittgenstein's view, is wrong with moral theorizing as standardly conceived; second, if ethics isn't that kind of theorizing, what is it?

Traditional moral philosophy comprises seeking clarification of the meanings of moral terms, such as 'good', 'right', 'ought' (metaethics) and the formulation and defence of principles for moral conduct. Wittgenstein has provocative things to say about both of these endeavours. He holds that the terms on which moral philosophers concentrate are not the ones that characteristically occur in moral discussions. And he holds that human beings are so diverse, and the complexities of the human condition are so rich, that no set of general principles could possibly serve as a guide to conduct.

If there is one facet of Wittgenstein's late view on ethics that is

191

absolutely clear, it is his insistence that 'right' and 'wrong', 'good' and 'bad' are *not* the terms which loom large in our everyday moral discussions. We don't see serious moral problems in terms of 'wrong' and 'right'. These concepts are just too thin. Early on in the 1938 *Lectures and Conversations on Aesthetics, Psychology and Religious Beliefs*, Wittgenstein makes the interesting observation that a child learns words like 'beautiful' and 'fine' not as evaluative adjectives but as interjections, and generally applies a word like 'good' first to food, and as a kind of gesture of approval (*LA*, §5).[32] These terms have a 'negligible place' in, are 'entirely uncharacteristic' of those adult activities in which we use language. Wittgenstein says that 'in real life, when aesthetic judgments are made, aesthetic adjectives such as "beautiful", "fine" etc., play hardly any rôle at all' (*LA*, §§8, 9, 12); where they play a prominent rôle is just in the interjections of 'people who can't express themselves properly' (*LA*, §9) and in 'the stupid kind of example which is given in philosophy' (*LA*, §36). Wittgenstein habitually treats aesthetics and ethics in parallel, and would make similar points about the terms upon which traditional moral philosophers are fixated. We must, of course, distinguish between theoretical, classroom discussions, and those that we have in real life; the latter, so Wittgenstein claims do not typically revolve around an agent asking: 'What is the morally right thing to do here?'

In describing a melody, we might use such epithets as 'springy', 'stately' or 'pompous' (*LA*, §9); we equally use a rich, thick vocabulary for talking about a suit (at least if we are tailors, or people who know clothes) (*LA*, §13) or about the behaviour of moral agents – or about the behaviour of immoral ones. Philosophers (perhaps one should exclude Aristotle and neo-Aristotelians) generally tried to squeeze discussion of moral issues into the framework of 'rights', 'obligations', 'duties' etc. ... a tightly circumscribed range of evaluative terms, whereas ordinary people talk of loyalty, of kindness, of feeling oppressed. Samuel Sheffler, speaking of the 'morality system' engendered by traditional theories, draws attention to the neglect of specific or 'thicker' ethical concepts, such as 'treachery', 'brutality' and 'courage', that people actually use in their moral evaluations. 'Such theories [the traditional ones] thereby impose an oversimplified structure on ethical thought, and overlook the variety and complexity of our ethical ideas. In so doing, they mirror the characteristic obsessions of the morality system itself, which seeks to represent all ethical conclusions as statements about people's *moral obligations*.'[33]

In experimental science, one can control the variables, prescind from the complexity of the world and focus on relationships between selected parameters (such as pressure, volume and temperature). Physics makes no mention of ordinary complex paraphernalia, such as tables and chairs; the vocabulary of physics includes 'electron', 'density', 'force', but not 'book', 'toothbrush', 'cheese slicer'. This is true, but notice how stupid a parallel characterization of morality would sound: in morality we prescind from the complexities of persons and their social relations; we ignore the ordinary terms we use for describing people's moral dealings, such as 'treachery', 'compassion', 'spite' and confine ourselves to expressions such as 'ought' and 'good'. It's absurd. The fact is that a rich moral vocabulary has evolved precisely to do justice to the richness of our moral lives and our urge to talk about moral situations: to ignore that vocabulary would be to turn one's back on the kind of people we are – what else could morality be about than *us* and our relations to the things around us?

There is, indeed, a danger in operating with the 'oversimplified structure' of which Scheffler speaks, for it serves to restrict our vision of moral behaviour, to reduce consideration of serious problems to sterile academic disputes. Mary Midgley makes the point well in a discussion of our treatment of animals. This debate bogs down if we view the problem in terms of 'rights' and of the question of whether animals have them. Midgley says: 'Debates about the word "rights" are a red herring in discussions about animals, a displacement activity invoked to help us avoid seeing the odious confusion of the gap between our theory and our practice' (Midgley, 1997). In certain cultures, the concept of a right does not even exist (Tao, 1996, p. 12), and, in those cultures, moral debates *have* to take a different form. A Samurai warrior, testing the sharpness of his sword by plunging it into an infant, would not regard himself as infringing an inalienable right possessed by that child; and neither should we. Midgley writes:

> For most of our activities the question 'have you a right to this?' does not arise. We use other forms of moral thought and language. Insistence on raising questions about rights distorts ordinary moral business by invoking the cruder methods of the law.[34]

One cannot imagine Wittgenstein giving up his fishing rights on Lake Eidsvandet for the reason that the fish had the right not to be fished.

A restricted moral vocabulary attenuates our moral discussion, and there is a danger that we shall equally do a disservice to serious thought about moral behaviour if we look to moral theory to deliver a set of principles for the guidance of our lives. We might enquire, for a start, who is supposed to be guided by such principles. Are they designed for a morally perfect agent in a community of equally morally perfect beings? If so, then the business of ethics becomes the rather mediaeval enterprise of eliciting the rules of behaviour for a community of angels. If, on the other hand, our perfect agent is conceived as a seeker of the good inhabiting a community of imperfect beings, then we are confronted with God's problem of advising his son Jesus how to behave. If God got it right, the principles are rather exacting and include the injunction to get yourself crucified if people don't follow your teachings. Once again we find ourselves formulating principles – this time for the guidance of a martyr, of a superhuman – that don't seem applicable to *ourselves*. Notice too, that the principle just mentioned is not an absolute one. It is the hypothetical: If you want to uplift others, to set a good example, to save their souls, then get yourself crucified. But can we *argue* for the claim that we ought to want to save the souls of other people?

Just which moral principles *are* absolute or axiomatic? Even so categorical a principle as that all non-defective adult humans ought to be treated the same, simply is not evident to all rational humans. And how would one convince the unconvinced? Not by considerations *more* fundamental, for *ex hypothesi* the principles we are reviewing are the most fundamental. Think of some other candidates for the axioms of morality. Daniel Dennett produces a list of them:

> Slavery is beyond the pale. Child abuse is beyond the pale. Discrimination is beyond the pale. The pronouncing of death sentences on those who blaspheme against a religion (complete with bounties or rewards for those who carry them out) is beyond the pale. It is not civilized, and it is owed no more respect in the name of religious freedom than any other incitement to cold-blooded murder. (Dennett, 1995, pp. 516-17)

Well, I do not dissent from any of the principles on Dennett's list, but it is self-evident that millions do. Dennett does not speak of *arguing* these people out of their views, and, if they just don't buy your principles and accept all the consequences of their own, what can you do? (Dennett says that 'we will be obliged, reluctantly, to cage or disarm' them.)

If these considerations point to the futility of traditional moral theory, then we can turn to the second of our questions: what is ethics; what should those with an interest in morality be doing? In Wittgenstein's opinion, our business, not just in ethics, but in philosophy in general, is not to theorize, but to describe. Perhaps confining oneself to *descriptions* of moral realities is unnecessarily restrictive. One should also consider *enactments* of real or fabricated events in drama and film. There is more to learn about morality from great poets and playwrights than from philosophers, because poets and playwrights capture those pleasures and pains and tensions in the human condition that make us the moral creatures that we are. Bernard Williams, in his early book, *Morality*, asks: 'Can the reality of complex moral situations be represented by means other than those of imaginative literature? [in particular, can *philosophy* address such situations?]. If not, can more schematic approaches represent enough of the reality? [i.e., is there anything to be gained by the philosophical study of artificial situations less complex than those we encounter in real life?] How much of what genuinely worries anyone is responsive to general theory?' (Williams, 1973, p. 11). In that early book, Williams indicates that he does not know the answer to these questions. In later writings, he, like Wittgenstein, gives negative or sceptical answers.[35]

If we find a play or a film morally uplifting, this will normally not be a matter of its making us aware of our moral obligations, or giving us an insight into the good.[36] The effect will rather be a transformation (perhaps only a very minor one) of ourselves – we may be made more sensitive to certain problems, more sympathetic to the plight of others, or we may be stirred when certain dormant feelings or sentiments are reawakened. This would imply that the rôle of moral discourse (thus broadly conceived) is to shape one's moral character rather than to furnish prescriptions on how to live. So this discourse need not be rational (reason-giving) discourse. In Wittgenstein's view, 'A typical American film, naïve and silly, can – for all its silliness and even *by means of* it – be instructive. A fatuous, self-conscious English film can teach one nothing. I have often learnt a lesson from a silly American film.'[37] One thing of which we can be sure is that the 'lesson' to which Wittgenstein is referring is not a lesson in moral theory. He once said: 'What is ethical cannot be taught. If I could explain the essence of the ethical only by means of a theory, then what is ethical would be of no value whatsoever' (*WVC*, p. 117; 17.12.30). When Martin Luther King invited his audience to share his dream of a world in which people are judged not by the colour of their skin but by the quality of their character, he was not teaching. But he made a contribution to moral enlightenment – after all, some people who heard him were morally enlightened by his words. But their attitudes were changed not by an argument or a set of deontological axioms, but by a vision, and they subsequently came to see things in a new light.

Williams (1994) is unapologetic about ignoring philosophical texts, and he certainly does not think that tragedy is proto-philosophy. The tragedies are not works of philosophy, but that certainly does not mean that what they reveal is not of great interest to philosophy. Wittgenstein, similarly, thinks that Tolstoy's novels are of great philosophical value, but he chides Tolstoy for 'bad theorizing' (*CV*, p. 58). To criticize a playwright for not expressing deep philosophical arguments is to misunderstand the contribution that literature can make. The late Sir Denys Page may have been confused on this score when he issued what Williams calls 'his remarkable end-of-term report on the author of the *Oresteia*': 'Aeschylus is first and foremost a great poet and a most powerful dramatist. The faculty of acute or profound thought is not among his gifts' (Williams, 1994, pp. 14-15). It is not the playwright's function to argue his audience towards a certain conclusion; nevertheless, by a sensitive depiction of some course of events, he may bring about a change in our moral attitudes and beliefs or a change of heart.

But why look to literature when we are seeking a reflective understanding of ethical life; why not take examples from life? 'It is a perfectly good question, and it has a short answer: what philosophers will lay before themselves and their readers as an alternative to literature will not be life, but bad literature' (Williams, 1994, p. 13). Williams is right about this tendency, and Wittgenstein too remarks (to Rhees in 1942) that it is 'strange that you could find books on ethics in which there was no mention of a genuine ethical or moral problem' (Rhees, 1965, p. 21). Moral philosophers often use contrived examples – thought experiments – which serve the purpose not of controlled experiments in science, where variables of particular interest to the investigator are isolated, but rather of *crude* experiments which mask important subtleties.[38] Wittgenstein himself, of course, had no need to invent examples of problematic moral situations. The biggest moral problem was his own life.

In a conversation with Waismann, Wittgenstein says: 'At the end of my lecture on ethics, I spoke in the first person. I think that is something quite essential. Here there is nothing to be stated any more; all I can do is to step forth as an individual and speak in the first person' (*WVC*, p. 117, 17.12.30). Considering the moral dilemma, raised by Rhees, of a man who has come to the conclusion that he must either leave his wife or abandon his work on cancer research, Wittgenstein says 'Here we may say that we have all the materials of a tragedy; and we could only say: "Well, God help you" ' (Rhees, 1965, p. 23). He says that this is a solution to an ethical problem, although for someone who has adopted (say) Christian ethics, it is not a problem. But, if one goes on to ask whether Christian ethics is the *right* ethics, Wittgenstein says (this is in 1945) that if you do say this, you are making a judgment of value which simply amounts to *adopting* Christian ethics. 'If you say there are various systems of ethics you are not saying they are all equally right. That means nothing. Just as it would have no meaning to say that each was right from his own standpoint. That could only mean that each judges as he does' (Rhees, 1965, p. 24). The man in Rhees' tragedy cannot look to Wittgenstein for an answer, nor to Christianity. He can, if he is a sufficiently reflective person who has learned what moral struggle is all about, look to himself. When Wittgenstein says 'God help you', he means, God help you to work it out, to reach a conclusion that only you, who have come to terms with your own beliefs, failings, prejudices and temperament, can reach. Ray Monk's characterisation of Wittgenstein's conception of ethics can't be bettered: 'He was arguing for a morality based on integrity, on being true to oneself, one's impulses – a morality that came from inside one's self rather than one imposed from outside by rules, principles and duties'.[39]

Some indication of how successfully Wittgenstein had worked on himself, can be seen from a kind letter he wrote, when he was nearly fifty years old, to Maurice Drury, one of the Cambridge undergraduates who had fallen under his spell and whom he had advised as to choice of career. Drury went into medicine after Wittgenstein warned him off becoming ordained as an Anglican priest. Walking one day with Wittgenstein in a Dublin park, Drury expressed his worry that taking up medicine might have been a mistake. He was then in his final year of training, working in the casualty department of a hospital, and was distressed by his clumsiness when performing his duties. In the letter he wrote to Drury next day, Wittgenstein offers some practical suggestions: 'Don't think about yourself, but think about others, e.g. your patients .... Look at people's sufferings, physical and mental, you have them close at hand, and this ought to be a remedy for your troubles. Another way is to take a rest whenever you ought to take one and collect yourself.' Addressing some of Drury's religious concerns, Wittgenstein continues:

As to religious thoughts I do not think the craving for placidity is religious: I think a religious person regards placidity or peace as a gift from heaven, not as something one ought to hunt after. Look at your patients more closely as human beings in trouble and enjoy more the opportunity you have to say 'good night' to so many people. This alone is a gift from heaven which many people would envy you. (Rhees, 1984, pp. 95-6)

197

This is a clear example of seeing a problem 'from a religious point of view'. Wittgenstein is here adopting Drury's perspective, although it is a way of looking at a problem that he himself also found quite natural. Winch notes that, although speaking as an outsider to religious faith, Wittgenstein is expressing a concern for Drury's *spiritual welfare*; the letter is infused with religious sensibility and the language used is 'poised on the edge of the religious' (Malcolm, 1993, p. 126). Towards the end of the letter, Wittgenstein writes: 'It is most important that we should not one day have to tell ourselves that we had wasted the time we were allowed to spend together.'

As to Drury's worry that he had made a mistake going into medicine, Wittgenstein says:

> You didn't make a mistake because there was nothing at the time you knew or ought to have known that you overlooked. Only this one could have called making a mistake: and even if you had made a mistake in this sense, this would now have to be regarded as a datum as all the other circumstances inside and outside which you can't alter (control).

Winch thinks that this is 'a major *philosophical* point' (op. cit., p. 126) but it is nothing of the sort. Translated into Agony Auntese, what Wittgenstein is saying is: 'It wasn't your fault: you did all you could. And there's no use crying over spilt milk'. The *content* of the letter is not particularly profound. Wittgenstein assembles some useful reminders, but it is not so much what he *says* that is important. Rather, the fact that he took the trouble to write at such length *shows* his concern, and this was much appreciated by Drury. Wittgenstein, in this letter, displays a level of decency which, though not very much out of the ordinary, is warming. For he had achieved it only through a lifetime's struggle for self-transformation.

This, in the end, is what I think distinguishes Wittgenstein from an ordinary man. Many of the people who knew him thought that he possessed an extraordinary purity of spirit. Von Wright writes: 'He certainly was no saint and I doubt whether one should say he was a "good" man. He had a passionate temper – and sometimes he lost his temper and did things which he then regretted. He was extremely sensitive to questions of right and duty and his search of truth was relentless to a degree which, I think, we do not find in many persons. He was in some sense a fearful man but also one for whom one could not fail to feel compassion and also love' (private correspondence, 1.11.95). Norman Malcolm speaks of his heroic striving for complete understanding and of his uncompromising integrity (Rhees, 1984, p. xiii). In his early life, Wittgenstein did hate himself venomously, was aware of his vile defects such as arrogance and vanity, and went to great lengths to eradicate them. What his late followers saw was a cleansed man battling to prevent himself sliding back into the cesspit.

Wittgenstein was inspirational because he achieved what few academics achieve: intellectual modesty. After coming to fully understand the folly of the grand *Tractatus* scheme, he recognised that the philosopher's task was primarily that of curbing extravagance. If a phenomenon is puzzling, then it is the philosopher's rôle to describe the situation as accurately as possible, to avoid generalization and speculation, and to expose the false preconceptions of theorists who rush in with 'explanations' of what they have yet to describe in an unprejudiced way. He reminds himself: 'Make sure you really do paint only what you see' (*CV*, p. 68). Once a phenonenon has been described properly, in all its richness and diversity, *then* relevant experts can come in and seek explanations – philosophical armchair theorizing is not to the point here. Part of his work consisted of helping to recover from the kinds of 'grammatical' error that lead psychologists, philosophers and others astray. Another part consisted of asking the right questions. These are the questions that provoke a genuine tension, where he felt a strong pull in one direction – and in the opposite direction too, and the truth is hard to come by. In his late, late period, he succeeds, I think, in rediscovering a childlike wonder. The questions that fill his very late works are not rhetorical or pointed, but genuine expressions of puzzlement. Commentators who read certain 'positions' into these late writings have failed to understand his character.

Notes

1. Method

1. For more on the difficulties that Wittgenstein had in getting the book published, see McGuinness (1988, pp. 296-9) and Monk (1990, pp. 169-84).

2. In a letter to Ludwig von Ficker of October 1919, Wittgenstein says of the *Tractatus*: 'The work is strictly philosophical and literary at the same time; however, there is no gassing in it' (*LF*, p. 94).

3. There are two standard translations of the *Tractatus*, the first by Ogden and Ramsey in 1922. I shall generally use the 1961 Pears/McGuinness translation (though I don't here). Ogden had some correspondence with Wittgenstein on the translation of the work – see *LO*.

4. This is the theme of Janik and Toulmin (1973); see p. 27. I argue, in Chapter 5, that to interpret properly Wittgenstein's writings, one needs to understand not only the background but also the man himself.

5. Hertz is mentioned at *T* 4.04, 6.361. Allan Janik argues that not just the *Tractatus*, but also the conception of philosophy embraced by Wittgenstein in his mature works are heavily indebted to Hertz's philosophy of science. See Janik (1994). For example, in the section of the 'Big Typescript' (TS 213) entitled 'Philosophy', written around 1933, when he was working out his later conception of philosophy, Wittgenstein writes 'As I do philosophy, its entire task consists in expressing myself in such a way that certain troubles //problems// disappear. ((Hertz.))'. (The word 'problems', indicated as an alternative by the double slashes, is also broken-underlined, indicating uncertainty.)

6. This name for Habsburg Vienna was coined by Robert Musil in his great novel *The Man Without Qualities*. It is both a play on its official title as kaiserlich-königlich (Imperial-Royal) abbreviated 'k und k', and on German Motherese, translating roughly as 'Shitville'. Wittgenstein had a deep reverence for the 'high' German culture of the nineteenth century. He felt himself to be out of tune with the culture – particularly with the musical culture – of contemporary Vienna.

7. See also David Pinsent's diary (Pinsent, 1990, p. 90), entry for Wednesday, 29 April, 1914: '... about a month ago Ludwig wrote to me that he had settled [the problems with Russell's Theory of] Types and in fact put the whole of Logic in order and was writing a book on the subject'. Contrast Terry Eagleton's tacky and ridiculously uninformed contrasting view in his introduction to the text of Derek Jarman's film *Wittgenstein* (Eagleton, 1993). Writing of the *Tractatus*, Eagleton proposes that '[i]ts true coordinates are not Frege or Russell or logical positivism but Joyce, Schoenberg, Picasso'. The great Alan Sokal Hoax will, one hopes, teach the likes of Eagleton that whereof they cannot speak thereof they ought to remain silent.

201

8. McGuinness (1988, pp. 73-6) suggests that Wittgenstein may have come upon either Russell's book or Frege's *Grundgesetze der Arithmetik* before his time in Manchester and (relying on an account given by Wittgenstein's sister Hermine) that he became violently gripped by reflection on philosophical problems during his time in Charlottenburg (1906-8).

9. The 'Notes on Logic' and the 'Notes dictated to G.E. Moore in Norway' are printed as appendices in *N*. A transcription of the 'Notes on Logic' (TS 201 in von Wright's Catalogue), produced by the Wittgenstein Archive in Bergen, is available on the World Wide Web at http://www.hd.uib.no/wab/sample/sample.htm#201a. For an account of the relation of the early manuscripts to the *Tractatus*, see McGuinness (1989).

10. The matter is complicated by the fact that 'analysis' is sometimes used to refer to the revealing of a perspicuous structure somehow underlying the surface appearance of everyday language, sometimes to refer to the *replacement* (for certain purposes) of everyday language, by a more perspicuous alternative – an 'ideal' or 'perfect' language. Frege adopted the latter approach. Although his writings became more generally known only after the First World War, Frege's ideas, and those of Peano, were a major source of inspiration for Russell's highly influential text *The Principles of Mathematics* (1903), which adumbrates the themes and methods of twentieth-century analytic philosophy.

11. The whole of Frege's text is reproduced in van Heijenoort (1967, pp. 1-82). In his introduction to (Bell and Cooper, 1990), David Bell suggests that we date the beginnings of analytical philosophy from Frege's *Grundlagen der Arithmetik*, which was published five years after *Begriffsschrift*. While it is true that the *Grundlagen* is devoted to showing that the laws of arithmetic are analytic judgements, the *methodology* of analysis is certainly adopted in *Begriffsschrift*. For a useful discussion of the relation of these two texts to each other and to Frege's *Grundgesetze der Arithmetik* (1893), see Dummett (1991), chs 1 and 2, esp. p. 11.

12. *Begriffsschrift* itself does not contain much of a philosophical defence of the *raison d'être* of the new logic, but the bulk of Frege's writing between 1879 and 1884 is devoted to just that, largely in response to unfavourable reviews. See Hovens (1997).

13. Wittgenstein told Russell that this theory was undoubtedly correct. Norman Malcolm recalls that Wittgenstein believed the Theory of Descriptions to be Russell's most important production (Malcolm, 1958, p. 68). It is almost certainly this theory that Wittgenstein has in mind when he says 'It was Russell who performed the service of showing that the apparent logical form of a proposition need not be its real one' (*T* 4.0031).

14. See Russell's paper 'On Denoting' which originally appeared in *Mind* (1905) and is reprinted in many places including Russell (1956). This quotation and those following are from pp. 43-4 of the latter.

15. For a particularly scathing review of one of the logic books of this period, see Wittgenstein's *RC*.

16. Letter dated 29.12.1912. The Russell-Morrell correspondence is housed in the Humanities Research Center, University of Texas.

17. Kant sought to establish, by a 'transcendental argument' what must be true for it to be the case that people have experiences. For an exploration of many of the connections between Kant's thought and Wittgenstein's, see Garver (1994).

18. I here use 'statement' as the translation of 'Satz', but in what follows, I shall often leave the German word untranslated, since there is no short English counterpart. Wittgenstein usually uses the word to mean 'what is produced in the performance of an act of speech' (e.g. a question is produced by someone who performs the speech-act of asking a question). Since the only speech act product discussed in Wittgenstein's early writings is the *statement*, I shall occasionally use 'statement' as the translation of 'Satz'. This translation is defended by D. Shwayder (1963). On the notion of the *product* of a speech act, see Achinstein (1977).

19. For the logically perspicuous rendering of the statement 'Nobody has just come into this room', we employ the functional expression 'x has just come into this room'. Thus: 'It is not the case that there is an x such that x has just come into this room.'

20. In a long piece (151 pp.) dating from 1904, to which editors have given the title 'Fundamental Notions', Russell gets rather close to Wittgenstein's *Tractatus* view. He writes: '... the postulate of functionality is embedded in the use of variables; hence it would seem to be presupposed in the notation, and therefore to be pre-formal' (Russell, 1994, pp. 251-2).

21. John Koethe (1996) argues that, in a variety of different forms, the doctrine of *showing*, of what can be seen or displayed but not said, pervades Wittgenstein's writings both early *and* late.

22. For a discussion of this matter, see Palmer (1996).

23. From now on, we are using 'argument' not as above when we were discussing Frege, but in the ordinary philosophical sense – in a typical argument, a conclusion is drawn from premises.

24. I here ignore refinements to this classical criterion of validity proposed by relevance logicians and others. The question to what extent Wittgenstein himself departed from classical logic will be touched on in Chapter 4.

25. It is highly probable that Wittgenstein was familiar with a famous puzzle about inference discovered by Lewis Carroll and published at the end of the nineteenth century (Carroll, 1895). Roughly speaking, a tortoise pesters Achilles to show him that a particular inference from premises 'P' ('Two things that are each equal to some other thing, are equal to each other' and 'The two sides of this triangle are each equal to some other thing') to conclusion 'C' ('The two sides of this triangle are equal to each other') is justified. Achilles gives, as justification, the law of inference 'P entails C'. This does not satisfy the tortoise, who wants now to know how the inference from 'P' and '(P entails C)' to 'C' is justified. So Achilles produces another law of inference: '(P and "(P entails C)" entails C'. And so on, *ad infinitum*. If Wittgenstein's point about the superfluousness of laws of inference is correct, that would solve Lewis Carroll's puzzle, for the inference from 'P' to 'C' is justified by inspection of the constituent propositions alone (*T* 6.122), or by observing that 'If P then C' is a tautology.

26. For some of the positivists, the appeal lasted little more than an instant, since there are several important conflicts between Wittgenstein's *Tractatus* views and the precepts of Logical Positivism. See Grayling (1988).

27. As I have interpreted Wittgenstein here, he is deriving ontological conclusions from considerations about the logic of language, despite the fact that the *Tractatus* begins with ontological doctrine. Others have suggested that the flow goes in the opposite direction (Goddard and Judge, 1982), (Pears, 1987). I am swayed by such (non-decisive) considerations as (i) Frege sets the example of deriving ontology from the logic of language. He says that objects just are the referents of singular terms, not that singular terms are the names of independently identifiable objects; (ii) Wittgenstein says that philosophy consists of logic and metaphysics, the *former* its basis; (iii) 'The world is the totality of facts, not of things' (*T* 1.1) *has* to be a conclusion rather than a premise or assumption – who would acept a bald statement like that without any support?; (iv) the *Philosophical Investigations* identifies as a crucial *assumption* of the *Tractatus* the 'crystalline purity' of *logic*. For further arguments on 'my' side, see Hallett (1977, p. 37). Epistemological considerations leading to an ontology of facts are adduced in McDowell (1994, pp. 3-45).

28. This was one of the first ideas on logic that Wittgenstein committed to paper. It is expressed in the 1913 TS 201a 'Notes on Logic' (from The Bertrand Russell Archives, McMaster University, Canada), catalogue number RA1.710.057822. This is a 7-page 'Summary', a typescript with many handwritten additions. On p. 5, Wittgenstein writes: 'Symbols are not what they seem to be. In "a R b", "R" looks like a substantive, but it is not one. What symbolizes in "a R b" is that R occurs between a and b .... Similarly in "φx", "φ" looks like a substantive but is not one; in "~p", "~" looks like "φ" but is not like it.'

29. We thus have a reflection of the real-world situation which contains not Angus, Brett and a 'being on top of' which binds them together, but just Angus and Brett combined in a certain way. As Russell says, in a 1904 MS 'On Functions', 'The mode of combination of the constituents of a complex is not itself one of the constituents of the complex. For, if it were, it would be combined with the other constituents to form the complex; hence we should need to specify the mode of combination of the constituents with their mode of combination' (Russell, 1994, p. 98). The new mode of combination would then, by the same token, be combined ... ad infinitum. This argument against admitting a mode of combination as a constituent object (on the grounds that doing so would require one to admit an infinite number of constituents in any given complex) is known as Bradley's regress.

30. *PI* §81. In two earlier drafts of this section, Wittgenstein says 'and did lead me in the *Tractatus*'.

31. For an interesting discussion of the demand for a logically perspicuous language ('logical perfectionism') and of the view that the presumptive role of words is to stand for or refer to things, and the presumptive role of sentences is to picture or represent how things stand to each other ('referentialism'), see Fogelin (1996).

32. By this time, 'metaphysics' had become a dirty word. Contrast the 1913 claim already cited (*N*, p. 93) that philosophy consists of logic and metaphysics.

33. For more on philosophy as grammar, see Rundle (1979), Garver (1996).

34. See McDowell (1994) for a criticism of Crispin Wright on this score. Peter Hacker, in the second edition of his *Insight and Illusion*, roundly castigates his first edition self for attributing to Wittgenstein a theory of anti-realism in the form of an assertion-condition semantics. One commentator who does take Wittgenstein's disavowal of theories absolutely seriously is Oswald Hanfling (1989). Of course, the difference between merely assembling reminders and advancing a theory is none too clear. Wittgenstein seems to be claiming that it is not the philosopher's task to propose generalizations or to test hypotheses.

35. Both to philosophers and to post-Chomskyan linguists. Kripke discusses Donald Davidson whose theory of meaning, when Kripke was writing, was certainly close to the *Tractatus* (Kripke, 1982, pp. 71-2, n. 60). Davidson is a particularly interesting case, because a sea change occurred in his outlook around 1986, and recent papers of his have been very much in the spirit of (and sometimes contain explicit discussions of) the *later* Wittgenstein.

2. Meaning

1. Signs for logical connectives would also not figure in a completely perspicuous language since, following *T* 4.442, any complex proposition can be written out in truth-tabular form.

2. 3.1432 is widely regarded as one of the 'difficult' remarks in the *Tractatus* and the interpretation I have offered, first defended, to the best of my knowledge, by Wilfrid Sellars (1962) is not without its critics.

3. Wittgenstein believed St. Augustine to be a 'great mind' (Malcolm, 1958, p. 71) and thought the *Confessions* 'possibly the most serious book ever written' (Rhees, 1984, p. 90). For an interesting account of St. Augustine's conversion as recorded in this work and of why Wittgenstein regarded St. Augustine as a fellow spirit, see Eldridge (1997, pp. 121-54). Eldridge writes: 'This picture of conversion is enormously attractive to Wittgenstein. It offers a way out of self-dissipation and into coherent self-unity' (p. 125). As we shall see in Chapter 5, Wittgenstein attached great importance to confession; and converting his own character in the way that St. Augustine succeeded in doing was, for him, a lifetime project.

4. What makes for confusion in the translation is that, in the *Tractatus*, Wittgenstein follows Frege in using the word 'Bedeutung' in a technical way, best translated as 'reference' – the thing to which the word points ('deuten' = 'to point, indicate'). He there says that Names have reference, but that propositions don't; the latter have meaning or sense (Sinn) (*T* 3.144).

5. Also *BB*, p. 5. Likewise, when confronted with the substantive 'I', we are tempted to ask what it stands for. One could argue that it cannot stand for my body, because I could change my body, but retain all my memories and psychological attributes by having them downloaded into the new brain. But this does not show, says Wittgenstein, that, besides A's body, there is something else, another object, such as an ego, which is A (Ambrose, 1972, p. 20). Wittgenstein's views on 'I' are extremely subtle and complex. See David Pears' intricate discussion (Pears, 1998).

6. *LA*, p. 2. Hacker cites Quine citing Dewey saying in 1925 that meaning is use (Hacker, 1996a, p. 189), but Hacker explains in n. 11 (p. 317) that Dewey's behaviourist conception is not Wittgenstein's position. Hacker usefully exposes many of the misunderstandings of Wittgenstein's claim that meaning is use, and responds to certain obvious objections such as that, in some circumstances, we cannot substitute 'meaning' for 'use' and *vice versa*. He himself favours Wittgenstein's 'more cautious' position that 'although not every feature of use is necessarily a feature of meaning, it is the use that determines the meaning of an expression, and every difference of meaning is a difference of use' (op. cit., pp. 244-9).

7. Many writers think that names do not have meaning, and Hacker criticises Wittgenstein for thinking otherwise (Hacker, 1996a, p. 249). I myself can see nothing wrong with Wittgenstein's view. Note that at *PI* §79, he speaks of the use *for me* of the name 'Moses' (my italics) again indicating that he has in mind speaker's meaning.

8. For a discussion of this issue, see *BB*, pp. 78-9; *PI* §§19-21.

9. The notion of a language-game occurs quite early in Wittgenstein's later

writings. In MS 113 (1931-2) he describes a language-game in which a a child is taught to say 'light' and 'dark' when an electric light is turned on or off (MS 113, pp. 88, 97-8).

10. Horwich (1995, p. 356).

11. The so-called 'redundancy' theory of truth is often credited to Frank Ramsey, but, many years before Ramsey, both Frege (1891) and Wittgenstein had stated the core of the 'redundancy' position. In (*N*, p. 9, entry for 6.10.14), Wittgenstein says ' "p" is true, says nothing else but p'. Here Wittgenstein is using the double quotation marks as a means of pointing to an arbitrary *proposition*; he is not using them to cite the letter 'p'. Peter Hacker points out that although at (*PI* §136) Wittgenstein claims that 'p' is true = p, he had argued in *Philosophical Grammar* that 'the quotation marks in the sentence " 'p' is true" are simply superfluous', since ' " 'p' is true" can only be understood if one understands the grammar of the sign "p" as a propositional sign, not if "p" is simply the name of the shape of a particular ink mark'. Like Ramsey, Wittgenstein had no qualms about propositional quantification, agreeing with him that 'What he says is true' = 'Things are as he says' (*PG* §79, pp. 123-4), i.e. 'For all p, if he says that p, then p' (Hacker, 1996a, p. 318). Wittgenstein's account of truth is minimalist or *deflationary*. Deflationism could be called the no-theory of truth, for it denies that truth is a substantive property, so we don't have a problem of characterising what property it is.

12. Wittgenstein frequently alludes to first language learning. Some commentators are under the impression that the empirical matter of how words are learned cannot have a very important rôle to play in his considerations (Baker and Hacker, 1983b, pp. 30-5; Hanfling, 1989, p. 92). They are wrong. Up until about the time of the composition of *PG* (1934), Wittgenstein does not appreciate the significance of first-language learning; subsequently he does. Of course, in some cases – e.g., when we are thinking of reacting to words as adjusting a mechanism to respond to a certain kind of influence, as happens at the very earliest stage of language-learning – it does not matter whether we think of those words as learned in the regular way or whether the ability to so react is innate (*PI* §495).

13. The classic source is Austin (1975), a work sadly neglected by philosophers, but which became a 'bible' for applied linguists. A student of Wittgenstein's, Wolfe Mays, comes up with an interesting suggestion as to the connection between Wittgenstein and speech-act theory: 'I can now see that Wittgenstein was stressing in his lectures much more the expressive side of communication, through gesture, etc., rather than the cognitive aspects which tend to give meaning an essentialist character. When his disciples took over this approach, they emphasised the speech act as a form of behaviour rather than gesture. Was this I wonder because it is bad form for English speakers to talk with their hands?' (Mays, 'Recollections of Wittgenstein' in Fann, 1978, p. 83).

14. There's a bothersome confusion of terminology that won't trouble us here. J.L. Austin, before settling on the terminology of 'locutionary', 'illocutionary' and 'perlocutionary' for describing various acts and effects that a speaker can achieve (Austin, 1975), used the expression 'performative' to refer to verbal performances in which something got done – for example, the vicar saying 'I wed you' is (under the right circumstances) wedding two people (to each other); if I say 'I promise you $10' then, in so saying, I make a promise. So Austin's performatives are acts done with words, whereas the performatives to which developmentalists refer are acts that are done wordlessly. The term 'communicative act' is used by developmentalists to embrace both speech acts and dumb performatives.

15. Exactly when to apply the term 'proposition' to the child's utterances seems an arbitrary matter. See Wittgenstein's discussion in *A*, pp. 11-13, which begins with the question: 'In teaching a child language by pointing to things and pronouncing the words for them, where does the use of a proposition start?'

16. For an account of the gestural development of young children, see Werner and Kaplan (1963). There is an interesting body of literature supporting the view that gesture was the primitive form of language from which speech evolved. See, for example, Harnad et al. (1976); Von Cranach et al. (1979).

17. In the case of some intonation patterns, no training may be required; there may be a universal, non-conventional connection between certain patterns and certain reactions. For example, as Jerome Bruner suggests, 'the fast-rising stress may have a "natural" power to attract an infant's attention' (Bruner, 1983, p. 73). However, the child's *production* of intonation patterns for affective purposes does seem to depend on the feedback supplied by the caregiver – see Galligan (1987).

18. Grice (1957). Certain alleged problems with this view are usefully cleared away in Bach (1987).

19. Bruner (1983, pp. 37-8). E.L. Kaplan described experiments showing selective responses among eight-month-old children to rising and falling intonation (Kaplan, 1969). In the same year, Menyuk and Bernholtz showed, by spectrograpic analysis, that the fundamental frequency contours for children's one-word utterances fall into distinct types (Menyuk and Bernholtz, 1969).

20. The expression 'gradual' as used to describe meaning-acquisition is potentially misleading for it is clearly not the case that there is some measure of a child's mastery of language in terms of which it would be correct to describe his or her progress as uniform or steady. A better picture would be that of clambering up a flight of wildly riser-variable steps. There are the large Piagetian leaps that Gopnik compares to conceptual revolutions in science (Gopnik, 1984), the jumps to recognition of broad categories such as SOURCE, and the subsequent resolution into narrower ones such as AGENT and CAUSE (Clark and Carpenter, 1989) and the smaller hops of adjusting extension to that of fully competent speakers in the vicinity. If among all this there are also brief periods of consolidation, then it might be appropriate to describe the acquisition process as one of punctuated dynamism. By calling this process 'gradual', I do not imply a smooth transition.

21. This stage of syllabic reduplication is reached at about the age of eight months, when the child is able to pick up objects with thumb and forefinger. The various stages of infant language and motor development, from age three months to four years, is charted by Farb (1975, pp. 247-9).

22. By 'stage', I do not intend to imply sudden transition; meaning acquisition is gradual. In the colour spectrum, there is likewise a gradual transition from red to violet, but we find it natural and convenient to divide it into 'stages'. For a good discussion of the multiple ambiguity of the phrase 'stage of language acquisition', see Ingram (1989, pp. 32-58).

23. For example, some psychologists, drawing on an extensive database (CHILDES) of children's utterances, contend that, before the age of three, children have our concept of *want* (*desire*), but do not yet have our concept of *belief*. See, for example, Wellman (1991). Regrettably, few philosophers have taken much interest in the empirical developmental literature. An exception is Andrew Woodfield, who addresses this question and the fundamental problem of what counts as the possession of a concept. See Woodfield (1996).

24. Susan Carey defends the view that some of the concepts possessed by children are incommensurable with those possessed by adults, and compares conceptual development in children with the development of scientific theories incommensurable with their predecessors (Carey, 1992).

25. For a clear introductory discussion, see Robinson (1992). It's a big question, of course, whether any future computer will be capable of possessing qualia. For speculative functional neuroanatomical discussion, see Dennett (1979, pp. 190-229).

26. For a critical review, see Sugarman (1987, pp. 50-55).

27. Davidson's well known view that thinking requires language (Davidson, 1975; 1982) just does not seem to square with our knowledge of the behaviour of animals and of prelinguistic children (Marcus, 1990). I think Davidson can be answered by pointing out that it is propositional attitude *reports* that are propositional; the attitudes themselves may be had by language-less creatures. As we have seen in the case of young infants, our reports must be pretty tentative. It may be anthropomorphic to say that the panting dog wants water (i.e H_2O), but it could be needlessly reticent to say only that it wants relief from thirst – perhaps it would turn its nose up at the offer of a Perrier. Quine usefully compares the infant's early holophrastic use of observation sentences with animal cries. Such cries are associated, by instinct or conditioning, only to ranges of sensory neural intake, *not* to partitionings of the external world (into mothers, slippers etc.) made available by an adult conceptual scheme (Quine, 1993, p. 111). For humans, a shared conceptual scheme and a public language come about only after a period of the right sort of engagement with the social world.

28. The 'Lexical Contrast Theory' (Clark 1983; 1990) depends on the concept of a *lexical contrast* introduced in Saussure's classic text (Saussure, 1968). The notion of a *basic contrast set* can be characterized as consisting of a linguistic expression L (the covering term) and a set of monolexemic expressions $E_1 \ldots E_n$ (the members of the set) such that the extension of each E_i is a subset of the extension of L, and the extensions of the E_i are pairwise disjoint. Two straightforward examples of such sets are <Parent: mother, father> and <Day: Monday, Tuesday ... Sunday>. Richard Grandy, echoing Clark, argues that 'part of what speakers know when they know the meaning of a word is the contrast set(s) to which it belongs, that the contrast sets are an essential part of the theoretical description of the meaning, and that this knowledge of contrast sets is evident in semantic memory' (Grandy, 1987, p. 261).

29. See Ritchie (1985) and Pinker's discussion of the possibility of a maturationally critical point in the development of lexical rules (Pinker, 1989, pp. 349-50). In working-class households, Latinate vocabulary is rarely used, which explains why middle-class children perform better at subjects such as chemistry and physics which are rich in Latinate terms, than do working-class children to whom the vocabulary seems alien and recondite. This is the thesis of Corson (1985).

30. Fodor (1975). In subsequent writings, Fodor has modified and refined his position considerably. One of his recent efforts (Fodor, 1994) to worm himself out of difficulties is particularly interesting. But these refinements have no direct bearing on the following discussion. For a clear exposition and sympathetic discussion of the Language of Thought hypothesis, see Crane (1990).

31. Fodor (1975, p. 82). Balzano and McCabe cite Fodor himself as terming his view 'mad-dog nativism'. They offer a critique of Fodor and advocate an 'ecological' account of concept acquisition which shares with the position I am advocating the idea that concepts *develop* under environmental pressures in response to the *needs* of a child at different stages of its early growth (Balzano and McCabe, 1986, p. 102).

32. Fodor is thus in bed with the *early* Wittgenstein (*T* 4.5). Quine too, without offering any supporting argument, claims that observation sentences are 'the child's entering wedge into cognitive language' (Quine, 1992, p. 39). That, as I have urged, is a mistake. The child does not begin its linguistic life by passing comments on the surrounding scene but by expressing its *wants*, and the same may be true of our near-relatives the bonobos – see Savage-Rumbaugh (1995). In a cartoon strip, a young yobbish father with his little yob baby on his knee, says to the baby, 'Hello son, and how've you been today?' The baby replies 'Piss off you bastard.' The yob, delighted, shouts to his wife 'Carole. Come quick, he's just said his first words' (Husband, *Private Eye* 736, 2 March 1990). Funny, right? – those couldn't be a baby's first words. Yet they are more likely candidates than the first words that Fodor or Quine want to put into babies' mouths.

33. Halliday says that much of the difficulty with language that a child experiences at school, for example, in the traditional first 'reading and writing' tasks, arises because such tasks are unrelated to what the child already knows about the nature and uses of language. The child 'is required to accept a stereotype of language that is contrary to the insights he has gained from his own experience' (Halliday, 1975, p. 11) This is the stereotype that Fodor apparently accepts. A similar criticism can be made of John McDowell, who believes that we can avoid attributing complex Gricean intentions to speakers if we view exercises of the linguistic repertoire as 'cognitive stand-ins for the states of affairs which they represent'. See McDowell (1980, p. 135). What state of affairs does an utterance of 'Mama' represent?

34. As a matter of interest, this account comes pretty close to what St. Augustine says in a passage immediately preceding the one that Wittgenstein attacks at the beginning of the *Philosophical Investigations* (§1). Augustine writes: 'It was not that grown-up people instructed me by presenting me with words in a certain order by formal teaching, as later I was to learn the letters of the alphabet. I myself acquired this power of speech with the intelligence which you gave me, my God. By groans and various sounds and various movements of parts of my body I would endeavour to express the intentions of my heart to persuade people to bow to my will' (Augustine, 1991, p. 10).

35. Our criticism of Fodor's theory of mental representations has been only from the point of view of its ability to contribute to a plausible account of language development. There is a vast literature criticizing Fodor's position as an account of linguistic competence, and interesting alternatives now on the market include connectionism and mental model theory. I recommend Bechtel and Abrahamsen (1991) for an introduction to the field, and McGinn (1989, ch. 3) for a critique of Fodor.

36. For a rather similar view on the criteria of identity for words, see Kaplan (1990).

37. The physical token, the syntactical element and the word (in the full sense) are almost exactly, respectively, J.L. Austin's phone, pheme and rheme, the constituents, respectively, of the phonetic act, phatic act and rhetic act (Austin, 1975, pp. 92-8).

38. For doubts about claims about chimpanzee language, see Pinker (1994, pp. 335-51); also Mithen (1996, pp. 85-8) who thinks that African Grey parrots are a better bet.

39. On some advantages of neural nets over the traditional symbolic paradigm as models of the human mind, see, for instance, Smolensky (1988), Clark (1989; 1993a), Hanson and Burr (1990), Elman (1995). Tim van Gelder lovingly describes James Watt's steam generator as an illustration of the crucial respects in which a dynamical state system such as a neural net differs from a symbol-processing device (van Gelder, 1995).

40. This is one strand of the so-called (but not by Wittgenstein) 'Private Language Argument' – see, for example, *PI* §293 – about which more in Chapter 3. It becomes especially poignant if one accepts the view that, in the *Tractatus*, Wittgenstein construes language as private: *'The limits of my language* mean the limits of my world' (*T* 5.6), and interprets him as holding that the Names of the language stand for private, subjective Objects.

41. The same problem which has caused so much excitement among the readers of Kripke's book had been discovered earlier and set out in a text by Robert Fogelin but, for some reason, Fogelin's discussion didn't raise a stir – see his n. 10 to the second edition of his book (Fogelin, 1987, pp. 241-6).

42. So Kripke's solution entails that meaning can exist only in a community of speakers; we can ascribe meaning only if there are, or were, more than one speaker (see p. 110). There is a scholarly controversy over whether a Robinson Crusoe, isolated from birth, could follow rules and speak a language, and there is dispute over which of these views Wittgenstein held, for there seems to be much evidence for *both* views in his writings. For a judicious attempt to reconcile these differences, see Canfield (1996).

43. This is brought out clearly by Baker and Hacker from a study of the location in the source manuscripts of the section which is now *PI* §201 (Baker and Hacker, 1984, pp. 11-21).

44. For related thoughts on natural or 'direct' computation, see Robinson (1995, p. 310).

45. The Shorter *OED* has as its fourth quotation 'She vomited some 24 pounds of fulsome stuffe of all colours (Robert Burton)'. I'm grateful to Ossie Hanfling for bringing this up.

3. Mind

1. This was in 1942-43 at the Royal Victoria Infirmary in Newcastle, England. For the story, see Monk (1990, pp. 444-53). Monk says that the report *Observations on the General Effects of Injury in Man* written by Wittgenstein's team 'had an effect that he hoped his philosophical work would have – namely, it put an end to many misguided lines of research' (p. 452)

2. See Drury (1984, p. 106). Wittgenstein also mentions that James' *The Varieties of Religious Experience* had done him a lot of good.

3. Wittgenstein appears to have begun reading Schopenhauer at about age 16. Schopenhauer was one of the few philosophers whom he read closely and upon whose ideas he drew extensively and, if von Wright remembers the conversation correctly, Wittgenstein said that his first philosophy was a Schopenhauerian epistemological idealism. See von Wright's 'Biographical

Sketch' in Malcolm (1958, p. 5). For contrasting accounts of the influence of Schopenhauer on Wittgenstein, see Hacker (1986, pp. 81-107); Janaway (1989, pp. 317-42); Wiener (1992).

4. The citation for the award is in the Kriegsarchiv in Vienna (McGuinness, 1988, p. 242).

5. In the *Tractatus* too, we find the claim that 'solipsism, when its implications are followed out strictly, coincides with pure realism' (*T* 5.64). It is hard to know what to make of this. Commentators tend to read it as a rejection of solipsism even though Wittgenstein does not actually say that solipsism is *superseded* by realism, and goes so far as to insist that 'The world is *my* world' – 'what the solipsist *means* is quite correct', although the doctrine is ineffable (*T* 5.62). One possibility is that Wittgenstein embraces solipsism and that therefore the Objects of the *Tractatus* are 'my' objects – subjective phenomenal entities. For more on Wittgenstein and solipsism, see Pears (1975), and essays (each very interesting) by Pears, William Child, David Bell, Lucy O'Brien, Peter Sullivan and Adrian Moore in *European Journal of Philosophy* 4/2 (1996).

6. That the mediation of Schopenhauer was minimal is the conclusion of Gudmunsen (1977, pp. 111-13).

7. True, at *PI* §360, Wittgenstein remarks that we can also say that it thinks 'of dolls and no doubt of spirits too', but, as he made clear at *PI* §282, this is 'thinking' in a secondary sense.

8. In the *Tractatus*, a thought is said to be a logical picture not of a proposition but of facts (states of affairs) – see *Tractatus* 3. It is not clear whether, in this *Notebook* entry, Wittgenstein is proposing a theory different from the *Tractatus* or whether he just dozed off for an instant. My own inclination is to think that 'of the proposition' is just a slip of the pen; he meant 'of the fact'.

9. It is a pity that, in his *Commentary*, Max Black passes over this 'hence' without any comment. The German word translated as 'privileged' is 'ausgezeichnet', which is commonly used as an interjection, meaning 'wonderful' or 'excellent'. The verb 'zeichnen' means 'to designate'. Wittgenstein appears to be making the point that no number has been designated (by God) as having an outstanding status. (None of this helps understand his 'argument', I'm afraid.)

10. By this, he does not mean a system of gestures, such as American Sign Language. 'Zeichensprache' is simply any language which makes use of words or other signs.

11. For further remarks in the same vein, see references supplied in Hallett (1977, p. 41).

12. This is in complete contrast to Frege's view. Frege maintained that thoughts are abstract entities, not sentences belonging to the world of physical objects nor subjective states belonging to the psychological world, but rather sempiternal existents occupying a distinct third realm. For more on the difference between Frege's view and Wittgenstein's, see Hacker (1996b, esp. pp. 245-6). Note also the contrast with the view commonly attributed to the early Wittgenstein by commentators to the effect that thought is prior to language, that only by performing a mental act of meaning can a speaker convert his Satzzeichen into a Satz. A clear exposition of this interpretative error is to be found in Mounce (1997).

13. Similarly, the sign 'Welcome' on a doormat doesn't say 'Welcome' unless someone put it there so intending to say that, as Mr. Mole tries to persuade Mr.

Rat in Brown (1996a). This sign resembles those frequently used to perform greetings and it is favourably located for such a use, but we should beware of what Dretske calls The Paley Syndrome – 'an irresistible tendency to use resemblance and placement [location] as a basis for attributing purpose and design' (Dretske, 1996).

14. There is a good discussion of Russell's views on this issue in McDonough (1986, pp. 145-58). One problem with the view that the mind contains mental copies of situations, in the form of images, or bunches of ideas, or strings of words in the head, is that it is difficult to see how these could help the thinker to think. When you take a picture with a camera, an image is formed on the film inside the camera, but that image doesn't enable the camera to see the world outside. Humans and other animals see; cameras do not. Even if there are inner inert pictures in the mind, the big question would remain as to how the thinker could access them or make any use of them – to 'see' them with an 'inner eye'. For an early highly entertaining and too little known attack on the 'theory of ideas' along these lines, see Reid (1975). See also Ishiguro (1994); Watson (1994). One of the running themes in the writings of the late Wittgenstein is a diatribe against 'inner objects'. Wittgenstein tries to show that the postulation of them has no explanatory value.

15. Aquila (1983, pp. 1, ix). For further discussion and development of Kant's view on this subject (at least, of the view of Kant's view that seems to me faithful to Kant's text), see Sellars (1968); McDowell (1994).

16. For a comparison of the two, see Brown (1996b). Brown argues that Occam's theory yields a more explanatorily powerful semantics, a better understanding of language understanding and a superior (though not satisfactory) means for handling the problems of opaque psychological contexts.

17. J.C. Nyiri takes this remark to be a *rejection* of Wittgenstein's old view, but, as I have tried to show, the remark exactly captures the *Tractatus* position. The 'breakthrough' of which Nyiri speaks occurs very soon *after* this remark. See Nyiri (1989).

18. Diane Proudfoot and Jack Copeland show how, in his later writings on the mind, Wittgenstein's attack on mechanistic theories applies not just to the Cartesian conception, but also to the modern computer version – the 'symbolic paradigm'. In a fascinating study of Alan Turing's little-known work on 'unorganized machines', they show that one of Turing's own 'most important but least appreciated achievments was to provide cognitive science with the conceptual resources for understanding how the mindbrain could *fail* to be equivalent to a Turing machine' (Proudfoot and Copeland, 1994, pp. 497-8).

19. A mistake made by many critics of Wittgenstein (including Russell and Popper) is to assert that, in his later work, Wittgenstein was not interested in getting clear about puzzling phenomena but only in the language we use for talking about the phenomena. For comparison: if we are interested in observing the wondrous world, we may use spectacles to help us, and it would be perverse to then spend all our time looking at the spectacles. But Wittgenstein is not guilty of this particular perversity, and the critics have misconstrued his method. In *NL* he writes (about the experience of fright) 'There is here again the queer case of a difference between what we say, when we actually see what happens, and what we say when we think about it (giving over the reins to language)' *PO*, p. 202. Again, 'Surely what puzzles us isn't a word but the nature of a phenomenon. To investigate the nature of a phenomenon is to *look closer*' (*LPP*, p. 5). As Marie McGinn has argued, Wittgenstein is certainly not saying that the investigation of the language in which we speak of a phenomenon such as colour replaces the scientific investigation of that phenomenon (McGinn, 1991, pp. 437-42).

20. J.L. Austin's so-called 'phonetic act' is the result of abstracting from a speech act everything *except* the sound. See Austin (1975, pp. 92-6).

21. For further development of this point, see Millikan (1991).

22. The Ballard case would not pose a problem for Jerrold Fodor. He would allow that a deaf-mute who'd had no contact with natural language can ponder questions of God and the origins of the universe, in virtue of being born with a language of thought containing words for God, universe, origin etc. We have already tried to cast aspersions on this suggestion in Chapter 2.

23. Already in the 1913 'Notes on Logic' (printed as Appendix 1 to *N*), Wittgenstein had insisted that the 'p' in 'A judges p' cannot be replaced by a proper name; it stands in the place of a *proposition*. This is demonstrated by the fact that 'A judges p' amounts to the same as 'A judges that p is true and not-p is false' (p. 96). If a person A judges that the Thames is longer than the Tiber, then, unless A is an idiot, he also judges that the Tiber is shorter than the Thames. We can say this in virtue of the fact that what A judges has a complex structure. But a proper name does not have any such complexity; it is just a label we attach to an individual. So there is no escaping the fact that 'A judges p', 'A believes p', 'A hopes p' *appear* to express relations between a proposition and an individual. The *Tractatus* project in the 5.54s is to show that this is *only* appearance.

24. My student Masaharu Mizumoto, in a forthcoming dissertation, pursues the intriguing idea that the disappearance of A is a requirement of Wittgensteinian solipsism.

25. See Sluga (1996) for a discussion of how this theory of Wittgenstein's represents both a repudiation of Cartesianism and an attack on a theory of judgment proposed by Russell in a book on the theory of knowledge, the writing of which he then abandoned under pressure of an uneasy feeling that Wittgenstein's criticisms were decisive (Sluga and Stern, 1996, esp. pp. 322-7). One of these criticisms was that Russell's theory does *not* explain why nonsensical judgments are impossible.

26. Important differences between 'Not-p and I believe that p' and 'p and I don't believe that p' are discussed in Williams (1982).

27. Acording to Wittgenstein, 'If there were a verb meaning "to believe falsely" it would not have any significant first person present indicative' (*PI*, p. 190). This view has been questioned in Crimmins (1992).

28. The qualifications 'normally' and 'usually' that I have attached to Wittgenstein's claim that 'I believe' is an avowal (Äußerung) of a belief rather than a description are important. Wittgenstein moves from a crude, unqualified claim in his *NL* to the position that sentences such as 'I am afraid' may be used in a variety of ways, *sometimes*, indeed, to describe a mental state (*PI*, p. 187). For a very good discussion of this movement in Wittgenstein's thought, see Malcolm (1986, pp. 140-1).

29. I am grateful to John Williams (*forthcoming*) for clarifying an earlier formulation of mine (Goldstein, 1993). For advocacy of Wittgenstein's solution, see Linville (1979); Goldstein (1988). Wittgenstein points out that, in normal utterances in the first person present, the use of 'believe' is quite different from its use in other persons and tenses. Jane Heal has used this point to refute functionalism. She says, 'It is very important to functionalism that the meaning of "believe" is uniform' (Heal, 1994, pp. 13, 18, 19) for functionalism defines belief that p just as a state which, together with a person's desires, will normally cause behaviour which satisfies those desires only if p. So, for a functionalist, the Mooronic assertion 'I believe that it is raining, and it isn't' would have the form 'There is some state within me, and there's something going on in the world outside'. In other words, if functionalism were true, then the Mooronic assertion would not be absurd. So, by *modus tollens*, Heal is able to refute functionalism, because, of course, the Mooronic assertion *is* absurd.

30. *A*, p. 139. Herbert Simon is reputed to have said that first-order logic is a dulcet language, but I don't know whether this was as a riposte to Wittgenstein.

31. Wittgenstein *PI* §108. The crucial passage is *RPP I* §488: 'It would produce confusion if we were to say: the words of the ... sentence ... have a definite sense, and the giving of it, the "assertion" supplies something additional. As if the sentence, spoken by a gramophone, belonged to pure logic; as if here it had the pure logical sense; as if here we had before us the object which logicians get hold of and consider – while the sentence as asserted, communicated, is what it is in *business*. As one might say: the botanist considers the rose *as a plant*, not as a decoration for a dress or for a room or as a delicate ornament. The sentence, I want to say, has no sense outside the language-game. This hangs together with its not being a kind of *name*. As though one might say " 'I believe ...' – *that's* how it is" pointing (as it were inwardly) at what gives the sentence its meaning.'

32. These three quotations are from, respectively, *OC* §155; Malcolm (1995); Albritton (1995). Wittgenstein, Malcolm and Albritton take the view that, in the absence of any background story which shows its point, a Mooronic utterance is an Unsatz, a view which I too defend in Goldstein (1988).

33. See Fraassen (1995, pp. 26-7), my own (1992c), where I point out that the doing/describing distinction applies to other speech-acts, and Gardies (1975, p. 157), in which credit is given to Husserl. For the latter reference, I'm very grateful to Daniel Schulthess.

34. *LRKM*, p. 177; *PI*, p. 190. See also *RPP I*, §§478, 493.

35. Stalnaker's remarks, for which I'm indebted, are taken from his response to a paper of mine at a conference in Caen, France, March 1995.

36. This is a point that Aristotle makes at *Categories* 12b5-12b15: 'For in the way an affirmation is opposed to a negation, for example "he is sitting" – "he is not sitting", so are opposed the actual things underlying each, his sitting – his not sitting.' For a fuller discussion of this point, see Chapter 4.

37. This example inspired the title of Van Fraassen's (1995) paper. The general principle that Van Fraassen defends in that paper is: 'My current opinion about event E must lie in the range spanned by the possible opinions I may come to have about E at a later time t, as far as my present opinion is concerned' (p. 16). His discussion has practical relevance to the problem of formulating a sensible policy on those wills wherein an agent requests euthanasia under specified future circumstances and that this request should over-ride any contrary wishes he expresses at that later time.

38. At *PI* §621, Wittgenstein raises the question of what is left over if I subtract the fact that my arm goes up from the fact that I raise my arm. Since there may be no observable difference between the rising and the raising, a theoretician will be inclined to suppose that the difference must be some inner state or process. Thus, in his chapter on the will, William James argues that, in voluntary movement, there must be 'passive sensations of movement'. He says: 'We may consequently set it down as certain that, *whether or no there be anything else in the mind at the moment when we consciously will a certain act, a mental conception made up of memory-images of these sensations, defining which special act it is, must be there*' (James, 1890, p. 1104). Wittgenstein, by contrast, points out that there are voluntary actions such as lying for which there are no associated sensations (*LPP*, pp. 75-81). He says that there is nothing 'inner' which distinguishes the voluntary from the involuntary, but that the voluntariness of an action is determined by its character and surroundings (*Z* §§577, 587). For useful discussion of Wittgenstein on the will, see Scott (1996).

39. Wittgenstein indicates that there are grave difficulties with the supposition that a language-learner can introspect a sensation and invent a name for it. He says that 'the whole business of "christening the sensation" is all off' (*LSD* in *PO*, p. 332). The point also emerges in *PI* §§257-63 (McGinn, 1997, pp. 132-41. McGinn regards this interpretation of that passage as in competition with an interpretation which sees Wittgenstein as insisting that there must be outward (visible, behavioural) criteria for the application of psychological concepts. But Wittgenstein's criticism of the traditional distinction between 'inner' and 'outer' is multi-pronged, and *both* of these considerations are present in this passage. Sections 243-315 of the *Philosophical Investigations* are commonly referred to as 'the private language argument' though, as David Stern has noted, Wittgenstein himself never uses this phrase (Stern, 1994, p. 29, n. 100). There is not just one argument here, but an amalgam of complementary considerations. *NPL*, written for a general audience, is a more straightforward, didactic presentation of several features of the discussion.

40. Toothache was Wittgenstein's own favourite illustrative example. It is treated extensively in MS 108, beginning with an entry dated 14 December 1929. Hanfling reports that Wittgenstein's class at Cambridge, after his return there in 1930, became known as 'the toothache club' (Hanfling, 1989, p. 95).

41. W.V. Quine gives his name to this verb by dint of the sparseness of his ontology. One might contrast Wittgenstein's position with that of Georges Rey who too opposes the reifying of sensations. Rey gives a functionalist construal of sensations as *judgments* within a language of thought. This is a more radical quining, since it seems to deprive sensations of their particular *feel*, effectively disqualifying them. See Rey (1991). Sextus Empiricus seems to side with Wittgenstein: 'When we investigate whether existing things are such as they appear, we grant that they appear, and what we investigate is not what is apparent but what is said about what is apparent (*Outlines of Scepticism* I.x.19).

42. For an exploration of the difference between a robot that might look as if it is experiencing pain and one that actually does, see Robinson (1992, ch. 4). For more on the difference between Wittgenstein's position and behaviourism, see Hutto (1995).

43. For information on this literature, see Hark (1990, p. 160, n. 2).

44. Hark (1990, p. 166) supplies evidence that Wittgenstein's discussions of seeing-as are primarily aimed at untangling the conceptual knots in the debate between Gestalt psychologists, represented by Köhler, and opponents such as William James and his followers who claimed that aspect change is a matter of the imagination acting on raw, unchanging sensation.

45. This provides a clue to how one might refute the epistemicist solution to the Sorites paradox, such as that defended in Williamson (1994), and points to the interesting idea that, in the Sorites, one doesn't have to judge that one sample looks different from its indistinguishable neighbour; one can judge a given sample to be F, and, in the next instant, judge *that same sample* to be not-F. But that is a story for a different occasion.

46. My translation of '*Die* würde der "Bedeutungsblinde" verlieren'. The Anscombe translation suggests that the meaning-blind *lose* the relation. But one can't lose what one didn't have.

47. This important exclamation mark has been left out of the English version – without it, some readers may not realize that Wittgenstein is using an idiom.

48. 'It is as if the word I understand had a definite slight aroma that corresponds to my understanding of it. As if two familiar words were distinguished for me not merely by their sound or their appearance, but by an atmosphere as well' (*RPP I* §243).

49. The remark 'What we call "understanding a sentence" has, in many cases, a much greater similarity to understanding a musical theme than we might be inclined to think' also occurs at *BB*, p. 167. At MS 180b, p. 6, Wittgenstein writes: 'Why should I say at all what meaning is? Why should I not say: Language, music and much that we call similar to language is meaningful?' Hark (1990, n. 7, p. 164, n. 18, p. 142) draws attention to Spengler who also emphasizes the musical aspects of language and distinguishes 'Ausdruckssprache' and 'Mitteilungssprache' (Spengler, 1923, pp. 693-4), and mentions a similar view in a work by Bühler, whom Wittgenstein knew well (Bühler, 1934, p. 28). At *RPP I*, §888, Wittgenstein writes 'Verbal language contains a strong musical element. (A sigh, the modulation of tone for a question, for an announcement, for longing; all the countless *gestures* in the vocal cadences).'

In his commentary (1996c, p. 330) on *PI* §527 (an earlier version of which occurs at *PG*, §4, p. 41) Hacker lets his pedantic Oxford ear get the better of him when he criticizes Miss Anscombe's translation of 'was das alles heisst' as 'what it's all about' on the grounds that a musical theme, the particular variation in loudness and tempo, isn't *about* anything. Hacker says 'The "semantic" connotations of "about" are out of place here'. But, in ordinary English, the phrase 'what it's all about' in a context like this has no such 'semantic connotations'; it just means 'what's going on'.

50. That this consciousness should not be construed as the introspective monitoring of private, inner states is argued by John Hyman, who draws upon the 'private language' considerations in *PI* (Hyman, 1991, p. 178).

51. For a review of the evidence, see Stoerig (1997). Stoerig discusses another example of the non-conscious processing of visual data: Subjects who have been blinded after an injury but who still have a small population of retinal ganglion cells intact can retain their proper circadian rhythm in harmony with the day and night cycle because, through the mediation of the suprachiasmatic nucleus of the hypothalamus, melatonin secretion is suppressed when bright light is incident on the retina.

52. Philosophers like to engage in 'thought experiments' since one can do these without inhaling formaldehyde and without even dirtying one's hands. Jackson is here simply experimenting with the thought that Mary knows *everything* about vision while, of course, recognizing that no actual scientist will ever have that knowledge. Wittgenstein himself was a fertile source of such

216

experiments. This does not conflict with his insistence that philosophy describe and not theorize. He often finds it instructive to describe fantasy situations in order to create objects of comparison and to break down over-rigid preconceptions.

53. Jackson (1986). Jackson's original presentation of his example about Mary is somewhat flawed, as is noted in Thompson (1995, p. 264). Jackson tells me that he now rejects the 'knowledge argument'. He now thinks that false 'memory' traces are sufficient for someone to know what feeling pain and seeing colour are like. This seems a poor reason for rejecting the argument to which he gave birth. If someone has only black-and-white vision, it is difficult to see what 'memory trace' could inform him what seeing red is like.

54. For elaboration on this point – that the dispositional theory does not account for the phenomenology of colour perception, see McGinn (1996). One might argue against McGinn that from the fact that, when we see a colour, it does not *strike us* as dispositional, it does not follow that colours are not dispositions (Pitson, 1997, pp. 251-3). The dispositional theory of colour, and the associated primary/secondary quality distinction are of no concern to Wittgenstein in *RoC* and seem to have nothing to say about what seeing colour is like. Wittgenstein's phenomenological enquiries have an interest which is quite independent of any such theory.

55. Goethe (1970). For a thorough account of Goethe's critique, see Sepper (1988). Wittgenstein said 'Colours spur us to philosophize. Perhaps that explains Goethe's passion for the theory of colours' (*CV*, p. 66). Some remarkable similarities of outlook and literary style between Goethe and Wittgenstein are described in Rowe (1991).

56. Immediately after the passage from the *Opticks* just cited, Newton continues 'in the rays [colours] are nothing but their dispositions to propagate this or that motion into the sensorium, and in the sensorium they are sensations of those motions under the forms of colours'. So a theory of colour is, for Newton, a theory not of light rays, but of visual sensation.

57. Escher writes: 'I am full of a color problem: a physical property ... of red to appear closer than blue, which manifests itself very strikingly in a shrill and (perhaps) tastelessly colored reproduction of one of my black-and-white woodcuts, which has been clandestinely printed by hippie admirers in California .... This color problem of the suggestion of a third dimension ... will perhaps lend itself for application to a future print' (Loeb, 1982, letter dated 13.7.1969).

4. Mathematics

1. See the 'Family Recollections' by Hermine Wittgenstein (Leitner, 1973, p. 17). For a brief account of Wittgenstein's fascination with machinery, see McGuinness (1988, p. 45).

2. For the story, see Bartley (1973, pp. 70-1).

3. But note the possibility, mentioned in Chapter 1, that Wittgenstein's interest in philosophy may have been awakened even earlier. The influence of *The Principles of Mathematics* on Wittgenstein's early thought is evident in the metaphysical section of the *Tractatus* in which the doctrine of simple Objects is canvassed (2.02-2.0272) – see Ricketts (1996). Anthony Grayling makes the point as strongly as this: 'It is clear ... that one of the first offshoots from Russell's work was Wittgenstein's *Tractatus*' (Grayling, 1996, p. 102). Grayling

Notes to pp. 124-132

also demonstrates the influence on Wittgenstein of Russell's manuscript *Theory of Knowledge* (1913) and his *Our Knowledge of the External World* (1914).

4. For the Russell-Frege correspondence on the paradox, see van Heijenoort (1967, pp. 124-8). Frege himself gives a clear, non-technical exposition of Russell's Paradox at the beginning of Appendix II of his *Grundgesetze der Arithmetik* (1893); see Frege (1964, pp. 127-8).

5. See Frege (1964, pp. 127, 72). In Frege's terminology, the statement 'The morning star is a planet' contains a proper name 'the morning star' (which stands for an object) and the concept-word 'planet' (which stands for a concept). A concept is a constituent of (in Frege's terminology) a 'thought' – what modern writers generally call a 'proposition'. The extension of the concept *planet* is all planets. See Frege (1892; 1918).

6. Here Wittgenstein echoes an objection of Poincaré's: 'Verification [what Wittgenstein would call proof in logic] differs from true demonstration precisely because it is purely analytic and because it is sterile. It is sterile because the conclusion is nothing but the premises translated into another language' (Poincaré, 1902, p. 33). For an able account of Poincaré's critique of logicism, see Detlefsen (1992).

7. Ivor Grattan-Guinness kindly transcribed for me the second half of this extract from Jourdain's manuscript (and I have expanded all Jourdain's contractions). The first half appears in Grattan-Guinness (1977, p. 114).

8. For a discussion of this solution, see Goldstein (1983).

9. Notice how inappropriate it is to classify Wittgenstein, as some do, as an 'ordinary language' philosopher: Whereas for that paradigmatic 'ordinary language' philosopher J.L. Austin, the foot of the letter is often the foot of the ladder, for Wittgenstein the foot of the letter is often to be found up to its ankle in mud.

10. For an excellent account of how the various major isms, such as logicism, intuitionism and formalism respond to Kant's *Problematik*, see Detlefsen (1996).

11. Well, you might want to say that the infant who refuses to crawl off the edge of a high table is already doing geometry but, if you go that route, you may soon find yourself attributing advanced mathematical knowledge to cats and dogs.

12. For a sophisticated modern defence of Platonism in mathematics, see Katz (1981, pp. 192-216). The Platonist, says Katz, 'explains the necessity in logic, mathematics and grammar on the grounds that the statements in these subjects are about abstract objects' (pp. 185-6).

13. See Brouwer (1975), especially the essay 'Intuitionism and Formalism' in Volume I.

14. I doubt whether Wittgenstein would much appreciate our careful positioning of his view with respect to intuitionism, for, in his typically measured and judicious style, he says that intuitionism is 'all bosh – entirely' (*LFM*, p. 237). He ventures a similar opinion on finitism and behaviourism (*LFM*, p. 111).

15. That this (standard) interpretation of Frege is wrong is argued by Joan Weiner (1991).

16. The editors of *PG* note that, according to C. Lewy (1967, p. 422), Wittgenstein wrote this (probably in 1923) in the margin of Ramsey's copy of the *Tractatus* at 6.02 (see *PG*, p. 296, n.1). This is in stark contrast to what Wittgenstein is saying at this point of *PG*, namely: 'Number is not at all a "fundamental mathematical concept". There are so many calculations in which numbers aren't mentioned.'

17. At *Tractatus* 4.126, Wittgenstein says that we can talk about formal concepts in the same sense that we speak of formal properties, and I have followed his characterization of formal properties at *Tractatus* 4.123.

18. N is the operation of 'joint denial'. Applying this operation to a set of propositions $p_1, p_2, \ldots p_n$ delivers a new proposition which is true if and only if all the p_i are false; otherwise it is false. For a thorough discussion of N, see Fogelin (1987, 54-85).

19. The ancient Greeks' way of representing numbers as arrangements of dots led to the Pythagoreans' earliest discoveries about the 'geometrical' properties of numbers.

20. For further arguments against Quine's position, see Field (1980, especially ch. 1.)

21. See also *PG*, p. 321.

22. Although he criticizes Formalism, it is only a caricature of that view which Wittgenstein addresses – the view that mathematics is about strokes of ink on paper (*WVC*, pp. 103-5). He says, 'to this I reply that it is so in just the sense in which chess is about wooden figures. For chess does not consist in pushing wooden figures ….' Obviously mathematics is no more about ink strokes than chess is about bits of wood. A *piece* in chess (which may be *made* of wood, plastic etc.) is identified not by the material from which it is made, but by the rules of the game, to which it is subject. 'The rules that hold of those structures … are what interests me about those structures' (*WVC*, p. 105). Now, as Frascolla has pointed out (1994, p. 55), exactly this analogy with chess was used by J. Thomae to *characterize* Formalism, in a passage, quoted by Frege, which was very likely known to Wittgenstein. If it was, then Wittgenstein, in persisting with the 'bits of wood' caricature, is here perpetrating a very cynical example of the Straw Man fallacy.

23. See Baker and Hacker (1985, p. 303) in which is cited a condemnation of negatives by Hamilton in 1837 and, from the pen of the great mathematician Blaise Pascal: 'I have known those who could not understand that to take four from zero there remains zero.'

24. The classical modern defence of this view is Kripke (1980) which includes a lively discussion of gold and tigers at pp. 116-21. For a Wittgensteinian critique of this view, see Chan (1997).

25. For a good explanation of this Tractarian position, see Frascolla (1994, pp. 21-2).

26. This classic theorem was proved many years after Wittgenstein's death. See Wiles (1995); Taylor and Wiles (1995).

27. Crispin Wright stresses the closeness of the connection between Wittgenstein's notion that proof involves concept-modification and his characterization of mathematics as invention rather than discovery. See Wright (1980, ch. 3).

28. For an interesting discussion of the Appel-Haken solution of the four-colour problem in relation to Wittgenstein's claim that a mathematical proof must be 'surveyable', see Shanker (1987, pp. 130-60).

29. Grelling's paradox is built around the predicate 'heterological'. A predicate is said to be heterological if it is not true of itself. Thus the predicate 'long' is heterological because it is not true that the word 'long' is long (in fact 'long' is a rather short word). Now ask whether the predicate 'heterological' is true or is not true of itself, i.e. whether the predicate 'heterological' is or is not heterologi-

cal. If the predicate 'heterological' *is* heterological, then it is true of itself – which means it is *not* heterological. But if it is *not* heterological, then it is one of those predicates which are not true of themselves, i.e., one of the predicates which *are* heterological!

30. Goldstein (1983) deals mainly with Wittgenstein's discussion of Russell's paradox. Wittgenstein's approach to the Liar and Moore's Paradox is the subject of Goldstein (1988) and this approach is extended so as to solve both the Paradox of the Surprise Examination and Kavka's Toxin Puzzle in Goldstein (1993).

31. Dialetheism has been defended most prominently in recent times by Graham Priest – see his (1987) and (1995). It is a difficult doctrine to attack because, if you prove to the dialetheist that the position leads to contradiction, he or she may cheerfully admit that it does, but point out that you can't draw any bad conclusions about dialetheism from that without begging the question at issue. Nevertheless, I have tried (1992a).

32. Monk speculates that Turing stopped attending Wittgenstein's 1939 lectures on the foundations of mathematics because he became 'convinced ... that if Wittgenstein would not admit a contradiction to be a fatal flaw in a system of mathematics, then there could be no common ground between them' (Monk, 1990, pp. 421-2).

33. That sense or *directionality* is essential to Sätze was a claim that Wittgenstein developed early (August 1913 or before) and one to which he attached great importance. See McGuinness (1972, p. 452).

34. This point is rediscovered and discussed in Lowe (1985).

35. In Lazerowitz (1937), the author argues that 'true' and 'false' must have deviant senses when applied to tautologies and contradictions, but he takes this to be an argument *against* Wittgenstein's position!

36. A similar claim is made about the logical insulation of mathematical Sätze from non-mathematical ones at *T* 6.211.

37. The principle of *reductio ad absurdum* also raises an apparent problem for the insulation doctrine, since the use of this principle seems to involve the derivation of a contradiction from contingent assumptions. Wittgenstein, however, denies that this is a correct description of the *reductio* method (*WVC*, pp. 179-81, 207-8).

38. W.D. Hart (1968, p. 25) comments that here language is disguising thought. This is, of course, a whimsical reference to *T* 4.002.

39. In a later work, Wittgenstein still has no problem with the idea that contradictions can occur in a calculus, but he does suggest that, where this happens, we should *not* accept as a rule of such a calculus *ex contradictione quodlibet* for 'if we allow contradictions in such a way that *anything* follows, then we would no longer get a calculus, or we'd get a useless thing resembling a calculus' (*LFM*, p. 243).

40. But what if there is a contradiction in the rules which has not yet been discovered? Wittgenstein says that such talk of hidden contradiction does not make sense, 'and the danger mathematicians talk about – as if a contradiction could be hidden in present-day mathematics like a disease – this danger is a mere figment of the imagination' (*WVC*, p. 174). The idea that where there is no procedure for discovering a contradiction then it is nonsense to say that a contradiction is there (*WVC*, pp. 120, 195-6) rests on a Principle of Verification with which Wittgenstein flirted during his transitional period, when the influence of Intuitionism on him was at its strongest. (In later years, he denied ever having espoused Verificationism (Gasking and Jackson, 1967, p. 54) and, as we have seen, declared Intuitionism 'all bosh'.)

41. At *T* 3.3 he does say 'Only statements have sense; only in the nexus of a statement does a name have meaning' but this probably means just that a name does not have any meaning outside the context of a statement, not that what meaning a name has depends on which statement it is embedded in.

42. *PI* §288; see also the example with colour words at *RFM* §§VI-28, 35.

5. Wittgenstein the Man

1. A highly readable long one is Monk (1990), and another, with less dash, but more detail, covering the first half of Wittgenstein's life is McGuinness (1988). Both are excellent. For short, I recommend Malcolm (1958); shorter (and sharper), Grayling (1988, pp. 1-11). The theme of Scharfstein (1980) is that childhood experiences may shape the content of a philosopher's writings. He discusses Wittgenstein at pp. 318-34.

2. For discussion in which the characterization of this approach emerged, I'm grateful to Anita Noguera. Mandy Rice-Davies made this remark in the course of giving evidence in the famous 1963 trial in Britain of Dr. Stephen Ward, a society osteopath who had rented his apartment to a beautiful prostitute, Christine Keeler, who was servicing both Captain Ivanov – a Russian diplomat – and John Profumo, the British Minister for War, with the attendant risk of compromising national security.

3. Monk (1990, p. xviii). Peter Winch too claims that 'we can sense in [Wittgenstein's philosophical works] a spiritual dimension seldom met in the works of "professional philosophers" ' (Malcolm, 1993, p. 129). See also Szabados (1995).

4. Wittgenstein's perfectionism and his fanatical attention to detail when working as an architect/engineer on the construction of his sister Gretl's house are legendary. He drove at least one of the workers to tears. His sister Hermine recollects: 'Perhaps the most telling proof of Ludwig's restlessness when it came to getting the proportions exactly right is the fact that he had the ceiling of one of the rooms, which was almost big enough to be a hall, raised by three centimetres, just when it was almost time to start cleaning the complete house' (Rhees, 1984, p. 8). Wittgenstein says that good architecture 'makes one want to respond with a gesture' (*CV*, p. 22). One can guess with what kind of gesture his workers would have wanted to respond to him. For more on Wittgenstein as architect, see Leitner (1973) and Monk (1990, pp. 235-8).

5. Such, anyway, was the opinion of Frank Ramsey, one of Wittgenstein's closest friends in the 1920s. See a letter of his to John Maynard Keynes, dated 24.3.24 (Nedo and Ranchetti, 1983, p. 191).

6. In an early draft found among his papers, Wittgenstein records thoughts of suicide at the age of 10 or 11. For more on his suicidal tendencies, see McGuinness (1988, pp. 48-50).

7. As Monk tells us: 'For both Rowland Hutt and Fania Pascal, listening to the [Wittgenstein] confession was an uncomfortable experience. In Hutt's case, the discomfort was simply embarrassment at having to sit in a Lyons cafe while opposite him sat Wittgenstein reciting his sins in a loud and clear voice. Fania Pascal, on the other hand, was exasperated by the whole thing. Wittgenstein had phoned at an inconvenient moment to ask whether he could come and see her. When she asked if it was urgent she was told firmly that it was, and could

not wait. 'If ever a thing could wait,' she thought, facing him across the table, 'it is a confession of this kind and made in this manner.' The stiff and remote way in which he delivered his confession made it impossible for her to react with sympathy. At one point she cried out: 'What is it? You want to be perfect ?' 'Of course I want to be perfect', he thundered (Monk, 1990, pp. 368-9). For Pascal's account of Wittgenstein's confession, see Rhees (1984, pp. 34-9). As she tells it, Wittgenstein did not 'thunder'; he 'pulled himself up proudly'.

8. Cited in McGuinness (1988, p. 52). Wittgenstein referred to his classmates as 'Mist', which McGuinness translates as 'What a shower'. This is undoutedly not sufficiently strong. The word means 'muck'. (Rolls Royce once planned to introduce a new marque with the name 'Silver Mist' until they learned that this was unlikely to encourage sales in Germany. 'Silver Shower' would, by contrast, be a fine name for a Rolls.)

9. Hitler has only got one ball,
Rommel's got two, but very small,
Mussolini, his two are teeny
And Dr. Goebbels has no balls at all.

10. Not wishing to be accused of sensationalism, I'll confine to an inconspicuous footnote Zemach's conjecture that what Wittgenstein confessed to was a homosexual sado-masochistic relationship with Hitler. We have the masochistic, self-loathing Wittgenstein who, according to Bartley (1973, p. 40) was later to roam the seedy Prater district of Vienna in search of rough, blunt homosexual youths, and the domineering, sadistic Hitler – who was not homosexual, though, as Zemach says, 'Wittgenstein's preferences would have suited him to a tee.'

11. It is not just the references to stammering and to Jews who disguise themselves as 'pure' Germans. Hitler talks of Jewish women marrying into Christian nobility (Hitler, 1969, p. 286). It was Princess Wittgenstein, to whom many thought Ludwig was related, who was the mistress of Franz Liszt, and Liszt's illegitimate daughter Cosima married none other than the musical Nazi Richard Wagner. So, as Cornish puts it, 'a "Wittgenstein" had an adulterous affair with the father of the wife of the man whom Hitler admired most for his Teutonic blood purity' (Cornish, 1997, p. 24). Further, after the *Anschluss*, Hitler singled out the *Neue Freie Presse* from the Jewish-owned newspapers and closed it down. Wittgenstein's father Karl was a contributor to the *Neue Freie Presse* and in 1901 published an article mooting the abolition of tariffs on imports, a move that could have had the effect of depriving some customs officials (such as Alois, Hitler's father) of their livelihood.

12. See von Wright (1990, p. 5), Pinsent's diary entry for Friday, 31 May 1912. Here Pinsent records that he has known Wittgenstein 'only for three weeks or so', but von Wright, in his Foreword (p. vii) suggests that they may have first met on 1 February, since Pinsent does mention having then met 'a young German attending Russell's lectures'. Von Wright may not have been aware that there were *two* Germans attending those lectures (Russell, 1992, p. 400, letter to Lucy Donnelly, 28.10.11).

13. Brilliant thinkers with whom Wittgenstein came in contact were swift to recognize his genius. For example, Russell describes him as 'perhaps the most perfect example I have ever known of genius as traditionally conceived, passionate, profound, intense and dominating' (Russell, 1975, p. 329); the philosopher-economist F.P. Ramsey wrote: 'He is great. I used to think Moore a great man but beside W!' (letter to his mother, 20.9.1923; (Monk, 1990, p. 217)).

Norman Malcolm, describing a session in 1939 at which Moore presented a paper and Wittgenstein spent at least two hours talking almost continuously, attacking Moore's position, writes: 'Wittgenstein's brilliance and power were impressive and even frightening' (Malcolm, 1958, p. 33).

14. Wittgenstein confides to his diary 'very sensual' thoughts about Pinsent (13.3.15; Monk, 1990, p. 127). He discussed frankly all manner of intimate subjects with his close friend Paul Engelmann – despair, suicide, religion etc. – but, writing after Wittgenstein's death, Engelmann explains that he can say nothing about Wittgenstein's sexuality since he and Wittgenstein 'did not discuss such things' (McGuinness, 1988, p. 292; Monk, 1990, p. 185). Writing of a later homosexual partner, Francis Skinner, Wittgenstein tells his diary of 1938 about his sensual desires, but this time is worried that these might be incompatible with love. It is probable that Pinsent was his first and only true love.

15. He got so far as taking her to Norway in 1931, as part of a spiritual preparation for marriage, and put her in Anna Rebni's farmhouse in Skjolden so that, in isolation, she might read the Bible and devote herself to reflecting on the nature of virtue and love. It soon became clear to Marguerite that what she expected of marriage was rather different from what he expected and, after two weeks, she left, determined, as Monk puts it 'that the one man she was *not* going to marry was Ludwig Wittgenstein' (Monk, 1990, pp. 238-40, 317-19).

16. For an attempt to see what Wittgenstein saw in Weininger, see Stern (1996).

17. Letters to Lady Ottoline Morrell, dated 1.6.12 and 18.3.12 respectively (Russell, 1992, pp. 432, 419).

18. In a letter to Lucy Donnelly, 19.10.1913, Russell writes: 'Now Wittgenstein, during August and September, had done work on logic, still rather in the rough, but as good, in my opinion, as any work that ever had been done in logic by anyone' (McGuinness, 1988, p. 184).

19. In a Letter to Moore, Wittgenstein drew a sketch of the location of his hut. See *LRKM*, p. 166.

20. And yet, sickeningly enough, Wittgenstein was prepared, in 1939, to connive at transferring a great deal of the family fortune into the Reichsbank in exchange for the Nazis' decreeing his sisters Hermine and Helene to be Aryan and allowing them to stay in Austria. See Monk (1990, pp. 399-400).

21. At the battlefront, to which he was posted at the end of March 1916, Wittgenstein volunteered to be stationed in the most dangerous position, the observation post, where he was often under enemy fire. He sought spiritual comfort both in God and in his own meditations. We saw, in Chapter 3, some examples of his Buddhistic wartime reflections. Compare his talk of 'one spirit common to the whole world' with the testimony of two of the political prisoners who suffered frequent horrendous torture at the Bago Bantay Detention Centre in Manila under the regime of Ferdinand Marcos. These prisoners were regularly visited by Sister Elaine MacInnes who taught them Zen meditation: 'I don't get obstructed by prison walls any more, nor am I anxious about how our case will eventually be settled. Through my prison window, I can see oneness pervades the whole universe and I am in my perfect place, moving along the way' (Boy Morales); 'The bars and stone walls do not really separate me from my loved ones, from my friends, from my people and from everything and everybody in the universe. In reality, I and the universe are one' (Marcello) (Middleton, 1997).

223

22. That Wittgenstein found Nietzsche's work stimulating is probably due to the fact that Nietzsche's outlook was in sharp contrast to the Tolstoyan Christian attitude that he had then made his own. See Monk (1990, pp. 121-3).

23. For the full list see McGuinness (1990, p. 207). McGuinness' ch. 7 (pp. 204-66) is a fine, detailed acount of Wittgenstein's war (against the enemy and himself).

24. Reports of those who stayed with him, or with whom he stayed (including Ramsey, Maurice Drury and Norman Malcolm) attest to the extreme frugality of his diet. He seemed to regard taking pleasure in eating as rather sinful. There are also many accounts of his generosity. For performing his miracle cure on the steam engine at Trattenbach he was rewarded with some linen. He gave this to some of the poorer children in the school.

25. I have heard Richard Hare remark that the Oxford of his day was a free port for ideas. Academics nowadays, under heavy pressure to publish and to make names for themselves, might see a failure to acknowledge intellectual debts as simply dishonest and cheap. Which it is. Yet people feel quite relaxed about retelling, without acknowledging a source, *jokes* that are not their own. So perhaps we should not be too hasty to accuse Wittgenstein of plagiarism – perhaps in his time, or in his mind, philosophy was not regarded as private property, but as ideas to be shared and enjoyed.

26. See Monk (1990, p. 184). The first premise of this 'unanswerable' argument is a tautology, something which, according to strict *Tractatus* doctrine, is senseless!

27. For example, at *RPP I* §903ff. (also *Z* §605ff.), Wittgenstein writes: 'No supposition seems to me more natural than that there is no process in the brain correlated with associating or with thinking ....' Numerous commentators have read this as an attack on physicalism, ascribing to Wittgenstein the position that 'one's nervous system could be just any way' (McGinn, 1984, p. 115), or that our thinking could take place without a brain. But in fact here Wittgenstein is attacking a specific psychophysiological hypothesis – the electric brain fields theory of Wolfgang Köhler (1938) which posits an isomorphism between psychological facts and macroscopic physiological states. See Hark (1995).

28. Skinner had taken a first class degree in mathematics at Cambridge but, on Wittgenstein's advice, abandoned academia and went to work as an apprentice factory mechanic, making screws. Wittgenstein then became infatuated with Keith Kirk, a man who worked at the same factory. Kirk was totally uninfatuated, but he was preparing for some examinations, and derived great benefit from the coaching, Socratic style, that Wittgenstein gave him. Finally, there was Ben Richards, a medical student some forty years younger than Wittgenstein about whose love Wittgenstein appears to have felt insecure.

29. See Hilmy (1987). Also Cooper (1997) on Heidegger, who shared Wittgenstein's loathing of the hegemony of science and the (alleged) consequent depreciation of wonder. Whether such an attitude is justified or paranoid would take a long time to discuss.

30. From a conversation with Maurice Drury (Rhees, 1984, p. 160). Interpreting this remark is the project of Malcolm (1993), a book which contains a response to the author by Peter Winch. Winch, it seems to me, comes much closer to seeing what Wittgenstein was getting at than does Malcolm.

31. '... I cannot imagine that Carnap should have so completely misunderstood the last propositions of the *Tractatus* – and hence the fundamental idea of the whole book' (Letter to Schlick, dated 8.8.32, in Nedo and Ranchetti, 1983,

p. 255). Who can blame Carnap? In the *Tractatus* itself, Wittgenstein himself says that the fundamental idea (Grundgedanke) of the book is that logical constants don't represent (*T* 4.0312).

32. In *Philosophical Investigations* §77, Wittgenstein makes the additional claim that, if we attend to the examples we were given when we were learning the meaning of the word 'good', to the different language-games in which the word featured, then we shall see that the word must have a family of meanings. Hence it would be futile to seek a *definition* of 'good'.

33. S. Sheffler, review of Bernard Williams' *Shame and Necessity* (Sheffler, 1996). Williams also discusses the thick/thin contrast in Williams (1995, p. 233ff.)

34. Midgley (1997). On the crudeness of basing our moral thinking about animals on their 'rights', see also Sorabji (1993). Midgley concludes her article by considering fox hunting and the question of whether such sport is tolerable. She notes that 'Charles Darwin, a passionate shooter of birds in his youth, thought not. When he grasped this point, he gave up shooting. There are always other sports to turn to.' That's how it might seem to nice Mary Midgley. The real problem, unfortunately, is that most such 'sportsmen', blinded by the lust for blood, will never grasp the point.

35. For example, in his excellent *Shame and Necessity*, Williams examines the morality of ancient Greece. He regards the aim of this book as 'a philosophical description of an historical reality' (Williams, 1994, p. 4), and he draws more on poets and the great tragedians of the fifth century BC than on Greek philosophers. There is good reason for so doing. One of Williams' themes is that perfectly clear notions of *action*, *deliberation*, and *akrasia* present in the early dramas later got distorted by poor psychologistic philosophy (see e.g., pp. 38-49). This, of course, echoes Wittgenstein's account of the genesis of our intellectual muddles.

36. Wittgenstein, in a conversation with Bouwsma in 1949, dismisses the possibility of someone, reflecting on what he ought to do, being guided by identifying 'the good'. Even if a definition of good were possible (and Wittgenstein, of course, thinks that the most one can do is describe certain aspects of the uses of the word 'good') what use could one make of such a definition? (Bouwsma, 1986, pp. 40-1). Has your own conduct ever been altered as a result of identifying or fixing on a definition of 'good'? Could it?

37. *CV*, p. 57. Roland Hall, in a message to the electronic list PHILOS-L, recounts how Wittgenstein fell out with Ryle on the question of whether there could *be* a decent English film.

38. This kind of criticism is pursued in Wilkes (1988).

39. Monk (1990, p. 44). Monk also reports Wittgenstein saying to Heinrich Postl, a coalminer whom he met during his schoolmastering days at Puchberg, 'Just improve yourself; that is the only thing you *can* do to better the world.'

Bibliography

Achinstein, P., 'What is an explanation?' *American Philosophical Quarterly* 14 (1977) 1-15.

Albritton, R., 'Comments on "Moore's Paradox and Self-Knowledge" ', *Philosophical Studies* 77 (1995) 229-39.

Ambrose, A., 'Ludwig Wittgenstein: a portrait', in A. Ambrose & M. Lazerowitz (eds) *Ludwig Wittgenstein: Philosophy and Language* (George Allen & Unwin Ltd., 1972) 13-25.

Anscombe, G.E.M., 'Review of S. Kripke, *Wittgenstein on Rules and Private Language*', *Ethics* 95 (1985) 342-52.

Aquila, R.E., *Representational Mind: A Study of Kant's Theory of Knowledge* (Indiana University Press, 1983).

Augustine, Saint, Bishop of Hippo, *Confessions* trans. H. Chadwick (Oxford University Press, 1991). Composed 397-400 AD.

Austin, J.L., 'The meaning of a word', in his *Philosophical Papers* (Clarendon Press, 1961) 23-43.

Austin, J.L., 'Truth', *Proceedings of the Aristotelian Society* supp. vol. 24 (1950) 111-28, reprinted in G. Pitcher (ed.) *Truth* (Prentice Hall, 1964) 18-31.

Austin, J.L., *How to do Things with Words* (2nd ed.) (Oxford University Press, 1975).

Bach, K., 'On communicative intentions: a reply to Recanati', *Mind and Language* 2 (1987) 141-54.

Baker, G.P. & Hacker, P.M.S., *An Analytical Commentary on Wittgenstein's Philosophical Investigations, Vol. 1* (Blackwell, 1983a).

Baker, G.P. & Hacker, P.M.S., *Wittgenstein: Meaning and Understanding* (Blackwell, 1983b).

Baker, G.P. & Hacker, P.M.S., *Scepticism, Rules and Language* (Blackwell, 1984)

Baker, G.P. & Hacker, P.M.S., *Wittgenstein: Rules, Grammar and Necessity (An Analytical Commentary on Wittgenstein's Philosophical Investigations*, Vol. 2) (Blackwell, 1985).

Balzano, G. & McCabe, V., 'An ecological perspective on concepts and cognition', in V. McCabe & G. Balzano (eds) *Event Cognition: An Ecological Perspective* (Lawrence Erlbaum, 1986) 93-112.

Barrett, C., *Wittgenstein on Ethics and Religious Belief* (Blackwell, 1991).

Bartley, W.W. III, *Wittgenstein* (J.B. Lippincott Company, 1973).

Bates, E., Camaioni, L. & Volterra, V., 'The acquisition of performatives prior to speech', in E. Ochs & B.B. Schieffelin (eds) *Developmental Pragmatics* (Academic Press, 1979).

Bechtel, W. & Abrahamsen, A., *Connectionism and the Mind* (Blackwell, 1991).

Bell, D. & Cooper, N. (eds) *The Analytic Tradition* (Blackwell, 1990).

Benacerraf, P., 'What numbers could not be', *Philosophical Review* 74 (1965), reprinted in P. Benacerraf & H. Putnam (eds) *Philosophy of Mathematics* (2nd ed.) 272-94.

Bermudez, J., Marcel, A. & Eilan, N. (eds) *The Body and the Self* (M.I.T. Press, 1995).

Biggs, M. & Pichler, A., *Wittgenstein: Two Source Catalogues and a Bibliography* (Wittgenstein Archives at the University of Bergen, 1993).

Bouwsma, O.K., *Wittgenstein Conversations 1949-1951* (Hackett, 1986).

Brouwer, L.E.J., *Collected Works, Vol. 1* (North-Holland, 1975).

Bibliography

Brown, D., 'A furry tile about mental representation', *Philosophical Quarterly* 46 (1996a) 448-66.

Brown, D., 'The puzzle of names in Ockham's theory of mental language', *Review of Metaphysics* 50 (1996b) 79-99.

Bruner, J., *Child's Talk: Learning to Use Language* (W.W. Norton and Co., 1983).

Bühler, K., *Sprachtheorie* (Gustav Fischer, 1934).

Candlish, S., 'Wittgenstein and the doctrine of kinaesthesis', *Australasian Journal of Philosophy* 74 (1996) 581-97.

Canfield, J.V. (ed.) *The Philosophy of Wittgenstein* (Garland Publishing Inc., 1986).

Canfield, J.V., 'The community view', *Philosophical Review* 105 (1996) 469-88.

Carey, S., 'The origin and evolution of everyday concepts', in Giere, R.N. (ed.) *Cognitive Models of Science* (University of Minnesota Press, 1992) 89-128.

Carroll, L., 'What the tortoise said to Achilles', *Mind* 4 (1895) 278-80.

Cassam, Q. (ed.) *Self-Knowledge* (Oxford University Press, 1994)

Chan, K.Y., *A Critique of Kripke's Theories of Names and Necessity – An Application of Wittgenstein's Later Methodology* (unpublished Ph.D. thesis, University of Hong Kong, 1997).

Choi, S. & Bowerman, M., 'Learning to express motion events in English and Korean: the influence of language-specific lexicalization patterns', *Cognition* 41 (1991) 83-121.

Churchland, P., *Neurophilosophy: Toward a Unified Science of the Mind / Brain* (M.I.T. Press, 1986).

Clare, G., 'Last waltz in Vienna: a postscript', in I. Oxaal, M. Pollack & G. Botz (eds) *Jews, Antisemitism and Culture in Vienna* (Routledge & Kegan Paul, 1987) 234-40.

Clark, A., *Microcognition, Philosophy, Cognitive Science and Parallel Distributed Processing* (M.I.T. Press, 1989).

Clark, A., *Associative Engines: Connectionism, Concepts and Representational Change* (M.I.T. Press, 1993a).

Clark, A., 'Minimal rationalism', *Mind* 102 (1993b) 587-610.

Clark, A., *Being There* (M.I.T. Press, 1997).

Clark, E., 'Meanings and concepts', in P.H. Mussen (ed.) *Handbook of Child Psychology, Vol. III. Cognitive Development* (John Wiley & Sons, 1983) 787-840.

Clark, E., 'On the pragmatics of contrast', *Journal of Child Language* 17 (1990) 417-31.

Clark, E. & Carpenter, K.L., 'The notion of source in language acquisition', *Language* 65 (1989) 1-30.

Cohen, L.J., *Belief and Acceptance* (Clarendon Press, 1993).

Cook, J., *Wittgenstein's Metaphysics* (Cambridge University Press, 1994).

Cooper, D.E., 'Wittgenstein, Heidegger and humility', *Philosophy* 72 (1997) 105-23.

Cornish, K., *The Jew of Linz* (Century/Random House, 1997).

Corson, D., *The Lexical Bar* (Pergamon, 1985).

Crane, T., 'The language of thought: no syntax without semantics', *Mind and Language* 5 (1990) 187-212.

Crimmins, M., 'I falsely believe that p', *Analysis* 52 (1992) 191.

Davidson, D., 'Thought and talk', in S. Guttenplan (ed.) *Mind and Language* (Oxford University Press, 1975) 7-23; reprinted in Davidson, 1984, 155-70.

Davidson, D., 'Rational animals', *Dialectica* 36 (1982) 317-27.

Davidson, D., *Inquiries into Truth and Interpretation* (Oxford University Press, 1984).

Davidson, D., 'Knowing one's own mind', *Proceedings and Addresses of the American Philosophical Association* 60 (1987) 441-58; reprinted in Cassam, 1994, 43-64.

Davidson, D., 'The second person', in P. French, T.E. Uehling & H.K. Wettstein (eds) *Midwest Studies in Philosophy, vol. 17* (Notre Dame University Press, 1992) 255-67.

De Boysson-Bardies, B. & Vihman, M., 'Adaptation to language: evidence from babbling and first words', *Language* 67 (1991) 297-319.

Dennett, D., *Brainstorms* (Harvester Press, 1979).

Dennett, D., *Darwin's Dangerous Idea* (Penguin, 1995).

Descartes, R., *Philosophical Writings of Descartes, Vol. 1*, trans. J. Cottingham, R. Stoothof & D. Murdoch (Cambridge University Press, 1984).

Bibliography

Detlefsen, M., 'Poincaré against the Logicians', *Synthese* 90 (1992) 349-78.

Detlefsen, M., 'Philosophy of mathematics in the twentieth century' in S. Shanker (ed.) *Philosophy of Science, Logic and Mathematics in the Twentieth Century* (Routledge, 1996) 50-123.

Donaldson, M., *Children's Minds* (W.W. Norton & Co., 1978).

Douglas, G., 'Why pains are not mental objects', *Philosophical Studies* 91 (1998) 127-48.

Dretske, F., 'Absent qualia', *Mind and Language* 11 (1996) 78-85.

Drury, M.O'C., 'Conversations with Wittgenstein' in Rhees, 1984.

Dummett, M.A.E., 'Frege and Wittgenstein', in I. Block (ed.) *Perspectives on the Philosophy of Wittgenstein* (Blackwell, 1981) 31-42.

Dummett, M.A.E., *Frege: Philosophy of Mathematics* (Duckworth, 1991).

Dummett, M.A.E., *Origins of Analytical Philosophy* (Duckworth, 1993).

Eagleton, T., *Wittgenstein, The Terry Eagleton Script, The Derek Jarman Film* (British Film Institute, 1993).

Eldridge, R., *Leading a Human Life: Wittgenstein, Intentionality and Romanticism* (University of Chicago Press, 1997).

Ellenbogen, S., 'On the link between Frege's Platonic-Realist semantics and his doctrine of private senses', *Philosophy* 72 (1997) 375-82.

Elman, J., 'Language as a dynamical system' in R. Port & T. van Gelder (eds) *Mind as Motion: Explorations in the Dynamics of Cognition* (M.I.T. Press, 1995) 195-225.

Engelmann, P., *Letters from Ludwig Wittgenstein. With a Memoir* (Blackwell, 1967).

Fann, K.T., *Ludwig Wittgenstein: The Man and his Philosophy* (Humanities Press, 1978).

Farb, P., *Word Play* (Knopf, 1975).

Fest, J., *Hitler*, English translation by R. Winston & C. Winston (Penguin, 1982).

Field, H., *Science Without Numbers* (Blackwell, 1980).

Fodor, J.A., *The Language of Thought* (Harvard University Press, 1975).

Fodor, J.A., *The Elm and the Expert: Mentalese and its Semantics* (M.I.T. Press, 1994).

Fogelin, R., *Wittgenstein* (2nd ed.) (Routledge & Kegan Paul, 1987).

Fogelin, R., 'Wittgenstein's critique of philosophy' in Sluga & Stern, 1996, 34-58.

Foley, R., 'Is it possible to have contradictory beliefs?', *Midwest Studies in Philosophy* 10 (1986) 327-55.

Frascolla, P., *Wittgenstein's Philosophy of Mathematics* (Routledge, 1994).

Frege, G., 'Function and concept' (1891), reprinted in Geach & Black, 1952, 21-41.

Frege, G., 'On concept and object' (1892), reprinted in Geach & Black, 1952, 42-55.

Frege, G., 'The thought: a logical inquiry' (1918), reprinted in Strawson (1967).

Frege, G., *The Foundations of Arithmetic* (2nd ed.) trans. J.L. Austin (Blackwell, 1959). Composed in 1884.

Frege, G., *The Basic Laws of Arithmetic*, ed. M. Furth (University of California Press, 1964). Composed in 1893.

Frege, G., *Posthumous Writings*, ed. H. Hermes, F. Kambartel & F. Kaulbach (Blackwell, 1979).

Frongia, G. & McGuinness, B.F., *Wittgenstein: A Bibliographical Guide* (Blackwell, 1990).

Gaifman, H., 'Pointers to truth', *Journal of Philosophy* 89 (1992) 223-61.

Galligan, R., 'Intonation with single words: purposive and grammatical use', *Journal of Child Language* 14 (1987) 1-21.

Gardies, J-L., *Esquisse d'une grammaire pure* (Vrin, 1975).

Garver, N., *This Complicated Form of Life* (Open Court, 1994).

Garver, N., 'Philosophy as grammar', in Sluga & Stern, 1996, 139-70.

Gasking, D.A.T. & Jackson A.C., 'Wittgenstein as teacher', in K.T. Fann (ed.) *Ludwig Wittgenstein: The Man and his Philosophy* (Dell Publishing Company, 1967) 49-55.

Gay, P., *Freud for Historians* (1985).

Geach, P.T. & Black, M., *Translations from the Philosophical Writings of Gottlob Frege* (Blackwell, 1952).

Geach, P.T., 'Assertion', reprinted in his *Logic Matters* (Blackwell, 1972) 254-69.

Geach, P.T., 'Saying and showing in Frege and Wittgenstein', *Acta Philosophica Fennica* 28 (1976) 54-70.

Bibliography

Geach, P.T., 'Kinds of statement' in C. Diamond & J. Teichmann (eds) *Intention and Intentionality* (Cornell University Press, 1979) 221-35.

Goddard, L. & Judge, B., *The Metaphysics of Wittgenstein's 'Tractatus'* (Australasian Philosophical Association, 1982).

Goethe, J.W., *Theory of Colours*, trans. Charles Lock (M.I.T. Press, 1970). First published in 1840.

Goldfarb, W., 'I want you to bring me a slab. Remarks on the opening sections of the "Philosophical Investigations" ', *Synthese* 56 (1983) 265-82.

Goldstein, L., 'Wittgenstein and the logico-semantical paradoxes', *Ratio* 25 (1983) 137-53, reprinted in Canfield, 1986.

Goldstein, L., 'The development of Wittgenstein's views on contradiction', *History and Philosophy of Logic* 7 (1986) 43-56.

Goldstein, L., 'Wittgenstein's late views on belief, paradox and contradiction', *Philosophical Investigations* 11 (1988) 49-73.

Goldstein, L., 'Smooth and rough logic', *Philosophical Investigations* 15 (1992a) 93-110.

Goldstein, L., 'Squash – what difference does a scoring system make?' *Australian Senior Mathematics Journal* 6 (1992b) 50-3.

Goldstein, L., ' "This statement is not true" is not true', *Analysis* 52 (1992c) 1-5.

Goldstein, L., 'Inescapable surprises and acquirable intentions', *Analysis* 53 (1993) 93-9.

Gopnik, A., 'Conceptual and semantic change in scientists and children: why there are no semantic universals', in B. Butterworth, B. Comrie & O. Dahl (eds) *Explanations for Language Universals* (Mouton, 1984) 163-79.

Grandy, R., 'In defense of semantic fields', in E. LePore (ed.) *New Directions in Semantics* (Academic Press, 1987) 259-80.

Grattan-Guinness, I., *Dear Russell – Dear Jourdain* (Duckworth/Columbia University Press, 1977).

Grayling, A.C., *Wittgenstein* (Oxford University Press, 1988).

Grayling, A.C., 'Wittgenstein's influence: meaning, mind and method', in A. Phillips Griffiths (ed.) *Wittgenstein Centenary Essays* (Cambridge University Press, 1991) 61-78.

Grayling, A.C., *Russell* (Oxford University Press, 1996).

Grayling, A.C., 'Wittgenstein on scepticism and certainty', in H. Glock (ed.) *Wittgenstein: A Critical Reader* (Oxford University Press, 1998).

Grice, H.P., 'Meaning', *Philosophical Review* 66 (1957) 377-88, reprinted in Strawson, 1967, 17-38.

Gudmunsen, C., *Wittgenstein and Buddhism* (Macmillan, 1977).

Hacker, P.M.S., *Insight and Illusion: Themes in the Philosophy of Wittgenstein* (rev. 2nd ed.) (Clarendon Press, 1986).

Hacker, P.M.S., *Wittgenstein, Meaning and Mind: Part I Essays* (*An Analytical Commentary on Wittgenstein's Philosophical Investigations*, Vol. 3) (Blackwell, 1990).

Hacker, P.M.S., *Wittgenstein's Place in Twentieth Century Analytic Philosophy* (Blackwell, 1996a).

Hacker, P.M.S., 'The rise of twentieth century analytic philosophy', *Ratio* 9 (1996b) 243-68.

Hacker, P.M.S., *Wittgenstein: Mind and Will: An Analytical Commentary on the Philosophical Investigations, Vol. 4* (Blackwell, 1996c).

Hallett, G., *A Companion to Wittgenstein's 'Philosophical Investigations'* (Cornell University Press, 1977).

Halliday, M.A.K., *Learning how to Mean* (Edward Arnold, 1975).

Hanfling, O., *Wittgenstein's Later Philosophy* (Macmillan, 1989).

Hansen, C., 'Language in the heart-mind', in R.E. Allinson (ed.) *Understanding the Chinese Mind* (Oxford University Press, 1989) 75-124.

Hanson, S. & Burr, D.J., 'What connectionist models learn: learning and representation in connectionist networks', *Behavioural and Brain Sciences* 13 (1990) 471-89.

Hardy, G.H., *A Mathematician's Apology* (Cambridge University Press, 1967). First published in 1940.

Bibliography

Hark, M.R.M. ter, *Beyond the Inner and the Outer: Wittgenstein's Philosophy of Psychology* (Kluwer Academic Publishers, 1990).

Hark, M.R.M. ter, 'Electric brain fields and memory traces: Wittgenstein and Gestalt psychology', *Philosophical Investigations* 18 (1995) 113-38.

Harnad, S.R., Steklis, H.D. & Lancaster, J. (eds) *Origins and Evolution of Language and Speech* (*Annals of the New York Academy of Sciences* vol. 280, 1976).

Hart, W.D., *Wittgenstein, Philosophy, Logic and Mathematics* (unpublished Ph.D. thesis, Harvard, 1968).

Hayek, F.A., 'Unfinished draft of a sketch of a biography of Ludwig Wittgenstein', written in 1953 for private circulation; with some later insertions and corrections.

Hayman, R., *Hitler and Geli* (Bloomsbury, 1997).

Heal, J., 'Moore's Paradox: a Wittgensteinian approach', *Mind* 103 (1994) 5-24.

Heath, T., *Mathematics in Aristotle* (Clarendon Press, 1949).

Hilmy, S., *The Later Wittgenstein* (Blackwell, 1987).

Hintikka, K.J.J., *Ludwig Wittgenstein: Half-Truths and One-and-a-Half Truths* (Kluwer Academic Publishers, 1996).

Hitler, A., *Mein Kampf* (Hutchinson, 1969).

Horwich, P., *Truth* (Blackwell, 1990).

Horwich, P., 'Meaning, use and truth', *Mind* 104 (1995) 355-68.

Hovens, F., 'Lotze and Frege: the dating of the Kernsätze', *History and Philosophy of Logic* 18 (1997) 17-31.

Huitfeldt, C., 'Computerizing Wittgenstein. The Wittgenstein Archives at the University of Bergen', in Johannessen, Larsen & Åmås, 1994, 251-73.

Hutto, D., 'Consciousness demystified: a Wittgensteinian critique of Dennett's project', *Monist* 78 (1995) 464-79.

Hyman, J., 'Visual experience and blindsight', in J. Hyman (ed.) *Investigating Psychology* (Routledge, 1991) 166-200.

Ingram, D., *First Language Acquisition: Method, Description and Explanation* (Cambridge University Press, 1989).

Ishiguro, H., 'On representations', *European Journal of Philosophy* 2 (1994) 109-24.

Jackendoff, R., *Consciousness and the Computational Mind* (M.I.T. Press, 1987).

Jackson, F., 'What Mary didn't know', *Journal of Philosophy* 83 (1986) 291-5.

Jakobson, R., 'Why "Mama" and "Papa"?', in his *Selected Writings* (Mouton, 1962) 538-45.

James, W., *The Principles of Psychology* (Henry Holt, 1890).

Janaway, C., *Self and World in Schopenhauer's Philosophy* (Clarendon Press, 1989).

Janik, A. & Toulmin, S., *Wittgenstein's Vienna* (Simon & Schuster, 1973).

Janik, A., 'How did Hertz influence Wittgenstein's philosophical development?', *Grazer Philosophische Studien* 49 (1994/5) 19-47.

Jetzinger, F., *Hitler's Youth*, trans. L. Wilson (Greenwood Press, 1956).

Johannessen, K., Larsen, R. & Åmås, K.O., *Wittgenstein in Norway* (Solum Verlag, 1994).

Kaplan, D., 'Words', *Proceedings of the Aristotelian Society* Supp. Vol. 64 (1990) 93-119.

Kaplan, E.L., *The Rôle of Intonation in the Acquisition of Language* (Ph.D. thesis) (Cornell University, 1969).

Katz, J.J., *Language and Other Abstract Objects* (Rowman & Littlefield, 1981).

Kim, J., 'The myth of nonreductive materialism', *Proceedings of the American Philosophical Association* 63 (1989) 31-47.

Koethe, J., *The Continuity of Wittgenstein's Thought* (Cornell University Press, 1996).

Köhler, W., *The Place of Value in a World of Facts* (Liveright Publishing Corporation, 1938).

Kober, M., 'Certainties of a world-picture: the epistemological investigations of On Certainty', in Sluga & Stern, 1996, 411-41.

Kripke, S., *Naming and Necessity* (Blackwell, 1980).

Kripke, S., *Wittgenstein on Rules and Private Language* (Blackwell, 1982).

Kuhn, T., *The Structure of Scientific Revolutions* (2nd ed., enlarged) (University of Chicago Press, 1970).

Langsam, H., 'Why pains are mental objects', *Journal of Philosophy* 92 (1995) 303-13.

Bibliography

Lazerowitz, M., 'Tautologies and the matrix method', *Mind* NS 46 (1937) 191-205.

Leitner, B., *The Architecture of Ludwig Wittgenstein* (Press of Nova Scotia College of Art and Design, 1973).

Lewy, C., 'A note on the text of the Tractatus', *Mind* 76 (1967) 417-23.

Linville, K., 'Wittgenstein on "Moore's Paradox" ' in G.B. Luckhardt (ed.) *Wittgenstein: Sources and Perspectives* (Harvester Press, 1979) 286-302.

Lock, A.J., *Towards a Theory of Language Development* (Ph.D. thesis) (University of Hull, 1976).

Loeb, A.L., 'On my meetings and correspondence between 1960 and 1971 with the graphic artist M.C. Escher', *Leonardo* 15 (1982) 23-7.

Lowe, E.J., 'If A and B, then A', *Analysis* 45 (1985) 93-8.

Luckhardt, C.G. (ed.) *Wittgenstein: Sources and Perspectives* (Harvester Press, 1979).

Malcolm, N., *Ludwig Wittgenstein: A Memoir* (Oxford University Press, 1958).

Malcolm, N., *Nothing is Hidden: Wittgenstein's Criticism of his Early Thought* (Blackwell, 1986).

Malcolm, N., *Wittgenstein: A Religious Point of View?* (ed. with a response by P. Winch) (Routledge, 1993).

Malcolm, N., 'Disentangling Moore's Paradox' in R. Egidi (ed.) *Wittgenstein: Mind and Language* (Kluwer, 1995) 195-205.

Marcus, R.B., 'Some revisionary proposals about belief and believing', *Philosophy and Phenomenological Research* 50 (1990) 133-53.

Mazurkewich, I. & White, L., 'The acquisition of the dative alternation: unlearning overgeneralizations', *Cognition* 16 (1984) 261-83.

McCarty, D.C., 'Review essay: on the failure of mathematics' philosophy', *Synthese* 96 (1993) 255-91.

McDonough, R., *The Argument of the Tractatus* (State University of New York Press, 1986).

McDowell, J., 'Meaning, communication and knowledge', in Z. van Straaten (ed.) *Philosophical Subjects* (Clarendon Press, 1980) 117-39.

McDowell, J., *Mind and World* (Harvard University Press, 1994).

McGinn, C., *Wittgenstein on Meaning* (Blackwell, 1984).

McGinn, C., *Mental Content* (Blackwell, 1989).

McGinn, C., *Problems in Philosophy: The Limits of Enquiry* (Blackwell, 1993).

McGinn, C., 'Another look at color', *Journal of Philosophy* 93 (1996) 537-53.

McGinn, M., 'Wittgenstein's *Remarks on Colour*', *Philosophy* 66 (1991) 435-53.

McGinn, M., *Wittgenstein* (Routledge, 1997).

McGuinness, B.F., 'Bertrand Russell and Ludwig Wittgenstein's "Notes on logic" ', *Revue Internationale de Philosophie* 26 (1972) 444-60.

McGuinness, B., *Wittgenstein: A Life. Young Ludwig 1889-1921* (Duckworth, 1988).

McGuinness, B.F., 'Wittgenstein's Pre-Tractatus Manuscripts', *Grazer Philosophische Studien* 33/34 (1989) 35-47.

McGuinness, B.F. & von Wright, G.H. (eds) *Ludwig Wittgenstein. Briefe* (Suhrkamp, 1980).

McGuinness, B.F. & von Wright, G.H., 'Unpublished correspondence between Russell and Wittgenstein', *Russell* 10 (1990) 101-24.

Menyuk, P., *Language Development: Knowledge and Use* (Foresman & Company, 1988).

Menyuk, P. & Bernholtz, N., 'Prosodic features and children's language production', *Research Laboratory of Electronics Quarterly Progress Reports, M.I.T.* 93 (1969) 216-19.

Middleton, C., 'Silent treatment', *Sunday Times 'Style' Magazine* (3.8.97) 34-5.

Midgley, M., 'The morality of creature comfort', *Times Higher Education Supplement* 1288 (11.7.97).

Millikan, R., 'Perceptual content and Fregean myth', *Mind* 100 (1991) 439-59.

Mithen, S., *The Prehistory of the Mind* (Thames & Hudson, 1996).

Monk, R., *Ludwig Wittgenstein: The Duty of Genius* (Macmillan, 1990).

Bibliography

Moore, A.W., 'Review of P.M.S. Hacker's *Wittgenstein's Place in Twentieth-Century Analytic Philosophy*', *Philosophical Books* 38 (1997) 242-5.

Mounce, H.O., 'Philosophy, solipsism and thought', *Philosophical Quarterly* 47 (1997) 1-18.

Mulhall, S., *On Being in the World: Wittgenstein and Heidegger on Seeing Aspects* (Routledge, 1990).

Musil, R., *The Man without Qualities*, trans. by E. Wilkins & E. Kaiser; 3 vols. (Secker & Warburg, 1953-60).

Nedo, M., & Ranchetti, M., *Wittgenstein: Sein Leben in Bildern und Texten* (Suhrkamp, 1983).

Newton, I, *Opticks, Or a Treatise of the Reflections, Refractions, Inflections and Colours of Light* [based on the fourth edition of 1730] (Dover Publications, 1952).

Nyiri, J.C., 'Wittgenstein and the problem of machine consciousness', *Grazer Philosophische Studien* 33/4 (1989) 375-94.

Ong, W., *Orality and Literacy: The Technologizing of the Word* (Methuen, 1982).

Palmer, A., 'The complex problem and the theory of symbolism' in R. Monk & A. Palmer (eds) *Bertrand Russell and the Origins of Analytical Philosophy* (Thoemmes Press, 1996) 155-82.

Pears, D., 'Wittgenstein's treatment of solipsism in the Tractatus', in his *Questions in the Philosophy of Mind* (Duckworth, 1975) 272-92.

Pears, D.F., *The False Prison Vol. 1* (Clarendon Press, 1987).

Pears, D.F., *The False Prison Vol. 2* (Clarendon Press, 1988).

Pears, D.F., 'Saying and doing: the pragmatic aspects of Wittgenstein's treatment of "I" ', in G. Dorn & G. Schurz (eds) *The Rôle of Pragmatics in Contemporary Philosophy* (Hölder-Pichler-Tempsky, 1998).

Pinker, S., *Learnability and Cognition. The Acquisition of Argument Structure* (M.I.T. Press, 1989).

Pinker, S., *The Language Instinct: The New Science of Language and Mind* (Penguin, 1994).

Pitson, T., 'The dispositional account of colour', *Philosophia* 25 (1997) 247-66.

Poincaré, H., *La Science et l'hypothèse* (Ernest Flammarion, 1902).

Price, H., 'Why "not"?', *Mind* 99 (1990) 221-38.

Priest, G., *In Contradiction* (Kluwer Academic Publishers, 1987).

Priest, G., *Beyond the Limits of Thought* (Cambridge University Press, 1995).

Priest, G., Routley, R. & Norman, G. (eds) *Paraconsistent Logic: Essays on the Inconsistent* (Philosophia Verlag, 1989)

Proudfoot, D. & Copeland, B.J., 'Turing, Wittgenstein and the science of mind', *Australasian Journal of Philosophy* 72 (1994) 497-517.

Quine, W.V., 'On what there is', in his *From a Logical Point of View* (Harvard University Press, 1953) 1-19.

Quine, W.V., *Word and Object* (M.I.T. Press, 1960).

Quine, W.V., 'Success and limits of mathematization', in his *Theories and Things* (Harvard University Press, 1981) 148-55.

Quine, W.V., *Pursuit of Truth* (Harvard University Press, 1992).

Quine, W.V., 'In praise of observation sentences', *Journal of Philosophy* 90 (1993) 107-16.

Radford, C., 'Wittgenstein on ethics', *Grazer Philosophische Studien* 33/34 (1989) 85-114.

Ramsey, F.P., *Foundations – Essays in Philosophy, Logic, Mathematics and Economics*, ed. D.H. Mellor (Routledge & Kegan Paul, 1978).

Redpath, T., *Ludwig Wittgenstein: a student's memoir* (Duckworth, 1990).

Reid, T., *Essays on the Intellectual Powers of Man* (originally published in 1785), in K. Lehrer & R.E. Beanblossom (eds) *Thomas Reid's Inquiry and Essays* (Bobbs-Merrill Co. Inc., 1975) 129-295.

Rey, G., 'Sensations in a language of thought' in E. Villanueva (ed.) *Philosophical Issues I: Consciousness* (Ridgeview Press, 1991) 73-112.

Rhees, R., 'Some developments in Wittgenstein's view of ethics', *Philosophical Review* 74 (1965) 17-26.

Bibliography

Rhees, R. (ed.) *Recollections of Wittgenstein* (Oxford University Press, 1984), originally published under the title *Ludwig Wittgenstein – Personal Recollections* (Blackwell, 1981).

Ricketts T., 'Pictures, logic, and the limits of sense in Wittgenstein's Tractatus' in Sluga & Stern, 1996, 59-99.

Ritchie, W.C., 'Word-formation, learnèd vocabulary and linguistic maturation', in J. Fisiak (ed.) *Historical Semantics and Historical Word-Formation* (Mouton, 1985) 463-82.

Robinson, W.S., *Computers, Minds and Robots* (Temple University Press, 1992).

Robinson, W.S., 'Direct representation', *Philosophical Studies* 80 (1995) 305-22.

Rowe, M.W., 'Goethe and Wittgenstein', *Philosophy* 66 (1991) 283-303.

Rundle, B., *Grammar in Philosophy* (Clarendon Press, 1979).

Russell, B.A.W., *The Principles of Mathematics* (George Allen & Unwin, 1903).

Russell, B.A.W. 'On denoting', *Mind* 14 (1905) 479-93; reprinted in Russell, 1956, 41-56.

Russell, B.A.W., 'Mathematical logic as based on the theory of types', *American Journal of Mathematics* 30 (1908) 222-62, reprinted in van Heijenoort, 1967, 150-82.

Russell, B. & Whitehead, A.N., *Principia Mathematica* (Cambridge University Press, 1910-13).

Russell, B.A.W., *Logic and Knowledge*, ed. R.C. Marsh (George Allen & Unwin, 1956).

Russell, B.A.W., *Autobiography* (George Allen & Unwin, 1975).

Russell, B.A.W., *Correspondence*, ed. N. Griffin (Houghton Mifflin, 1992).

Russell, B.A.W., *The Collected Papers of Bertrand Russell, Vol. 4*, ed. A. Urquart (Routledge, 1994).

Ryle, G., *The Concept of Mind* (Hutchinson, 1949)

Saussure, F., *Cours de Linguistique Générale* (Payot, 1968; originally published in 1916).

Savage-Rumbaugh, S., *Language Comprehension in Ape and Child* (University of Chicago Press, 1995).

Scharfstein, B-A., *The Philosophers: Their Lives and the Nature of Their Thought* (Oxford University Press, 1980).

Schilpp, P.A., *The Philosophy of Rudolf Carnap* (Open Court Publishing Company, 1963).

Schulte, J., *Wittgenstein: An Introduction* (SUNY Press, 1992).

Scott, M., 'Wittgenstein's philosophy of action', *Philosophical Quarterly* 46 (1996) 347-63.

Searle, J., 'Minds, brains and programs', *Behavioral and Brain Sciences* 3 (1980) 417-57.

Searle, J., *Minds, Brains and Science* (Penguin, 1984).

Sellars, W.S., 'Naming and Saying' in his *Science, Perception and Reality* (Routledge & Kegan Paul, 1962).

Sellars, W.S., *Science and Metaphysics: Variations on Kantian Themes* (Routledge & Kegan Paul, 1968).

Sepper, D.L., *Goethe contra Newton: Polemics and the Project for a New Science of Color* (Cambridge University Press, 1988).

Shanker, S.G., *Wittgenstein and the Turning-Point in the Philosophy of Mathematics* (Croom Helm, 1987).

Shanker, S.G., 'Wittgenstein versus Russell on the analysis of mind', in A. Irvine & G. Wedeking (eds) *Bertrand Russell and Analytic Philosophy* (University of Toronto Press, 1993) 210-42.

Shanker, S.G. (ed.) *Philosophy of Science, Logic and Mathematics in the Twentieth Century* (Routledge, 1996) 50-123.

Shanker, S.G. & Shanker, V.A., *A Wittgenstein Bibliography* (Croom Helm, 1986).

Sheffler, S., 'Review of Bernard Williams' *Shame and Necessity*', *Times Literary Supplement*, February 16 1996, 13-14.

Shwayder, D., 'Critical review of Stenius', *Mind* 72 (1963) 275-88.

Simmons, K., *Universality and the Liar* (Cambridge University Press, 1993).

Sluga, H., ' "Whose house is that?": Wittgenstein on the Self ', in Sluga & Stern, 1996, 320-53.

Sluga, H. & Stern, D.G. (eds) *The Cambridge Companion to Wittgenstein* (Cambridge University Press, 1996).

Bibliography

Smolensky, P., 'On the proper treatment of connectionism', *Behavioural and Brain Sciences* 11 (1988) 1-74.

Sorabji, R., *Animal Minds and Human Morals: The Origins of the Western Debate* (Duckworth/Cornell University Press, 1993).

Spengler, O., *Der Untergang des Abendlandes* (Deutscher Taschenbuch Verlag, 1923).

Stern, D., *Wittgenstein on Mind and Language* (Oxford University Press, 1994).

Stern, D., 'The availability of Wittgenstein's philosophy', in Sluga & Stern, 1996, 442-76.

Stern, D.G., 'Why did Wittgenstein admire Weininger's *Sex and Character*?', unpublished TS, presented at the APA Eastern Division Meeting (1996b).

Stoerig, P., 'Phenomenal vision and apperception: evidence from blindsight', *Mind and Language* 12 (1997) 224-37.

Strawson, P.F., 'On referring', *Mind* 59 (1950) 320-44.

Strawson P.F. (ed.) *Philosophical Logic* (Oxford University Press, 1967).

Stroll, A., *Moore and Wittgenstein on Certainty* (Oxford University Press, 1994).

Sugarman, S., *Piaget's Construction of the Child's Reality* (Cambridge University Press, 1987).

Szabados, B., 'Autobiography and philosophy: variations on a theme of Wittgenstein', *Metaphilosophy* 26 (1995) 63-80.

Tao, J., 'The moral foundations of welfare in Chinese society: between virtues and rights', in G. Becker (ed.) *Ethics in Business and Society: Chinese and Western Perspectives* (Springer Verlag, 1996).

Thompson, E., *Color Vision* (Routledge, 1995).

Taylor, R. & Wiles, A., 'Ring-theoretic properties of certain Hecke algebras', *Annals of Mathematics* 142 (1995) 553-72.

van Fraassen, B.C., 'Belief and the problem of Ulysses and the Sirens', *Philosophical Studies* 77 (1995) 7-37.

van Gelder, T., 'What might cognition be if not computation?', *Journal of Philosophy* 92 (1995) 345-81.

van Heijenoort, J., *From Frege to Gödel: A Source Book in Mathematical Logic, 1879-1931* (Harvard University Press, 1967).

Vendler, Z., 'Goethe, Wittgenstein and the essence of color', *Monist* 78 (1995) 391-410.

Verheggen, C., 'Davidson's second person', *Philosophical Quarterly* 47 (1997) 361-9.

von Cranach, M., Foppa, K., Lepennies, W. & Plogg, D., *Human Ethology: Claims and Limits of a New Discipline* (Cambridge University Press, 1979).

von Wright, G.H., 'The Wittgenstein papers', in his *Wittgenstein* (Blackwell, 1982) 35-62, reprinted in Shanker & Shanker (1986) 1-21.

von Wright, G.H. (ed.) *The Diary of David Hume Pinsent* (Blackwell, 1990).

Vygotsky, L.S., *Thought and Language* (M.I.T. Press, 1962).

Watson, R., 'Having ideas', *American Philosophical Quarterly* 31 (1994) 185-98.

Weiner, J., *Frege in Perspective* (Cornell University Press, 1991).

Weininger, O., *Sex and Character* (Heinemann, 1906).

Wellman, H.M., 'From desires to beliefs: acquisition of a theory of mind' in A. Whiten (ed.) *Natural Theories of Mind* (Blackwell, 1991) 19-38.

Werner, H. & Kaplan, B., *Symbol Formation: An Organismic-Developmental Approach to Language and the Expression of Thought* (John Wiley & Sons, 1963).

Westphal, J., *Colour: Some Philosophical Problems from Wittgenstein* (Blackwell, 1987).

Wiener, D., *Genius and Talent: Schopenhauer's Influence on Wittgenstein's Early Philosophy* (Association of University Presses, 1992).

Wiles, A., 'Modular elliptic curves and Fermat's Last Theorem', *Annals of Mathematics* 142 (1995) 443-551.

Wilkes, K., *Real People* (Oxford University Press, 1988).

Williams, B.A.O., *Morality* (Cambridge University Press, 1973).

Williams, B.A.O., *Shame and Necessity* (Cornell University Press, 1994).

Williams, B.A.O., 'Truth in ethics', *Ratio* NS 8 (1995) 227-42.

Williams, J.N., 'The absurdities of Moore's Paradoxes', *Theoria* 48 (1982) 38-46.

Williams, J.N., 'Wittgensteinian accounts of Moorean absurdity', forthcoming.

Bibliography

Williamson, T., *Vagueness* (Routledge, 1994).

Winch, P., 'The expression of belief', *Proceedings and Addresses of the American Philosophical Association* 70 (1996) 7-23.

Woodfield, A., 'Which theoretical concepts do chidren use?' *Philosophical Papers* 25 (1996) 1-20.

Wright, C., *Wittgenstein on the Foundations of Mathematics* (Duckworth/Harvard University Press, 1980).

Zemach, E., 'Meaning, the experience of meaning and the meaning-blind in Wittgenstein's late philosophy', *Monist* 78 (1995) 480-95.

Ziff, P., 'Linguistic and communication systems', *Philosophia* 18 (1988) 3-18.

Index

a priori 17, 35, 86, 90
Abrahamsen, Adele 209n35
absurd, absurdity 101, 145
act (of speech) 39, 49-50, 92, 102, 203n18, 206nn13&14
action 85, 102, 105, 186, 215n38
activity 32, 39, 42, 45-6, 54, 57, 63, 85, 91, 93, 137, 144, 159, 192-3
aesthetics 22, 48, 110, 115, 163, 183-4, 187, 192
Albritton, Rogers 214n32
Åmås, Knut vii
Ambrose, Alice 205n5
analysis, analytical 3, 10-15, 17, 23, 26, 28-9, 39, 96-8, 129, 202n10,11
animal 71, 80, 83, 90, 208n27, 225n34
Anscombe, Elizabeth 76, 216nn46&49
anticipation 52-4, 105
apply (employ), application 87, 112, 126, 134, 155
Aquila, Richard 88, 212n15
Archilochus 185
architecture 163, 181, 185, 221n4
Aristotle 15, 158, 192, 214n36
arithmetic 46, 73, 124-5, 129-30, 133-4, 138, 148
arrogance 7, 169, 183, 199
arrow 68, 112, 151, 156
artificial intelligence (AI) 55, 89, 118
aspect, aspect-blind, aspect-switch 109-12
assertion 100-1, 103-5, 214n31
atmosphere 114, 158, 216n48
Augustine, Saint, Bishop of Hippo 40, 205n3, 209n34
Austin, J.L. 43, 88, 206nn13&14, 209n37, 213n20, 218n9
Austria 10, 164, 176-7, 180, 182, 223n20
avowal 105, 108-9, 213n28
awareness 89, 109, 117
Azzouni, Jody 134
Bach, Kent 207n18
Baker, Gordon 44, 206n12, 210n43, 219n23
Balzano, G. 209n31
Barrett, Cyril 110
Bartley, William 22, 182, 217n2, 222n10

Bates, E. 49
Bechtel, William 209n35
beetle 107
behaviourism 4, 98, 108, 205n6, 215n42, 218n14
belief 4, 23, 33, 80, 85, 95-105, 129-30, 207n23, 213nn26-9
Bell, David 202n11, 211n5
Benacerraf, Paul 135, 137
Bergen vii, 202n9
Berlin, Sir Isaiah 185
Bermudez, José x
Bernholz, N. 207n19
Black, Max 18, 19, 211n9
blindsight 117-18
Bolstad, Arne 175
Bolzano, Bernard 9
Bolzmann, Ludwig 9
Bosanquet, Bernard 176
Bouwsma, O.K. 225n36
Bowerman, Melissa 55
Bradley, F.H. 14, 204n29
Brahms, Johannes 8, 167
brain 51, 55, 75, 81, 91-2, 107, 109, 117-18, 144, 205n5, 212n18, 224n27
Broad, C.D. 15
Brouwer, L.E.J. 130-1, 185, 218n13
Brown, Deborah x, 212nn13&16
Bruner, Jerome 50, 207nn17&19
Buddhism 80, 82, 223n21
Bühler, Karl 216n49
builder 45, 55, 67
Burali-Forti, Cesare 126
Burr, D.J. 210n39
calculus 27-8, 89, 125-6, 132, 144, 149, 154-5, 220n39
Camaioni, L. 49
Camestres 151
Candlish, Stewart x, 115
Canfield, John 210n42
Cantor, Georg 5, 128, 146
Carey, Susan 208n24
Carnap, Rudolf 115, 128, 178, 183-4, 224n31
Carpenter, K.L. 207n20
Carroll, Lewis 203n25

237

Index

Hespe, Franz vii
heterological 160, 219n29
Hilmy, Stephen 224n29
Hintikka, Jaakko viii
Hitler, Adolf 164-9, 185, 222n9-11
Hitler, Alois 222n11
Hobbes, Thomas 65
homosexual 162, 171, 22n10, 223n14
hope 4, 33, 82, 97-8
Horwich, Paul 47, 206n10
Hovens, F. 202n12
Huitfeldt, Claus vii
human 16, 35, 83, 85-6, 89, 172, 191, 197
Husserl, Edmund 214n33
Hutt, Roland 221n7
Hütteldorf 183
Hutto, Daniel 215n42
Hyman, John 216n50
hypothesis 46, 60, 74, 103, 142-4, 204n34
I 71, 80, 83, 104-5, 117, 205n5
idealism 82, 210n3
identity 15, 32, 113
image 43, 51, 88, 92, 95, 106, 120-1, 212n14, 215n38
imagine, imagination 64, 94, 107
infer, inference 21-2, 90, 100, 126, 149, 152-4, 203n25
infinite, infinity 75, 77, 108, 128, 151
Ingram, D. 207n22
innate 60, 62, 206n12
inner 4, 30, 60, 71, 86, 90, 101, 103, 105, 107-9, 120-1, 212n14, 214n38, 215n39
institution 69-70
integrity 197-9
intend, intention 49-50, 54, 64, 70-1, 73, 90, 151, 189, 209n34
internal 62, 72, 75, 81; relation 110-11, 120
interpret, interpretation 31, 63, 68-9, 72, 76, 112, 161-2
intuitionism 130, 218nn10,13&14, 220n40
Ishiguro, Hidé 212n14
Jackendoff, Ray 43
Jackson, A.C. 221n40
Jackson, Frank 118, 121, 216n52, 217n53
Jakobson, Roman 52-3, 55
James, William 45, 79, 94-5, 108, 115, 210n2, 214n38, 215nn38&44
Janik, Allan 201nn4&5
Janaway, Christopher 211n3
Jarman, Derek 201n7
Jaskowski, S. 155
Jastrow, Joseph 110
Jetzinger, F. 165
Jew, Jewish 163, 165-9, 222n11
Johanneson, K. 171, 173, 176
joke 32, 46, 102
Jourdain, Philip 126, 218n7

Judge, Brenda 203n27
justify, justification 22, 76-7, 149, 158
Kant, Immanuel 9, 17, 88, 129-31, 179, 202n17, 212n15, 218n10
Kaplan, B. 207n16
Kaplan, David 209n36
Kaplan, E.L. 207n19
Kasparov, Gary 91
Katz, Jerrold 218n12
Kavka, Gregory 220n30
Keynes, J.M. 178, 221n5
kinaesthesia 115-18
King, Martin Luther 195
Kirk, Keith 82, 224n28
Klimt, Gustav 8
Klingenberg, Hans 172-3
knowledge 96, 105, 116, 124, 129, 131, 204n27, 213n25, 218n11
Kober, Michael viii
Koethe, John 203n20
Köhler, Wolfgang 79, 215n44, 224n27
Kraus, Karl 9
Kripke, Saul 72-6, 79, 162, 204n35, 210nn41&42, 219n24
Kripkenstein 72, 76, 156
Krüger, Wilhelm vii
Kuhn, Thomas 145
Langsam, Harold 108
language, linguistic 3, 4, 7, 11, 15, 16, 17, 19, 20, 23, 25, 27-9, 29, 31-2, 34, 35, 37-40, 44-7, 52, 54, 58, 60-2, 66, 71-2, 85-6, 88-90, 92-4, 101-2, 115, 127-8, 135, 141, 156-7, 159, 182, 192, 210n10, 207n15, 208n27, 209nn32&33, 210nn38&40, 211n10, 216n49, 220n38; artificial 11; formal 12-13; ideal 28, 202n10; logically perspicuous 15, 39; mental 89-90; primitive 45, 48; sign 16, 86
language acquisition 48-62, 206n12, 207nn20&22, 209n35, 215n39
language-game 45-9, 60, 66-7, 77, 101, 104, 107, 109, 112, 115, 139, 155, 157-8, 182, 206n9, 214n31, 225n32
Language of Thought 60-3, 69, 89, 209n30, 215n41
Lau, Joe x
Lazerowitz, Morris 220n35
learn, learning 40, 48, 51, 61, 63-4, 66, 70-2, 92, 114-16, 182, 206n12, 225n32
Leibniz, Gottfried 11, 76
Leitner, B. 177, 181, 217n1, 221n4
Lessing, Gotthold 9
Lewis, C.I. 153
Lewy, Casimir 218n16
Li, Loletta x
life 43, 163, 187-8, 192-3, 196

240

241

Index

Newton, Sir Isaac 82, 119, 146, 217n56
Nida-Rümelin, Martine x
Nietzsche, Friedrich 177, 224n22
Nobel, Alfred 173
Noguera, Anita 221n2
nonsense, nonsensical (*unsinnig*) 3, 16, 20, 25, 98-9, 139, 145, 172, 184-5, 189-91, 213n25, 220n40
Norman, Jean 155
normative 28, 66, 71, 92, 140
Norton, H.T.J. 15
Norway vii, 9, 10, 20, 80, 170-3, 202n9, 223n15
number 4, 5, 19, 25-6, 42, 78, 86, 127-9, 133-8, 218n16, 219n19
Nyiri, J.C. 212n17
object 19, 23-5, 37, 39-40, 42, 56, 86, 93, 96-7, 106-9, 129, 131-2, 135, 137, 140, 203n27, 210n40, 211n5, 217n3
O'Brien, Lucy 211n5
Occam, William of 19, 89, 107, 137, 212n16
Ogden, C.K. 87, 201n3
Ong, W. 65
ontology, ontological 23, 38, 129, 159, 203n27, 215n41
operation 132-3
ostensive definition 39
Oxaal, Ivar 173
pain 33, 71-2, 83, 106-9, 116, 157, 215n42, 217n53
Palmer, Anthony 203n22
paradigm 141, 145-6
paradox 12, 32, 66, 68-9, 76, 148, 160; Liar 102, 127, 148, 160, 220n30; Moore's 4, 99-105, 148, 156, 220n30; Russell's 124-7, 148, 218n4, 220n30; Sorites 216n45; Zeno's 156
parrot 35, 92, 210n38
Pascal, Blaise 219n23
Pascal, Fania 221n7
Peano, Giuseppe 12, 131, 202n10
Pears, David 87, 201n3, 203n27, 205n5, 211n5
perceive, perception 110, 116, 118-19, 163
phenomenology 55, 113, 120-1, 217n54
philosophy 1-3, 12, 16, 22, 25, 27-8, 30-5, 43, 162-4, 170, 184, 191-2, 194-6, 199, 204nn27,32&33, 217nn52&55
Piaget, Jean 49, 55-6, 207n20
picture 35-40, 51, 77, 85-6, 88-90, 128, 133, 151, 204n31, 211n8
picture theory 9, 23, 26
Pinker, Steven 57-9, 208n29, 210n38
Pinsent, David vii, 9, 79, 123, 170-1, 179-80, 201n7, 222n12, 223n14
Pinsent, Ellen 179-80
Pitson, Tony 217n54

Plato, platonistic 28, 92, 129, 131, 134, 138, 140, 185, 218nn11&12
play 46, 56, 69, 104, 144
Poincaré, Henri 218n6
Popper, Sir Karl 212n19
Postl, Heinrich 225n39
Price, Huw 159
Priest, Graham 155, 220n31
private 24, 62, 69-71, 105-7, 210n40, 215n39, 216n50
probability 7
project, projection 37, 88-9
proof 5, 127, 130, 140-7, 149, 153-4, 219n27, 28
proposition *see* statement
Proudfoot, Diane 212n18
pseudo-proposition 17, 19, 25
psychology, psychological ix, 4, 11, 32, 35, 63, 79-80, 85-7, 91, 96-7, 109-10, 120, 181, 188-9, 199, 205n5, 211n12, 212n16, 215nn39&44, 224n27, 225n35
Putnam, Hilary 134
Pythagoras 138, 146, 219n19
quale 55, 106, 108, 121
queer, queerest 31, 64, 77, 114, 157
quietism 3, 138
Quine, W.V. 55, 108, 131, 134-5, 205n6, 208n27, 209n32, 215n41, 219n20
quus 74-7
racism 163, 169, 185
Radford, Colin x, 190-1
Ramsey, Frank 28, 151, 162, 178, 201n3, 206n11, 218n16, 221n5, 222n13, 224n24
Ranchetti, M. 178, 221n5, 224n31
Raubal, Geli 167
react, reaction 49, 52, 68-71, 112, 206n12, 207n17
reading 33, 46, 209n33
realism 82, 136, 211n5
reality 23, 35, 37, 64, 138, 140, 150-1
Rebni, Anna 223n15
Redpath, Theodore 168
Reeves, Basil 27
refer 49, 58-60, 65, 68, 71, 92, 137, 205n4
regularity 44, 66, 69
Reid, Thomas 212n15
relation 24, 37-38, 86-7, 88-9, 96, 100, 105
religion 23, 110, 128, 148, 166, 184-5, 187, 190, 194, 197-8
Rembrandt van Rijn 120
represent, representation 36-9, 50-1, 73, 88, 120, 129, 204n31, 209nn33&35, 225n31
Requate, Angela vii
Rey, Georges 215n41
Rhees, Rush 162, 168, 176, 184, 196-7, 199, 205n3, 221n4, 22n7, 224n30

242